GODDESS ASTROLOGY

GODDESS ASTROLOGY

Elisabeth Brooke

AEON

First published in 2022 by
Aeon Books

British Library Cataloguing in Publication Data

A C.I.P. for this book is available from the British Library

ISBN-13: 978-1-91350-491-5

Typeset by Medlar Publishing Solutions Pvt Ltd, India
Printed in Great Britain

www.aeonbooks.co.uk

FSC
www.fsc.org

MIX
From responsible
sources
FSC® C109576

Dedication for EFB

ὃ δ᾽ ὄλβιος, ὅν τινα Μοῦσαι φίλωνται: γλυκερή οἱ ἀπὸ στόματος ῥέει αὐδή.

*"Women who are pirates in a phallocratic society are involved in a complex opera-
tion. First, it is necessary to plunder-that is, righteously rip off gems of knowledge
that the patriarchs have stolen from us. Second, we must smuggle back to other
women our plundered treasure."*

Mary Daly

"When the whole world is silent even one voice becomes powerful."

Malala Yousefzai

CONTENTS

NOTES ON SOURCES

Homer: (c800–700 BCE) believed to be either a poet from Ionia or a name for a collection of oral poems sung accompanied on the lyre, by wandering minstrels. The poems (written in dactylic hexameters) were written down in the time of Peisistratus (561–527 BCE). The books, the *Iliad and the Odyssey* are partly set in Mycenaean times and centred around the Trojan War and its aftermath. Emily Wilson's (2018) translation of the Odyssey shows a woman's perspective rather than some of the gung-ho Victorian translations.

The Homeric Hymns are a collection of invocations to the gods, written in the 6th and 7th centuries BCE, by unknown authors. They were written to be performed accompanied by the lyre. These are among the earliest sources for the Greek Myths and in many cases show the move from pre-Hellenic to Hellenic theogony. The history of this takeover is discussed in the introduction.

Hesiod: (c700 BCE) was a Boeotian (Central Greece) poet and farmer who wrote *Theogony* and *Works and Days*. *Theogony* provided another framework for Greek mythology. His work is notoriously misogynist but is a good source material for mythology.

Sappho: (b.612 BCE) of Mytilene, Lesbos. A female poet and perhaps a priestess of Aphrodite, and composer of lyric poetry. Little of her work survives, fragments are still being discovered in the rubbish tips at Oxyrhynchus in Egypt, and as mummy wrappings. It is believed early Christian fathers ordered her books to be destroyed. Much of her work was quoted by later authors commenting on her poetic style, e.g. Horace the Roman poet. Plato called her the Tenth Muse. She wrote love poetry, choral hymns which were probably performed by young women in rituals for Aphrodite and wedding songs.

Aeschylus: (525–456 BCE) Athenian tragic dramatist, author of over ninety plays, seven of which survive. He wrote the *Oresteia* which was a trilogy of plays performed at the Dionysia dramatic festival in Athens. The last play of the trilogy, *The Eumenides,* explores the hounding of Orestes by the Furies, the Pythia at Delphi and the supplanting of mother-right by father-right (see: Mars the Furies and Pisces the Pythia).

Herodotus: (484–425 BCE) Ethnographer, historian (said to be the first) and geographer from Halicarnassus (Bodrum, Turkey) who wrote *The Histories*, the first major work in prose. He travelled extensively around Greece, Egypt and Asia Minor and recorded the customs and stories from the places he visited in a non-judgemental, accessible style. He was later attacked for making things up, like snowy mountains in Africa, but has subsequently been proven right (Mount Kilimanjaro) on several counts.

Sophocles: (496–406 BCE) Tragic playwright and friend of Herodotus. Most famous for his three Theban plays, one of which, *Electra* shows her revenge on their father's murder by their mother Klytemnestra (Clytemnestra).

Euripides: (480–406 BCE) Athenian dramatist who wrote tragedies including, *Medea, Hippolytus, the Suppliants, Hecuba, The Trojan Women, Iphigenia in Taurus, Phaedra, Phoenician Women. The Bacchae.* His portrayal of women, for example in *Medea*, and *Hecuba* is sympathetic.

Aristophanes: (450–385 BCE) Greek comic playwright whose works were performed in Athens, his play *Lysistrata* details the religious life of Athenian women and girls. His best known works are hilarious satire on Athenian life and notables, including Socrates, in *The Clouds*. Other well-known plays include, *Frogs, The Birds* and *The Wasps*.

All the translations from the Greek are mine, unless otherwise stated. It felt important to go back to the source, particularly as many of the texts were translated by 'Victorian Gentlemen scholars' who had a particular mindset, which is reflected in their choice of words, although new translators are also guilty of this. (see Amazons fn xxxviii for an example).

I also wanted to look especially at pre-Homeric texts, The Homeric Hymns, Sapho and Hesiod, as they sometimes relate a time before the Hellenic invasion of Greece which overthrew the native goddesses by 'marrying' them and absorbing their powers and spheres of influence.

I have chosen to reframe Greek myth as this is where my interest lies. This process can be repeated for any tradition looking at written sources, pottery, art, stories, legends and conversations with elders.

INTRODUCTION

This book came about through serendipity. I was asked to run a workshop and it could be about anything. Having run workshops all over the world the past forty-five years, I decided to do something new and wondered how the Greek goddesses would work with all the Astrological signs.

Of course, there was Venus and the Moon, but to my mind these are, or rather were, hackneyed archetypes of women's experience. We are not all breeders, and love, as portrayed by ordinary astrology, was a kind of dumb, saccharine experience. All of this bore little relation to women's lives in the twenty-first century. Also, some planets were problematic, Mars for example; there are women who fight, but this is not what most women can identify with.

This led me into the pre-patriarchal world of Crete and the Minoans and older writing, like the *Homeric Hymns* to see what they had to suggest. It was important for me to do the translations myself, as a lot of these texts were translated by Victorian and Edwardian 'Gentlemen Scholars' who generally had a patriarchal mindset. Most of what is known as Greek myth comes from Ovid, *Metamorphoses*. Ovid was a Roman writer of the first century CE, so a late source and a Romanised one.

Of course there was a time before, if not a matriarchy, at least not a patriarchy. A time before war, male domination, violence and rape were institutionalised, a time before the Aryans from Mongolia with their horses, sky gods and brutalist culture conquered the matriarchal culture of Old Europe.

This book then, is my research, offering another perspective of different female archetypes, illustrated by the lives of extraordinary women both alive and dead.

The book begins with a look at the context of history to see how Goddess worship developed and later, how it declined. It is chilling reading.

Then follow the chapters on each of the twelve astrological signs, each with a meditation, some background to the myths and examples of two women.

This is followed by a look at the seven traditional planets, again with examples of notable women.

Then I look at the Houses, and Aspects to see how the signs and planets express themselves in the horoscopes I introduced in the twelve Astrological Signs and the Seven Traditional planets.

Transits and cycles discusses how the movements of the planets affect our actions, again looking at the twenty-eight women I have previously discussed.

The Appendix shows all the horoscopes arranged alphabetically for ease of use, and also some key words for each sign.

I chose to use Greek Mythology, because those are the myths which speak to me, not because they are in any way better. I hope my work will be continued by other women from other Goddess Traditions who can widen the field. I felt it was better to study one system in depth rather than write about traditions I do not resonate with.

The book can be read straight through as an exploration of the Goddess and Astrology, and also as a reference book for both astrological studies and goddess lore. It was incredibly difficult to choose the example lives, there were so many women's stories I wanted to tell, but again, it felt better to study fewer women in more detail, than many superficially.

I would like to thank Oliver Rathbone and Melinda McDougal of Aeon Books for their forbearance in waiting for this book, written as it was during the plague years of 2020–21. Doing the research was challenging, the libraries I usually used were closed, with the exception of the Classical Association Library in the University of London where the super helpful librarians stoically remained open for book borrowing and study, hats off to them! I would also like to thank everyone in London who kept the show on the road, delivering food, and parcels and keeping this city alive. Especial thanks to EFB who was my lockdown companion and whose music and humour was a delightful diversion during this trying time.

Fitzrovia, Lamas 2021

HISTORICAL BACKGROUND

"Eurynome[1] Goddess of all things rose naked from Chaos but found nothing substantial to rest her feet upon and so she divided the sea from the sky, dancing alone upon its waves. She danced towards the south, and the wind set in motion behind her seemed something new and different, with which to begin a work of creation. Turning around she caught hold of the North Wind, rubbed it between her hands, and created the great serpent Ophion.

Eurynome danced to warm herself, spinning wildly, until Ophion, excited, coiled about those divine limbs and was moved to couple with her.[2] Eurynome fell pregnant.'

Next, she assumed the form of a dove,[3] brooding on the waves and, in due process of time, laid the Universal egg. At her bidding, Ophion coiled seven times about this egg, until it hatched and split in two. Out tumbled all things that exist, her children: sun, moon, planets, stars, the earth with its mountains and rivers, its trees, and herbs, and living creatures.

Eurynome and Ophion made their home on Mount Olympus, where he vexed her by claiming to be the author of the Universe. Forthwith she bruised his head with her heel, and kicked out his teeth, and banished him to the dark caves beneath the earth."

Pelasgian Creation Myth[4]

The Palaeolithic period is said to have been between 50,000–30,000 BCE when the glaciers which had covered much of Europe and Asia began to disappear and *Homo Sapiens* appeared. Steppe replaced the barren ground and herds of horses, cattle, and bison grazed. Between 20,000 BCE and 15,000 BCE steppe gave way to thick forest. The herds moved eastwards, settlers grouped around rivers and lived in nearby caves. For at least 20,000 years (approx. 30,000–10,000 BCE) people lived, worshipped and decorated these caves.[5]

Some of the most spectacular cave paintings and sculptures have been discovered in the Dordogne, France. Deep within these caves, sacred space was created. Some had underground labyrinths (Tuc d'Audoubert and Les Trois Frères). Lamps of hollowed out stone with juniper twig wicks and oil from animal fat, lit passages two to three kilometres long which opened out into caverns richly decorated with animal paintings (Lascaux). Stones believed to represent the souls of the dead and goddess figurines designed to rest on cave shelves or stuck in the ground at the cave entrances have been found. Many of these goddess figures were sprinkled with red ochre, probably representing blood, they were often pregnant with enhanced breasts and bellies.[6]

At Laussel, a figure of a woman (Fig. 1) 43cm tall, cut from limestone is holding a crescent shape (perhaps a horn, perhaps the crescent moon) which has thirteen notches on it. The figure points to her swollen belly. The crescent could also have been a lunar calendar, there are thirteen days of the waning moon and thirteen months in a lunar year. Previously these figurines were called 'Venus figures' or 'fertility idols', downplaying their importance as the symbol of the pregnant woman, the mother, who sustains the tribe, bringing new life into it and the Mother or life itself, and her rhythms and cycles.

The Neolithic period (stone age) followed, (around 10,000–3500 BCE). As the weather became more settled and predictably, agricultural communities were established, leaving cave life behind. The forests provided timber to build houses, crops were sown, and animals were domesticated. Instead of hunting and gathering

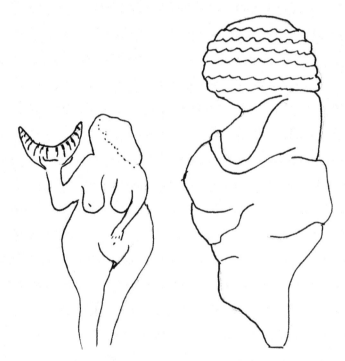

Fig. 1 Goddess of Laussel 22,000–18,000 BCE and Goddess of Willendorf c 20,000–18,000 BCE.

and living in caves to conserve warmth, people built houses, made pots to store food, and cook with. Houses, temples, and villages were built. It is believed the sowing of grain, harvesting, bread making, making of pots, weaving fibres for lighter clothes now the frost had gone, using plants for remedies, dyes and sacred ritual were all done by women, while men still fished and hunted to supplement their diet. A more reliable source of food and the means to store it through winter would have allowed for more leisure time, so artwork developed in complexity. Images of the goddess appear with more intricate patterns, four-armed crosses, snakes, cross-hatching, meanders, labyrinths, geometric designs and bird-like heads (Fig. 2).

Marija Gimbutas[7] unearthed treasures of the Neolithic period in an area she called 'Old Europe' which stretched from Kiev and Southern Italy, to Malta, Northern Greece to Crete and Anatolia. Her study of the art shows its transmission to Bronze Age Crete and Greece. Around 30,000 miniature sculptures from marble, clay, bone, copper, and

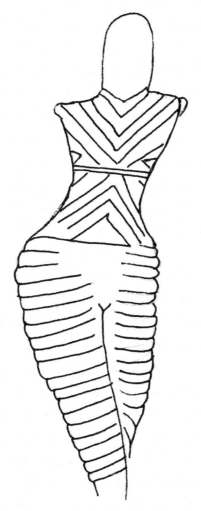

Fig. 2 Geometric figure: bird snake goddess, 5,000 BCE.

gold have been found in over 30,000 sites, including ritual vessels, shrines, altars, painted vases, implements, clay models of temples and houses. Central to this was the Great Goddess, "incarnating the creative principle as Source and Giver of All."[8]

Over time some of these settlements grew into communities housing several thousand people. In Vinca in Yugoslavia (5300–4000 BCE) towns were discovered with streets lined with spacious houses constructed beside rivers, extending over twenty acres (8 ha).[9] The inhabitants appear to have lived in peace and prosperity, no fortifications or weapons have been discovered, nor images of battle. Burial sites are arranged in a non-hierarchal way, suggesting there were no absolute leaders or ruling classes.[10] Instead, images of nature show their aesthetic sensibilities and love of a peaceful, wholesome life. Female statues of the goddess have been found with exaggerated breasts and buttocks.[11] Gimbutas writes in *The Language of the Goddess:*

> "The Goddess in all her manifestations was the symbol of the unity of all life in Nature. Her power was in water and stone, in tomb and cave, in animals and birds, snake and fish, hills, trees and flowers."[12]

Old Europe flourished for 2,000 years from around 6500–4500 BCE until a cataclysm occurred. Aryan (Indo-European)[13] tribes from the East (perhaps Mongolia) arrived. They were nomads and worshipped sky gods, rode horses, and wielded the axe.

> "Millennial traditions were truncated: towns and villages disintegrated, magnificent painted pottery vanished; as did shrines, frescoes, sculptures, symbols and script. The taste for beauty and the sophistication of style and execution withered. The use of vivid colours disappeared in nearly all Old European territories except Greece, the Cyclades, and Crete where old European traditions continued for three more millennia to 1500 BC."[14]

The Bronze Age followed the Neolithic from (circa 3500–1100 BCE). Bronze, an alloy of copper and tin, was developed. Bronze made longer lasting, stronger tools and weapons. Writing appeared. Shrines and temples were raised with images carved on them. These hieroglyphs told the stories which previously had been part of an oral tradition. Clay tablets and papyrus were used for record keeping and setting down the myths and stories of their culture. In them emerges a picture of one Great Mother Goddess who is the beginning of all life, she is the goddess depicted on the statues and wall painting of the Palaeolithic and Neolithic ages. She has many names, has a daughter and son or consort from whom she becomes separated. She is called Inanna in Sumeria, Ishtar in Babylonia, Isis in Egypt, Demeter in Greece.

These stories tell of the cycle of the moon, its bright fullness, its sharp new crescent, and the time when it disappears, and the long nights are dark. The loss of the daughter or consort represented both the dark moon and the dark, non-fertile winter months. There was a continuity between darkness and light, a sacred cycle, both lunar and solar. Life is seen, then as a continuum, the sacred rhythm of the great Goddess, she embodies all life.

Three main centres of this Great Goddess cult in the West were, Crete, Sumeria and Egypt. Similar myths of the Goddess are found in India, the Indus Valley, China and the Americas, Africa and Australasia, everywhere. There have been found a continuity of early goddess images from Anatolia to the Indus valley. As well as the sacred numinosity of life, there was an outflowing of learning; with writing came mathematics, and astronomy, which began in the temples and eventually spread to the populace at large.

Life was mostly lived in small settlements or larger towns, with the temples or shrines as a focal point. Small scale agriculture sustained the population, harvests were celebrated in the temples and grain stored there for the long, barren winter months. Astronomy linked the heavens to the land and the lives of people and gave a sacred rhythm to all human endeavour.

Crete; the Minoans

"There is a land called Krete, in the middle of the wine-dark sea, a fair, rich land, surrounded with water, and countless people live there in ninety cities and the languages are mixed: there are Achaeans, native Kretans, long-haired Dorians and Pelasgians. Knossos is there, a mighty city." Homer *Odyssey:* 19:174–8

The Minoan civilisation was believed to have begun with migration of people from Asia-Minor across the Aegean Sea to Crete. Its flowering was 1600–1400 BCE. Around 1400 BCE Crete suffered a series of fires and her power waned as the Mycenaeans from mainland Greece grew in power. The Mycenaeans may have destroyed Minoan culture or earthquakes destroyed it, or that its ending was a combination of these factors. Excavations have revealed palace-temples which were destroyed by earthquakes in 1450 BCE and 1700 BCE. Certainly, in Thera (nearby Santorini) murals and frescoes show devastating earthquakes which are dated 1600 BCE. It may be that these caused the disappearance of the Atlantis that Plato wrote about, and maybe Atlantis was Thera.[15]

Krete (Zakiriti) was self-sufficient. It had great oak, cypress, and fir forests with which they built their houses and temples. There was abundant water from melted snow from the mountains, and food from the rich alluvial plains. There were domesticated animals, sheep, pigs and oxen as well as olive oil, honey, fish from the sea, fruit and aromatic herbs which were exported around the Mediterranean and the Near East.

The palace-temple complexes were large, complex buildings, used to store food, house people and perform rituals. Houses could be several stories high and the walls were painted with brightly coloured murals. The greatest of the temple-palaces was at Knossos. The myth of the labyrinth may have been based on the meandering nature of the buildings within the palace compound. Knossos had no walls or other defences, suggesting Krete was such a powerful country there was no need for defence.

Krete had writing; Linear A (2000–1600 BCE) which has not yet been deciphered, but from what can be deduced, it was a non-military culture, that valued nature and the natural world. Linear B was also used; it is an early form of Greek (used around c1500 BCE) which the Aryan Mycenaeans from mainland Greece who traded with the Kretans used. In Linear B (deciphered in 1953) we find rituals and offerings to the goddess,

"To the Lady of the Labyrinth, a jar of honey., 'To the mistress A[t]hena …"[16]

Krete was a sea-power.[17] Excavated Minoan manufactured goods suggest there was a network of trade with mainland Greece, especially to Mycenae, Cyprus, Syria, Anatolia, Egypt, Palestine, Mesopotamia, Sumeria, Malta and as far west as the Iberian Peninsula.[18] Thucydides (c460–400 BCE) writes of the Kretan navy,

"When the navy of Minos was established, sailing then became safe for other people. For the wrongdoers from the islands left because of him, and when many of the men of the sea [Kretans] settled, they grew wealthy and lived a stable life."
The History of the Peloponnesian War: 1:8:2[19]

Phaistos was another large building complex[20] The number of sleeping rooms in the building suggest an extended family or community lived there. There were large storage areas probably both for grain and other produce like wine and oil. A complex system for food distribution fed craft workers, temple workers and administrators. On wall paintings and pottery, women were represented as ceramic and textile craftworkers.[21]

The Goddess was worshiped in temples, in caves and on the mountainsides. She was Goddess of the trees, mountains, of the sea, the harvest and the animals. She is shown in statues, wall paintings and jewellery adorned with serpents sometimes holding the double axe or *labrys*. These paintings depict a brightly coloured, highly decorated world filled with doves, poppies, the saffron harvest, lilies, birds, bees, dolphins, serpents, mountain lions and all the wide natural beauty of the island. There is a joyous, celebratory quality to all Kretan art-work. The bull was sacred to the Kretans, and bull horns, or 'horns of consecration, perhaps representing the crescent moon, were represented in artwork. Earth Goddess(es) were at the centre of Minoan religious life.[22] (Illustration: Fig. 3)

Fig. 3 Snake Goddess Minoan Phaistos 1800 BCE.

No image of a god has been found in Neolithic Krete, but young male figures appear as consorts or helpers of the priestesses. Minoan religion is focused on female deities, with women priestesses. While historians and archaeologists are sceptical of a historical matriarchy, the predominance of female figures in authoritative roles and lack of male ones, indicates that, at the very least, in Minoan society women held positions of sacred and temporal power.[23]

> "The male deity is, however, of rare occurrence and his position is a distinctively inferior one. His advent is late, and he may indicate that already the northern influence of the Achaeans was causing their god to be accepted by the Minoans, though always as subordinate to the indigenous goddess."[24]

Chronologically Minoan Crete lies with the timeline of the Bronze Age but it remained Neolithic in character, except for the use of writing. Krete gives a glimpse into the Neolithic culture described by Gimbutas.

The old European serpent goddess also appears in Krete. She appears holding up snakes in her hands, her bare breasts showing to indicate nurture and life. These statues often have a trance-like face, suggesting they were ritual objects. The lion cub/owl/cat sits on her head, reminiscent of the goddess figurines of Sumeria, Egypt and Anatolia. (Fig. 4)

Fig. 4 Snake Goddess Knossos 1600 BCE.

The 'horns of consecration' are identical to those found in Vinca around 5000 BCE and Catal Huyuk, Turkey circa 7000 BCE.

The *labrys* is found in the Palaeolithic cave of Niaux in France and the Neolithic Tell Halaf culture in Iraq.[25] In Krete some of these double-headed axes were 2m (6'5") high and stood on either side of altars, marking the entrance to sanctuaries. Goddess/priestess figures held them in their hands or on their heads Fig. 11 (Baring: p114). It has been suggested the *labrys* represented the butterfly and was an image of the soul, the word for soul and butterfly is the same in Greek (psyche, ψυχη).[26] Although they are called axes it is doubtful they were weapons. A vase from circa 1400 BCE (Fig. 5) has the *labrys* surrounded by flowers, perhaps roses, or marigolds and lilies, which suggests they were ceremonial and peaceful, especially as they are never shown held by a man. Perhaps they were used to kill the sacrificial bull, or to cut down the sacred tree which appears in so many images. (Fig. 6)

Fig. 5 Minoan vase with labyrinth 1500 BCE.

Fig. 6 The Sacred Tree Minoan, Mycenae 1500 BCE.

The Labyrinth may refer to the place of the *labrys*, a shrine or sacred space where rituals involving the *labrys* were carried out. A labyrinth was drawn on the floor at Knossos which may have been a dancefloor, many of the figures in the gold seals appear to be dancing with their arms raised. (Fig. 7)

Fig. 7 Aidonia Ring Knossos 1500 BCE.

Odysseus' visit to the Phaeacians (*Odyssey:* 7:81–239) is believed to be an account of (then) ancient Krete. Homer describes orchards, bronzed lined palaces, golden vessels and happy and prosperous people. The Queen Arete (Gr. Αρητη: goodness, excellence) addresses him directly, signifying her power and authority (Greek women were forbidden to mix socially with men, let alone speak to male strangers directly).

Kretan women were elegantly dressed, they wore embroidered boleros and were bare-breasted, with many layered flounced skirts or perhaps wide trousers. The pattern on their skirts may be a spider's web, suggesting the warp and weft of life, the seven layers of the skirt may refer to the seven planets of antiquity. They wore a sacred knot in their hair as a headband or perhaps necklace (Fig. 8). The sacred knot may be what the Greeks recorded as Ariadne's thread, which could have been untied during ritual and dance.[27] The women are depicted with self-confidence and dignity as equal members of their society.

Fig. 8 Sacred Knot Knossos 1500BCE.

Priestesses conducted religious ceremonies, often depicted holding snakes in their hands or coiled around their arms and headdress. Holding the sacred serpents shows their power and sacredness in manipulating both the spirit and natural world. These figures often have staring eyes as though in a trance like state. Images of poppies and crocus suggest they may have taken mind altering substances. The snakes may represent life and death, as snake shed their skin, snake venom is a known neurotoxin, it may have been used for sacred journeying or trance work. (Fig. 9)

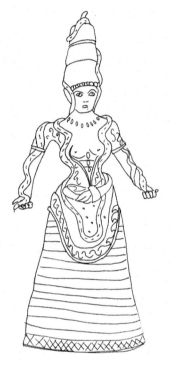

Fig. 9 Snake goddess Knossos 1600 BCE.

Krete remained safe until the Dorian invasion around 1200 BCE when it was finally destroyed.

The Mycenaean age: invasion of the sky-god

The Mycenaeans took much of their culture from the Minoans, we know this because their artwork shows similarities. The Mycenaean culture to some extent can be linked with the Homeric poems, the *Iliad and Odyssey*, which are believed to have been written down around 725 BCE, but which concern events around 1250 BCE, the beginning of patriarchy. The Minoans had their mother goddesses without a male counterpart, while Zeus brought the rape culture of the Hellenes. There is a massive difference between the orgiastic, mystical, earth Mother-goddess such as Demeter at Eleusis, where there is a mystical union between goddess and worshippers through ecstatic dance, clashing music and nature worship and probably mind altering herbs,[28] and the Achaean gods of Homer who are simply more powerful, who help or hinder mortals on a whim, and are jealous and vengeful.

> "The Achaean warrior did not seek to be born again from the bosom of Hera. He was indeed the reverse of a mystic by temperament."[29]

During the Bronze age people began moving into larger settlements, life became less peaceful and walls and defences grew up around towns and cities. There was an invasion of Indo-Europeans from both the north and east around 2000 BCE. Huge numbers of migratory tribesmen, with their sky gods of thunder, lightning and fire and storm, brought with them the glorification of war. They invaded Canaan and Mesopotamia from the Syro-Arabian desert (Semitic tribes); Hittites in Anatolia and Syria, Aryans in the Indus Valley, Mittani in Mesopotamia and Achaeans and Dorians in Greece, (who brought the Greek language and their sky-god, Zeus). They left devastation in their wake, in Anatolia 300 cities were sacked and destroyed, including Troy (2300 BCE). The Aryans were nomadic, warriors, tent dwellers, patriarchal and filthy. They prohibited writing, their culture was an oral one, a Sumerian scribe described them,

> "A host whose onslaught was like a hurricane, a people who had never known a city."[30]

In Sumeria, and then in Egypt the concept of the Father-god emerges and then dominates. A separation occurs between Earth and Heaven. The Great Goddess is replaced by Father-god who 'creates' rather than gives birth to the world. This sets humankind apart from nature for the first time and lead to a tendency to call Spirit-higher and Nature-lower, creating a hierarchy of values. Similarly, the idea of the 'hero' who can shape events becomes dominant, the man heading his tribe or ruling others who have less 'value' than he does.

There is evidence of debasement of nature, the invaders were not farmers but pastoralists, perhaps due to harsh conditions in both desert and steppe. The cult of war brings with it a nihilism and deep insecurity, life may be violently disrupted at any time for no reason. The warrior becomes all important, to defend the city, while the farmer is now a serf or slave.[31]

> "The tribal migrations changed the character of the early Bronze Age and had a lasting effect on the evolution of consciousness in the civilisations that followed them. Their legacy lives on in pervasive attitudes and structures of response to life that have not been questioned and still have a controlling influence on the psyche today."[32]

Now there was no unity, but separation, dark from light, sky from earth, male from female. Conquest and destruction rather than co-operation and non-violence. Naturally, this affected the status of women. There is evidence to suggest that previously, women owned property, ran businesses, were protected by law and culture, and were active in public life. After 2300 BCE in Sumeria their status deteriorated. In the Sumerian north (Babylonia) women became possessions of men, who had the power of life and death over them, including the right to sell them into slavery.[33]

The barbarism of the second and first millennium BCE brought with it the terror of invasion, or death or slavery. This heart-breaking lament of a queen encapsulates the times. (Figs. 10, 11)

'Alas! That day of mine, on which I was destroyed.
Alas! That day of mine on which I was destroyed.
...
For on it he came hither to my house,
for on it he turned in the mountains,
into the road to me,
for on it the boat came on my river towards me,
for on it, (heading) towards me,
the boat moored at my quay,
for on it the master of the boat came inside to me,
for on it he reached out his dirty hands towards me,
for on it he yelled to me 'Get up! Get up on board!'
For on it the goods were taken aboard in the bow.
For on it I, the queen, was taken on board in the stern.
For on it I grew cold with the most shivering fear.
The foe trampled with his booted feet into my chamber!
That foe reached out his dirty hands toward me!
He reached out the hand toward me, he terrified me!
The foe reached out his hand toward me,
Made me die with fear.[34]

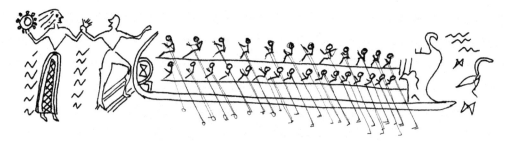

Fig. 10 Spouter Krater, Thebes, 900–700 BCE.

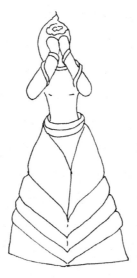

Fig. 11 Minoan, bronze 1600–1500.

Iron age

The changeover from the mystical, immanent goddess to the hierarchical, punishing gods mirrored what happened in the culture. As we move nearer the Iron Age there is a change in the relationship between people and animals. Initially they were benign; snakes wrapped around the body, lions adoring goddesses (Fig. 12). Lucy Goodison argues that the demotion of the goddess and her replacement by masculine gods was part of the debasement of the feminine. Where once the earth and those who lived on it were sacred, now the sky became separate and superior and[35]

> "Many of the creatures prominent alongside the [female] sun symbolism of the Bronze Age became discredited and monstrous." (Goodison 1989:176)

Fig. 12 Ecstatic dancer and lions Knossos 1500 BCE.

Snakes, once sacred to the Minoan goddess, became loathsome dragons, who needed to be destroyed. The sacred animals of the Kretan goddess are demonised; dogs (Cerberus), lions, goats, snakes, and the sphinx, and killed by 'male heroes' such as Pegasus, Bellerophon and Heracles. Goodison, (1989:114–5) argues that the old respect for nature, and closeness to animals was lost. Animals become 'the enemy' to be exploited and killed.

The nature of the gods also changed. For example, Athene's association with the snake, the olive tree and the owl are all found in Minoan religion as the domestic snake cult (house snakes), the tree cult, and the birds as divine messengers. Athene's association with warfare develops in the Mycenaean period. (Willets.1962:278).

Now war becomes a way of life, with male rulers, a strict hierarchy related to wealth and power as well as physical strength. Work is divided into female and male work, with male work privileged. There is an increased activity in religion by men for the first time, male priests officiating. In material culture, imagery of hunting, weapons and soldiers replaces images of nature and women.

> "There can be no doubt that in the very earliest ages of human history the magical force and wonder of the female was no less a marvel than the universe itself; and this gave to woman a prodigious power, which it has been one of the chief concerns of the masculine part of the population to break, control and employ to its own ends." Joseph Campbell, *The Masks of God: Primitive Mythology.*

The sacred becomes personified in named Gods, and is removed from nature, which it previously embodied. Gods and priests carry weapons or take an aggressive stance (Fig. 13) and are increasingly found, not in nature but in huge buildings which dwarf humans to emphasise their powerlessness against divine wrath. (Goodison 197–9).

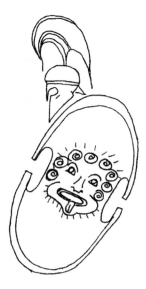

Fig. 13 Male warrior 530 BCE.

We have been led to believe that the values of these nomad-warriors are 'human values' and this remains largely uncontested. The values, beliefs, and ways of living prior to these invasions are seen as a 'lesser stage of evolution' or a fantasy past. As I write now, (2021) these values are hurtling us towards annihilation, but their proponents hang on grimly in the face of disaster, in the true 'heroic' way. And if you think, well this was in the long past, remember *Daesh* (*Isis*) rounding up the women of Iraq recently and using/selling them as slaves, the dead hand of patriarchy is everywhere.

Why does this matter? Because there was a time before.

Notes

1. The entomology is interesting: ευργνομε possibly from ευπυθμος-in good time, orderly, graceful, or wide wandering-ευρυνω
2. Myths of the union of sky and earth abound are found all over the world, see: https://www.perseus.tufts.edu/hopper/text?doc=Perseus%3Atext%3A1999.01.0022%3Atext%3DLibrary%3Abook%3D1%3Achapter%3D1 for a few. Apollodorus. Apollodorus, The Library, with an English Translation by Sir James George Frazer, F.B.A., F.R.S. in 2 Volumes. Cambridge, MA, Harvard University Press; London, William Heinemann Ltd. 1921. Includes Frazer's notes.
3. The Sumerian universal goddess was Iahu (exalted dove) Graves 2011, p.28. The dove was also sacred to Aphrodite, love, which suggests Love was concerned with creation, see Venus p.xx.
4. Graves, Robert. 2011. *The Greek Myths*. Penguin Books, London. p.27.
5. Cave dwellers were found worldwide, as the discovery of fantastic cave paintings in the Amazon show. Editorial, 4·12.2020. *The Guardian view on Amazonian Cave Art: a story about the environment too*. The Guardian newspaper. https://www.theguardian.com/commentisfree/2020/dec/04/the-guardian-view-on-amazonian-cave-art-a-story-about-the-environment-too accessed 6.12.2020.
6. Baring & Cashford, 1993. *The Myth of the Goddess*. pp.15–18.
7. See Gimbutas, Marija. *Goddesses and Gods of Old Europe* and *The Language of the Goddess*.
8. Gimbutas, *Goddesses of Old Europe*, preface.
9. Baring & Cashford,1993. *The Myth of the Goddess*. p.55.
10. Eisler, Riane *The Chalice and the Blade*, p.18
11. See Sjoo, Monica. *The Great Cosmic Mother*. 1987. Harper Collins, New York.
12. Gimbutas, 1989. p.321.
13. They were neither Indian nor European, Gimbutas calls them the Kurgan (Barrow) people, believed to have come from the steppes between the Dneiper and Volga rivers, Baring & Cashford, *The Myth of the Goddess*. 1993 p.79.
14. Gimbutas, *The First Wave of Eurasian Steppe Pastoralists into Copper Age Europe*, 1977.
15. Morford, 2015.*Classical Mythology*. Oxford University Press. Oxford. p.42.
16. Baring & Cashford, *The Myth of the Goddess*. 1993, p.108.
17. Thucydides *The Peloponnesian* War. 1.8.2 http://www.perseus.tufts.edu/hopper/text?doc=Perseus%3Atext%3A1999.01.0199%3Abook%3D1%3Achapter%3D8   accessed 8.8.2020.

18. Baring & Cashford, *The Myth of the Goddess*. 1993, p.109.
19. https://www.perseus.tufts.edu/hopper/text?doc=Perseus%3Atext%3A1999.01.0247 %3Abook%3D1%3Achapter%3D8 accessed 1.9.2020.
20. Knossos and the other large building complexes are called 'palaces', we do not know they were or that there was a royal family, they may have been large communal living areas, temple complexes or other types of building.
21. Nikolaïdou, Marianna (2012), *"Looking for Minoan and Mycenaean Women"*, A Companion to Women in the Ancient World, Blackwell Publishing Ltd, pp.38–53.
22. See, Max Dashu, www.supressedhistories.net for many examples of Minoan art.
23. Lee, Mireille M. (2000), *Deciphering Gender in Minoan Dress, in Rautman, Alison E (ed.), Reading the Body, University of Pennsylvania Press p.111–123* https://penn.degruyter.com/view/book/9781512806830/10.9783/9781512806830-011.xml accessed 8.8.2020.
24. Nilsson, Martin, P. (1968) *The Minoan-Mycenaean Religion and its survival in Greek Religion*. C.W.K. Gleerup. Lund. p.405.
25. Baring & Cashford, *The Myth of the Goddess*. 1993, p.1112.
26. Gimbutas, 1982, p.186
27. Baring & Cashford, *The Myth of the Goddess*. 1993, p.121.
28. Poppies are shown in many Minoan images, we can imagine they were for ritual use, likewise saffron. See, Max Dashu, www.supressedhistories.net for many examples of Minoan art replete with women and goddesses dancing, invoking animal and tree spirits and carrying sacred herbs.
29. W.K.C. Guthrie, *The Greeks and Their Gods*. 1955, Beacon Press, Boston. p.31
30. Piggott, Stuart. *Prehistoric India* p.329.
31. This is covered in great detail in Baring & Cashford, *The Myth of the Goddess*. 1993, pp.155–7
32. Baring & Cashford, *The Myth of the Goddess*. 1993, p.157.
33. Baring & Cashford, 1993, p.159.
34. Jacobsen, *Treasure of Darkness*, 1976, p.77 (Reproduced with permission of The Licensor through PLSclear).
35. Goodison, Lucy. *Death Women and the Sun. Symbolism of Regeneration in Early Aegean Religion* 1989. University of London, Institute of Classical Studies, London.

Aries the Amazon[1]

You stand on a plain. It is dawn, the warm rays of the rising sun bathe the surrounding mountains crimson. The plain is barren desert, the earth parched and cracked. Far in the distance, emerging from the darkness, you see a small flame, you mount your horse and trot, then canter, then gallop towards the light.

You feel the wind rushing through your hair, your body tense and alert, exhilarated as you ride faster and faster, the ground speeds below your feet and sweat breaks out on your forehead, wets your back.

You arrive. Your horse stops and you slide down from the saddle, your legs trembling from the ride.

The flame burns brightly in an iron bowl, you pick it up, your hands are warmed by the heat.

You stand and look around to the four corners of the earth. Which way will you go? Where will you take this flame?

You understand it does not matter if you go East or West, North or South.

You carefully mount your horse holding the flame and chose, excited and impatient for the adventure ahead.

We start not with a goddess, but by the mythical, or not,[2] tribe of Amazons. Herodotus (*The Histories*: 4:110–117) relates his story of the Amazons.

"The Greeks after their defeat the Amazons, who the Skythians call man-killers, (for they call *oior*-man and *pata*-killer) at the battle of Thermodon, they took them captive on three ships and sailed away. At sea, the Amazons set upon the men, cutting them down. But they knew nothing about boats, nor did they possess any knowledge of sailing, rudders, sails, or rowing. But since they had killed the men, they were carried by the waves and the wind and landed at Lake Maietidis on Kremni, in the land of the free Skythians.

Disembarking they walked towards human habitation and they seized the first horses they came across. Mounted on horseback they plundered everything they could of the Skythians. The Skythians were baffled by these people, not recognising their language nor their clothes, they wondered where they came from. They supposed the women to be youthful men. They fought and examining some of the dead, the Skythians discovered they were women. (iv:111)

Debating among themselves, the Skythians decided to stop attacking them and instead send young men to approach then and find out how many there were of them and they should camp near to them and to mimic what the women were doing. And if they [the Amazons] pursued them, to run away rather than fight. This the young men did ... When the Amazons saw they meant them no harm, they left them in peace and allowed these youths to camp nearer to them each day. (112)

The Skythians noticed that at midday the women left the camp in ones and twos to relieve themselves, so they did this themselves. A solitary woman was approached by a young man, she did not push him away but saw his desire and met it.[3] Afterwards the woman gestured she would return to this spot with another woman and that the man should bring a friend also. This they did. When the other men found out about this, they won the affection of the other Amazons.[4] After this meeting, the two camps begun living together, each woman with her original partner. The men were unable to learn the language of the women, so the Amazons took on the men's tongue. (113)

In time the men suggested the women return with them to their tribe to become their wives. The women responded,

> "We would not be able to live among your women. Because we do not share the common customs of these women. For we use the bow and arrow and throw spears and we ride horses. We have never learnt women's work. These women of yours do none of the things we spoke of, they stay in the waggons all the time and do not hunt. We would not be able to live with those women, but if you wish to have us as partners and want to be fair, go to your parents, take your share of the goods and come and live with us elsewhere." (114)

The men were persuaded. When they returned the women said they should leave the area to avoid any trouble (they had been pillaging after all). They did this and settled three days march north from the lake Maietidis.

From that time to this, the Sauromatian women are in the habit of hunting on horseback with and without their menfolk and go where they please and dress the same as the men. And they speak like the Skythians as they learned the language from their men. No woman might marry until she has killed a man in war, should they be unable to do this they remain unmarried." (115–17)

Herodotus expresses the goddess nature of Aries. First, they are fighting, Aries loves a scrap, particularly if they are coming to help a neighbour or ally, (they see themselves as the avenging Hero). When captured, they do not take their fate passively but rise up as one and kill their captors (Aries has a can do attitude and will fight to the death for their freedom). Once free they allow the winds to take them to a new land, (Aries are brave, fearless, open to new experiences, trust their luck will get them out of difficult situations, and it often does, as victory favours the brave) where they carry on their pillaging lifestyle. Horses, although associated with Sagittarius, are the vehicle which carries them quickly about the countryside, and represent freedom, mobility, speed and manoeuvrability.

An Amazon's horse is something she alone is in control of, and of course they are exciting, which is crucial, boring is death to an Aries. They are open to new experiences and casting their eye on fit young men who do not want to harm them, would naturally lead them to be sexually curious, "What would sex be like with them?" Aries, although often loners, are collegiate, naturally they would want to share this experience, if not the partner in question. They like everyone to share in their latest enthusiasm, and as a cardinal fire sign they have a lot of sexual energy. Some Aries women might have been socialised out of their fiery libido, but in their natural state I think they would be gung-ho for some action.

When the men suggest they go back to the tribe and enter domesticity, the women are realistic, this is non-negotiable. There is no way they want the lives of those women, stuck inside all day. They want freedom, autonomy, and excitement, not boring 'women's work'. The core principle is freedom or agency. Aries need to go their own way. An Aries woman needs to live her life according to her own rules and will not easily accept the imposition of the rules of others. They cannot and will not change their ways to fit in. Aries won't compromise if it means losing their liberty. They would rather walk away from everything and everyone, than give up their self-determination.

Interestingly, the young men agree. They would either prefer the nomadic life or they really like the Amazons who, unlike their own women, have spirit, liberty and self-sufficiency, which makes them attractive, exciting, and perhaps they are liberating for the men too. This is classic Aries territory, 'My way or the highway.' If the men fitted in with them, they were happy, but they were not prepared to alter their customs to accommodate the men. Aries are often loners, not because they cannot co-operate with others but because they will not compromise their values to do so. They would rather be alone than lose their freedom.

The Amazons are fair, though. They suggest the men take their share of the tribal wealth and forward thinking, imagining that if they settled there, the locals might later decide they didn't want such 'disruptive' women on their doorstep, especially as they have 'stolen' all their young men. Tactically, they avoid conflict and move away.

This is also an Arian trait. Although they will fight, they do not look for trouble, and would rather have a quiet life than endless battles. Aries often ends up alone, no company being better than bad company. They have little patience for time wasters, fools and bores, if they consider someone is not worth the bother, they leave.

Their restlessness prevents them hanging around and hoping people or situations will change. They are more black and white; if it doesn't work for them then it is no use and they will be off after the next thing. For this reason, they can be seen to be cruel, they dismiss and cut ties and can belittle people who fail to make the grade. Being on the receiving end of an Arian tongue lashing is an experience few would forget.

Notice the Amazons do not suggest that the two groups of women reach an accommodation, although Aries can be fair, they will not negotiate their core principles. For them, the life of these women is untenable and completely uninteresting, and if the men won't go with them, they will leave them behind. The Arian need for excitement, challenge and freedom will top any offers of stability and routine, let alone social acceptability.

The men are persuaded. Aries, with her passion, energy and sharp mind is a formidable debater, her enthusiasm is infectious, and people get swept along with their passion.

The loyalty of fire is strong in Aries, they will risk their lives in defence of a loved one or a beloved cause. Equally though, if they are betrayed or let down, they will ruthlessly either strike back or cut the person from their life.

In another story, Herodotus describes the encounter of Amazon Queen Tomyris of the Massegetans with the Persian king Cyrus. Her army was tricked by Cyrus, who got them drunk at a feast and then slaughtered them (they were unused to alcohol) and took her son hostage. She sent a messenger to Cyrus saying,

> "Blood drinker never sated! Proud are you, Cyrus, of your day's work? Well you should not be. The fruit of the vine, which bloats you Persians to the point of frenzy … was the poison you deployed, in your underhand way, scorning the honest test of battle … I swear by the sun, the lord of the Massagetans, that, ravening blood-drinker though you may be, yet I will glut your taste for blood." (*Histories* 1:212)
>
> "Tomyris assembled all the forces she could muster and met with him in battle. The resulting clash, I believe, was the most terrible ever fought between two barbarian armies." (1:214)

The battle came down to hand to hand combat with daggers. Cyrus was killed. Tomyris found his corpse and filled a wineskin with human blood, cut off his head and pushed it into the wineskin saying,

> "I threatened then I would glut your thirst for blood. Now have your fill." (1:214)

Fig. 14 Amazon 500 BCE.

Note that the Greeks underestimated the Amazon fighters, which is why they were able to overpower them, in the same way Cyrus did. (Fig. 14 Amazon)

There is a tradition that the wearing of trousers came from warrior women. Queen Semiramis (ruled c810–805 BCE) rode her horse into battle disguised as a man wearing a long-sleeved tunic and trousers. This proved so comfortable that the Persians and the Medes adopted the style.[5] Amazons had tattoos, did not cut off one breast, but may have had a type of armour which aided fighting while riding. They had sex with partners of their choosing, for reproductive purposes or for pleasure. They drank fermented mare's milk and inhaled the smoke from the seeds of hemp plants (*Kannabis*, incidentally a Herb of Mars).[6]

> [They] "take the seeds of a cannabis plant, crawl in under the felt (possibly a yurt—they are usually made from felt) and throw the seeds onto hot stones where they smoulder and release smoke. The Scythians howl with pleasure from this vapour which no Greek steam bath could compare with." (Herodotus, 4:75)

They shot arrows long distances and wielded battle-axes, which appear similar in shape to the Kretan labrys and used swords and spears.[7]

The many images of Amazons in Greece might represent the Hellenic invasion of Attica and their resistance to these invaders (see Introduction). Males seeking dominance create a discourse of aberrant, savage, barbarian and monstrous women (representing the male terror of loss of power and the need to control) and in the case of their women, to brainwash them into obedience. Amazons also represent of the 'other', namely women, barbarians, animals and the natural world, which the 'rational' Greeks needed to tame and control.[8]

Aries is one of the two signs that lives in the future (Aquarius is the other one) they are often way ahead and may or may not wait for other people to catch up with them. Often, when people have caught up, Aries has already moved on. They live in the moment; the past is of no use to them. Aries travel at high speed and can be careless and impatient, leaving a trail of wreckage behind them.

Aries is the seed but not the gardener, the spark but not the hearth, the idea but not the plan. In Western culture, Aries woman is often unpalatable as they reject domesticity, and the conventional straitjacket women are forced into. They are outspoken, fearless, and dismissive. Within patriarchy, this does not go down well.

For all the bluster, Fire signs can be extinguished. Trap an Aries and you will find a depressed woman, a bitter woman, who is passive aggressive and may self-harm in the myriad of ways available to us; drink, drugs for the excitement, overwork and risk, in order to feel alive, destruction for its own sake. If all that energy and willpower are directed towards the negative, they can be cruel, lashing out and wounding, like a trapped animal.

The idea of the heroic, the strong, the noble warrior is attractive to an Aries, they need to have their armour buffed up, by being courageous, taking risks. They can be found on the front line, and have sympathy for the underdog, the marginalised and will speak truth to power. Unafraid of authority, they will happily take on the corrupt and can be accused of tilting at windmills when everyone else wants a bit of peace and quiet. Like Scorpio they have a bad reputation, (both these signs are ruled by Mars) because the idea of fighting women is anathema to our culture.

Excellent in an emergency, they find daily routines stultifying. Aries always needs a challenge, something new and shiny to reach for. Boredom is their enemy, as are details, planning, caution and restraint, and many of the 'grown up' qualities. They can be both childlike and childish. They find delayed gratification baffling, there is no sense in waiting if it can be grabbed right now and if it can't, why bother? They get on well with children and young people whose energy and enthusiasm they admire.

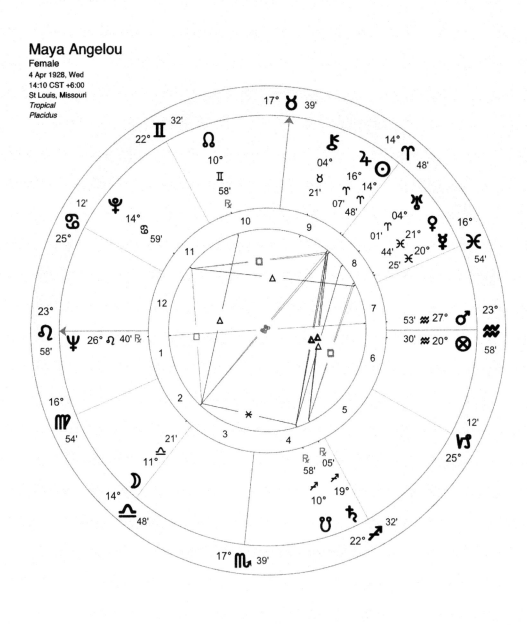

Maya Angelou
Female
4 Apr 1928, Wed
14:10 CST +6:00
St Louis, Missouri
Tropical
Placidus

Maya Angelou: Activist/writer, breaking through barriers
4 April 1928. (14:10) St Louis MI

"I've learned that people will forget what you said, people will forget what you did, but people will never forget how you made them feel."[9]

Maya Angelou was an American poet, writer and civil rights activist. She published seven autobiographies, three books of essays, several books of poetry.

Maya Angelou has a powerful, hopeful, Sun, Jupiter conjunction in Aries opposite a fine, intellectual Moon in Libra. Her warm Leo Ascendant with Neptune has perhaps allowed her to make peace with her challenging childhood through her writing and activism. Most of all, she shows her Aries courage and hope (Jupiter),

"Courage is the most important of all the virtues, because without courage you can't practice any other virtue consistently. You can practice any virtue erratically, but nothing consistently without courage."[10]

Her mutism followed the murder, by family, of the man who raped her at age six. She understood then the power of the word, that telling had killed the man, that her words were lethal. During this period of silence Angelou developed her extraordinary memory, her love for books and literature, and her ability to listen and observe the world around her.[11]

"I thought, my voice killed him; I killed that man, because I told his name. And then I thought I would never speak again, because my voice would kill anyone."[12]

In 1960 Maya met Martin Luther King and became an activist for civil rights in the US and begun her pro-Castro and Anti-Apartheid work. She lived in Ghana for five years, working as a journalist, broadcaster and actor. She met Malcom X in Ghana and returned to the USA in 1965 to help him build a civil rights organisation.

"Develop enough courage so that you can stand up for yourself and then stand up for somebody else."[13]

When Malcom X was assassinated, Maya was devastated. She was asked by MLK in 1968 to organise a march but, for various reasons, it was delayed. MLK was murdered shortly afterwards, on her birthday. For many years she did not celebrate the day but sent flowers to Corretta King, his widow.

"All my work, my life, everything I do is about survival, not just bare, awful, plodding survival, but survival with grace and faith."[14]

9

Devastated, she was encouraged by friend James Baldwin to write a ten part documentary series, *Blacks, Blues, Black* for PBS (despite having had no experience writing for TV). In the same year, at a dinner party, she was challenged by Random House editor, Robert Loomis, to write her autobiography. *I Know Why The Caged Bird Sings* was published in 1969 and brought her worldwide fame.

> "Nothing so frightens me as writing, but nothing so satisfies me. It's like a swimmer in the [English] Channel: you face the stingrays and waves and cold and grease, and finally you reach the other shore, and you put your foot on the ground—Aaaahhhh!"[15]

The ruler of her seventh house of friends and colleagues is Uranus in Aries in the eighth, showing their radicality and sadly also their violent death. Despite this, her gentle, kind, spiritual Venus and Mercury in Pisces allowed her to absorb the heartbreak and carry on.

Her ground-breaking poem *And Still I Rise* (1978) encapsulates that Aries fighting spirit where she notes her attackers but dismisses them as inconsequential and remains undefeated in the light of her inexhaustible joie de vivre:

> You may shoot me with your words,
> You may cut me with your eyes,
> You may kill me with your hatefulness,
> But still, like air, I'll rise.[16]

Maya uses the language of the sage warrior, Sun/Jupiter/Aries, who understands that life's trajectory is not without dark times, but that keeping on is the only way.

> "We may encounter many defeats, but we must not be defeated."[17]

Other activists:
Valerie Solanas, (see Mars, the Furies). Wangari Maathai 1 April 1940 (no time) Nyeri, Kenya. (Sun conjunct Jupiter in Aries).
Gloria Steinem, 25 March 1934. (22:00) Toledo, OH. (Sun conjunct Mars in Aries).
Vivienne Westwood, 8 April 1941. (01:00) Glossop, UK. (Sun conjunct Venus in Aries).
Other creatives:
Celine Dion 30 March 1968. (12:15) Quebec, Canada. (Sun, Midheaven, Saturn, North Node and Moon in Aries).
Lady Gaga 28 March 1986 (09:53) New York, (Sun, Venus in Aries).

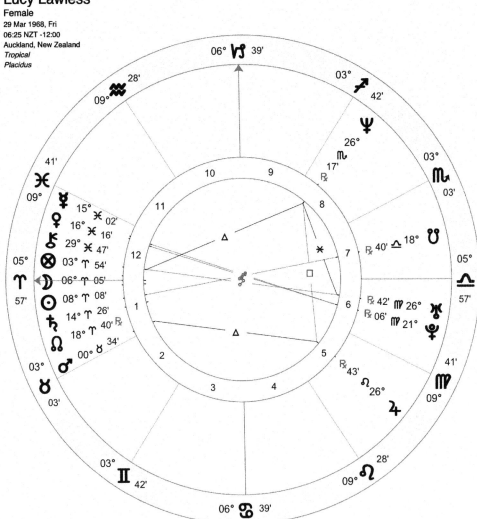

Lucy Lawless

Female
29 Mar 1968, Fri
06:25 NZT -12:00
Auckland, New Zealand
Tropical
Placidus

Lucy Lawless: Playing the part, Xena warrior princess
29 March 1968. (06:25) Auckland NZ

You could not make this up! Lucy Lawless (what a name) played the role of Xena Warrior Princess for six years. In the series, she was initiated into the Amazons and wore body sculpting armour. In the show Xena, also known as the Destroyer of Nations, was a legendary figure in ancient Greece and throughout the Known World. As a warlord, she was the leader of one of the world's most ruthless and destructive armies.

You can see from her astrology how this part was made for her; Sun, Moon and Ascendant in Aries, she is the epitome of a woman warrior. Of course, this was TV and the plotlines were a mishmash of Greek and Roman and made up myths but, as an archetype, Xena gave girls in the nineties a role model for powerful female warriors, who won (unlike the Greek myths, where they were always defeated by the men!)

In May 2009 Lucy became a 'climate ambassador' for Greenpeace. In February 2012 Lucy and six other activists boarded an oil drilling ship at Port Taranaki, New Zealand and climbed a drilling tower on the vessel *Noble Discoverer*, which was bound for the Arctic, to protest against oil exploration there. She spent four days on top of the 174-foot (53-meter) tower, camping and blogging about her experiences, to prevent the boat leaving port. Afterwards Lucy said, "For the first time in my life, I put my body and reputation on the line to stand up for my beliefs and do the right thing … I hope I've encouraged other people to do the same."[18]

(see Transits for details.)

When a new dwarf planet was discovered by Michael E. Brown he nicknamed it Xena rather than the official name of 2003UB313. There was a poll in the New Scientist to name this new planet, and Xena came fourth. It was eventually called Eris (discord). Lucy rang Brown in December 2005 and thanked him for his "senseless act of beauty" saying, she "Never dared hope the name would stick."[19]

Notes

1. Graves, (2011 p.355) writes that Amazon is believed to be an Armenian word meaning 'moon women'. The entymology of the non-Greek word Amazon is unknown. There are several theoriesincluding the Circassian *a-mez-a-ne* meaning forest or Moon Mother, to the ancient Iranian *ha-mazon* or warrior (Mayor, 85–88, 234–46).

2. Endless debate about their existence, see: https://www.sacred-texts.com/wmn/ama/ama03.htm Deipenbroek, Martine. (https://www.academia.edu/20830667/SEARCH-ING_FOR_AMAZONS Ustinova, Yulia. Amazons East and West. 2019. https://www.academia.edu/37537856/Amazons_East_and_West_A_Real_Life_Experiment_in_Social_Cognition. Mayor, Adreinne. 2014. *Amazons: Lives and Legends of Warrior Women across the Ancient World*. Princeton University Press, Princeton & Oxford. Discovery of a warrior woman's grave, complete with bows and arrows: Williams, Doug. July, 1, 2020. https://www.outdoorrevival.com/news/amazon-warrior.html.

3. 113: here it might be useful to note other translations, which imply the Amazons who were skilful, seasoned warriors, 'let him have his way with her' (Holland: 2013. p.303) and 'a young man laid hold of one of them, and the woman did not resist but let him do his will' (Goodley, A.D. 1920: iv:113:1). Passively, asexually, just like the ideal Victorian women on whom I suppose this translation was based. Ridiculous, demeaning, patronising, and misogynist, as if women have no desire of their own. It is important (if possible) to do your own translations, because men writing about women have so much patriarchal baggage, their work should be scrutinised.

4. My translation (iv:113), of εκτιλωσαντο 3 pl aorist from κτιλοω, 'won the affection of' [Liddell, Scott 1944:396] compare this with Holland, p.303 'broke in' emphasises the need to check translations.

5. Mayor, Adrienne. *Amazons in the Iranian World* Encyclopaedia Iranica, online edition, 2017. http://www.iranicaonline.org/articles/amazons-ii accessed 25.8.2020.

6. See Brooke, Elisabeth. 2019. *Traditional Western Herbal Medicine.* Aeon Books, London. p.86.

7. Mayor, Adrienne. 2014. *The Amazons: Lives and legends of Warrior Women across the Ancient World.* Princetown University Press. Princetown NJ. p.145–51, 170–84, 191–208, 209–33.

8. Ustinova, Yulia. *Amazons East and West A Real Life Experiment in Social Cognition* 2019. *https://www.academia.edu/37537856/Amazons_East_and_West_A_Real_Life_Experiment_in_Social_Cognition* Access 24.8.2020.

9. https://wisdomquotes.com/maya-angelou-quotes/ accessed 26.8.2020.

10. https://wisdomquotes.com/maya-angelou-quotes/ accessed 23.8.2020.

11. Gillespie, Marcia Ann, Rosa Johnson Butler, and Richard A. Long. (2008). *Maya Angelou: A Glorious Celebration.* New York: Random House, p.22.

12. "Maya Angelou I Know Why the Caged Bird Sings". World Book Club. BBC World Service. *October 2005.*

13. https://wisdomquotes.com/maya-angelou-quotes/ accessed 26.8.2020.

14. McPherson, Dolly A. (1990). *Order Out of Chaos: The Autobiographical Works of Maya Angelou. New York: Peter Lang Publishing.* pp.10–11.

15. Toppman, Lawrence (1989). "Maya Angelou: The Serene Spirit of a Survivor", in *Conversations with Maya Angelou,* Jeffrey M. Elliot, ed. Jackson, Mississippi: University Press. p.145.

16. Maya Angelou discusses the poem, https://www.youtube.com/watch?v=JqOqo50LSZ0.

17. https://wisdomquotes.com/maya-angelou-quotes/ accessed 26.8.2020.

18. Perry, Nick. Associated News, Wellington New Zealand. 4.6.2012. http://abcnews.go.com/Entertainment/wireStory/actress-lucy-lawless-pleads-guilty-trespass-16562451 accessed 19.4.2021.

19. https://skyandtelescope.org/astronomy-news/all-hail-eris-and-dysnomia/ accessed 19.4.2021.

Taurus: Aphrodite Kore

You are in a meadow. It is a warm, Spring day. All around, nature is waking from winter's deep sleep. You feel your bare feet on the cool, moist, earth. You wriggle your toes and smell the blossom as it blows in the breeze. You look around and see butterflies emerging into the sunlight, drying their wings in the warmth, rabbits frolicking in the long grass, birds singing out to one another from the bright green budding trees.

You feel your body, strong and soft and solid, your feet firm on the damp ground. You breathe in the beauty, colours, scents and sensations.

Far away you hear music and begin to step out in dance. You tread the earth and dance slowly, catching the rhythm, holding your arms high above your head. Your body is clothed in beautiful fabric, it slides on your skin as you move, soft and silky.

You feel delicious, sensual and physically alive.

Your sisters come, you hold hands and dance around and through the trees, flowers in your hair.

You are one with the song, with the plants and animals and insects, the sunlight, the soft grass and your companions. In this moment there is nothing else but your body, your voice and the tender embrace of Mother Nature.

The earthy Aphrodite is Taurus. Known as Aphrodite Pandemos, (πανδημος-for all the people). In early versions, Demeter and Kore/Persephone are fatherless, although it has been argued that the background of her myth was originally matriarchal. (Willetts, 1962, 150) Because Aphrodite who came from the east as Ishtar and Astarte was not Hellenised, she was treated with little respect by the Hellenes, and the Great Goddess is reduced to a sexy thing with a cruel humour and a jealous, libidinous nature.

Homer (*Iliad* 5.370–417) writes that Aphrodite was born from a union with Zeus and Dione.[1] Dione was the pre-Hellenic goddess whose priestesses kept her shrine at Dodona, where the cooing of doves or the rustling of oak leaves, or the clanking of bronze vessels hung from tree branches were used for divination (Graves, 2001:178.) Like other shrines, Dodona was seized by Zeus who absorbed her cult by 'marrying' Dione and becoming the 'father' of Aphrodite.

Dione was a Titan goddess, the daughter of Oceanus and Tethys, which may explain Aphrodite's birth in the sea. Aphrodite was born naked from the foam of the sea and came to land riding on a scallop shell. She first stepped ashore on the island of Cythera,[2] but eventually went to Paphos,[3] Cyprus which became the centre of her cult. Grass and flowers sprang from the soil wherever she trod.

> "Aphrodite smiled as she went to Kyprus, to the island of Paphos, where she had a fragrant altar and sanctuary. The Graces bathed her there and massaged her with the sacred unguents which shimmer upon the immortals, and they dressed her in sumptuous robes. She was a marvel to behold." (Homer, *Odyssey*, 8, 360–365)

Aphrodite takes to the air in a golden chariot drawn by doves and sparrows. The dove was commonly associated with Minoan goddesses. Aphrodite had a magic girdle which could make anyone fall in love with her. According to the patriar- chal myth, she refused to lend it to anyone because she wanted all the power to herself, but perhaps she only gave it to those who would not abuse the power of love. A lover of many, Aphrodite was able to renew herself by bathing in the sea at Paphos.[4]

So, Aphrodite Pandemos or Kore (the maiden) is connected with nature and the sea. She loves beauty and adornment. She is self-sufficient and self-nurturing. Aphrodite was also Goddess of the Wild Things.

> "She came to Ida, mountain of the many springs, the mother of all wild beasts and she walked straight to her mountain home and fierce grey wolves clustered around her and lions, and bears, nimble leopards ravenous for deer came. And her heart was delighted when she saw them and she cast longing in their hearts and spirits and at once, all in pairs, they lay down with one another in the shady hollows."
> (5:68–74) *Homeric Hymn to Aphrodite*[5]

Aphrodite Pandemos is the goddess of fertility and lovemaking. She is also Spring, renewal, nature, prophecy, song and dance. Small gold signet rings found in Knos- sos show women and goddesses worshipping on mountainsides, dancing with trees, ecstatically invoking the goddess, venerating her with flowers and serpents and dressed or transformed into bee-women.[6] (Fig. 15)

Fig. 15 Tree dancing signet ring, Mycenaean, Tholos 1450 BCE.

"Wreathe your shiny hair with garlands, Dika,
Weave stems of anise with your soft hands.
The Graces love to see you garlanded with flowers,
But they will turn away from an unadorned head."

Sappho 81[7]

Kore is the maiden who, dancing in the fields picking wildflowers is kidnapped by Hades. In Krete *Antheia* (the flower goddess) perhaps related to Aphrodite, was worshipped at Knossos. She was associated with apples, myrtle, poppy, rose and watermint. Sappho invokes Aphrodite,

"… down from the mountain-top …
Come now from Krete, I invoke you.
Come to your sacred temple,
your grove of apple trees,
and your altars fragrant with incense."

Sappho, 2.[8]

Aphrodite makes the morning dew.[9] Venus is the morning and evening star. At sunset, the sky is red, green and yellow, like a fruit laden apple tree and the Sun, cut by the horizon like a crimson half apple. When the sun has gone Hesperus, the star sacred to Aphrodite, appears.

"Hesperus, you are
The most beautiful of stars.
What bright dawn scattered
You bring back,
The lamb, the kid
And the child to her mother."

Sappho (104i)

The apple was the gift given by Aphrodite's priestesses to the Sun King to distract him before his death. Cut in two crosswise the core of the apple reveals the pentagram or five-pointed star, Aphrodite's symbol. (Graves, 2011:129–30)

Central to Aphrodite's cult was dance.[10] In the *Iliad* (18:590–606) Homer describes the public dances in Knossos.

"... On the one, [dance floor] Daedalus made for Ariadne of the beautiful hair. There, young men and desirable maidens, dance with one another, holding hands by the wrist, the girls wearing delicate, fine linen and the boys, gleaming with a little [olive] oil, in well spun tunics. The maidens wear beautiful headdresses and the boys' golden sacrificial knives hang from their silver belts. They skip around with their skilful feet, effortlessly ... while at other times they dance in rows opposite one another. While a great crowd stands around the delightful dance, charmed. Then a pair of acrobats take the lead, spinning around in the middle of the dance."[11]

Willets, (1962,123) suggests this passage is a reference to the Labyrinth and the dance is a sacred one, twisting and turning perhaps on a tiled floor with a labyrinthian design. Dance was integral to worship of the goddess on Krete, there are innumerable representations of women, and only women, dancing with their arms raised high or their legs bent and their hair flying behind them. One form of dance, the *geranos* was called the crane dance, but it has been suggested that it is a mistranslation, as it is also the word for 'to wind' as the dancers formed two rows winding backwards and forwards, sometimes changing direction as if in a maze. Perhaps the dance was in honour of the serpent as it mimicked its movement. The dance was performed by both men and women who stepped out in interweaving lines holding ropes or cords and branches. The *geranos* was performed during the *Hekatombaion*, a festival in July, at night, in torchlight. Night rituals honour the chthonic (underworld) goddesses, snakes are considered creatures of the Underworld.[12]

Sappho writes, extract 50.[13]

"Thus sometimes, the Kretan women, tender footed, dance in measure round the fair altar, crushing the fine bloom of the grass."

Ariadne gave Theseus Aphrodite's statue when he fled Krete. Landing on Delos, Theseus sacrificed to the Goddess Aphrodite and led the Crane or winding dance with the young men in front of a horned altar (the horns of consecration). According to Homer the dance was a *himerois* (ἵμερος) a dance of longing for a person, yearning and desire, a love dance. The songs they sang during these dances, were invocations to Aphrodite.

In the patriarchal myth, Kore is tricked by beauty and captured by the dark forces of the Underworld, her 'marriage' to Hades is brutal. (see Scorpio, Persephone for what happens next.)

> "Lovely haired Demeter, August Goddess. I begin to sing of her and her daughter with the slim ankles ... dancing and singing with the nymphs of Oceanus in flowing robes she was picking blossoms, red roses and meadow saffron and beautiful, sweet violets in the soft, grassy meadow and purple iris and both hyacinth and narcissus. Gaia decided to deceive this blushing maiden, granting the wishes of Zeus to please the All-Receiver Hades. An extraordinary iridescent flower, a shimmering blossom, an object of wonder, seen by all the immortal gods and humankind. And from this root a hundred fragrant flower heads had blossomed, an aroma of sweetness, that all the wide upper air above the whole earth and the salt waves of the sea delighted in. Kore was bedazzled and, stretching out with both her hands she picked the beautiful flower, and the wide earth broke open along the Nisian Plain."
> The *Homeric Hymn to Demeter* (2:1–19)[14]

Kore, as the maiden, is shown as a nature goddess, beguiled by beautiful flowers, singing and dancing in a luscious meadow with the Oceanids, children of the Titans Oceanus and Tethys. Like her mother Dione they personify rivers and streams. Kore evokes the deep nature of Taurus, dance, beauty, song, female companionship, flowers and the natural world.

Many of the goddess/priestess figures engraved in the gold signet rings from Krete are shown dancing, holding aloft flowers, particularly poppies and crocuses. In Akrotiri,[15] there are recovered wall paintings showing women wearing brightly coloured skirts, bare breasted, on mountaintops bringing in the saffron harvest. (Fig. 16). It can be supposed that saffron was both a culinary/medicinal herb. Saffron was sacred to the goddess Astarte, a Phoenician goddess resembling Aphrodite. Taurus loves to dance, whether it is swaying alone in the kitchen or slow dancing with a lover. Ecstatic dance is a way to connect with the Earth, through our feet, and Spirit by counter-intuitively letting go of our bodies. Dance increases our Vital Spirit—in short it makes us happy.

Most Taureans have beautiful voices, soft, melodious, and some, like Kore's reach up to the highest mountain peaks and the depths of the ocean.

> "And from the mountain peaks and the depths of the ocean rang out with the sound of her immortal voice and her august mother heard her." *Homeric Hymn to Demeter*: 38–9

Being soft voiced also makes Taurus a natural diplomat, they know how to speak gently to power and sweetly get their own way. Song and chanting of course, is another form of ecstasy and calling out to Spirit is as old as the hills.

Fig. 16 Saffron harvest Akrotiri wall painting, Thera 1700 BCE.

Hades realises he can trick Kore with beauty; why Gaia (her grandmother) agreed to produce this one hundred-headed flower to tempt Kore is unclear, but tempted she is. For the love of beauty, the pursuit of beauty, the owning of beauty can make people reckless, greedy and avaricious. Think of the miserly billionaire who hoards precious artworks. Fashion is an expression of beauty and no surprise that many Taureans, like Donatella Versace, work in the industry. Taurus is interested in the sensuality of fabric and her eye gladdens at the sight of colour. Negatively, a love of fashion and beauty can fuel her already acquisitive nature and bring consumer madness or the empty accumulation of material goodies for their own sake.

The love of beauty together with practical skills and routine, makes Taurus a great artist. Inspiration is never enough; artists must have a practice, the daily grind, which as an earth sign, Taurus is great at just getting on with it, for example, Bridget Riley, Lee Miller, Rachel Whiteread.

Taurus then, embodies spring, nature, fertility, the maiden, dance, beauty. The earthy Aphrodite is just that, connected to the earth, the abundance of Gaia, blossom, birds and animals. She embodies all the beauty and celebration of the physical world. Her voice and music is soft, powerful and deep, she loves beauty and celebrates all nature's bounty. Like nature she moves in her own time at her own rhythm. There is a dignity and both a softness and a strength, like the sacred cow Io, deep, limpid eyes, a powerful presence and persistent like nature, and stubborn like a bull.

This Aphrodite will show her love through sensuality, the physical body and pleasures of the senses like food, nature, alcohol and care. All earth signs have a leaning towards service, and as the first, Taurus is found cooking, gardening, sewing, making medicines and cosmetics. She will be like nature, frugal, caring for the earth's precious resources by recycling, buying products which are harmless and caring for the environment and animals.

The flip side is a lack of trust in the earth's bounty; meanness and hoarding are shadow sides of this Aphrodite. This merges into her emotional life; if there is lack of trust there can be jealousy, clinging behaviour or extremes such as stalking or shadowing, or staying in situations long beyond necessary.

Like nature, this Aphrodite likes routine and ritual and easily falls into both, this can be positive and negative. Good rituals and routines like heathy eating, exercise and meditation, self-care, and bad ones like over-eating, laziness and greediness.

Her practicality means she becomes an excellent businesswoman, as she digs deep for more ways to express her talents and get paid for them. Usually physically strong, Taurus loves to work hard and see their gardens grow. Stopping is an issue for all earth signs,[16] once in motion, they can be an unstoppable force, long beyond what is healthy for their bodies, which are stronger than those of the other elements. But because of this inflexibility, when they are exhausted, they can shatter.

Ella Fitzgerald

Female
25 Apr 1917, Wed
12:30 EST +5:00
Newport News, Virginia
Tropical
Placidus

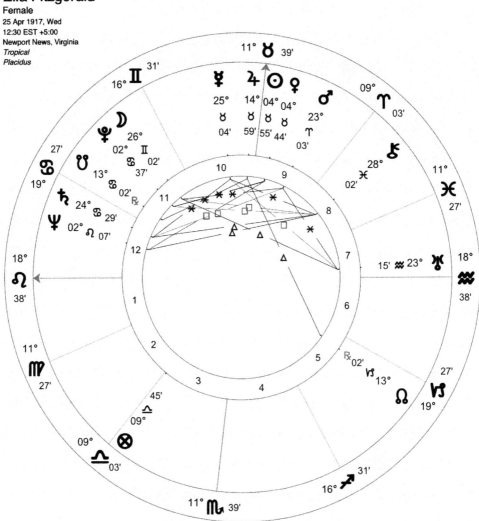

Ella Fitzgerald: Singer, the divine voice
25 April 1917. (12:30) Newport News, VA.

"I guess what everyone wants more than anything else is to be loved. And to know that you loved me for my singing is too much for me. Forgive me if I don't have all the words. Maybe I can sing it and you'll understand."[17]

Ella was an American jazz vocalist, often called 'The Queen of Jazz'. Ella had a tough childhood and may have spent some time in care and living on the streets in Harlem. She loved to dance and entered a talent competition on 21 November 1934 at the Apollo Theatre in New York when she was seventeen. Originally, she planned to dance, but she saw a previous dancing act and felt intimidated so she sang instead. She won first prize, but the Apollo did not offer her a week's residency as promised, because of her impoverished appearance.

"Just don't give up trying to do what you really want to do. Where there is love and inspiration, I don't think you can go wrong."[18]

In January 1935 she was hired by Chick Webb to do a gig at Harvard; she was a hit with the audience, and her musical career had begun.

After the decline of the Big Bands, Ella moved on to bebop, singing with Dizzy Gillespie and developing her scat style by imitating the horn section,

"I stole everything I ever heard, but mostly I stole from the horns."[19]

Ella had a vocal range spanning three octaves (D♭3 to D♭6) and was praised for her purity of tone, impeccable diction, phrasing and intonation. Her 1945 scat recording of *Flying Home* was described by *The New York Times* as,

"One of the most influential vocal jazz records of the decade … Where other singers, most notably Louis Armstrong, had tried similar improvisation, no one before Miss Fitzgerald employed the technique with such dazzling inventiveness."[20]

Like many Taureans, Ella was incredibly hardworking and serious about her work., and for many years spent forty to forty-five weeks a year on tour. Over the course of her sixty year recording career, she made over seventy albums, sold forty million copies, and won fourteen Grammy Awards.

"She brings out the best in everybody, making everyone work that much harder to keep up with her." Andy Williams[21]

Ella moved on from bebop to recording the *Cole Porter Songbook* which she referred to as the turning point in her life.[22] It was the first time a songwriter had been the focus of one album, she went on to record seven other *Song Book* sets between 1956 to 1964 each one focussed on particular composers and lyricists such as Gershwin, Irving Berlin and Duke Ellington, who played on the recording.

> "She is amazingly creative, bringing so much more to a song than just a singer. She is a first-class musician and the most gracious person in the world." Marty Paich.[23]

In her personal life she was quiet and shy, with a small group of long standing friends, as you would expect with a modest Taurean Sun. Her fine Leo Ascendant came to the fore when she stepped out on stage and she became the Queen of Jazz.

> "I know I'm no glamour girl, and it's not easy for me to get up in front of a crowd of people. It used to bother me a lot, but now I've got it figured out that God gave me this talent to use, so I just stand there and sing."[24]

Ella married perhaps twice or maybe three times,

> "I've had some wonderful love affairs and some that didn't work out."[25]

Ella has the sweet-voiced Venus in Taurus conjunct her Sun, as well as the lucky, expansive Jupiter in Taurus conjunct her MC which shows a huge career, one that would bring her a great deal of wealth. Music was her identity and her life's work, but also her joy.

> "Music comes out of her. When she walks down the street, she leaves notes." Jimmy Rowles.[26]

Other musicians:
Adele 5 May1988, (08:19) London (Sun conjunct Jupiter in Taurus).
Barbara Streisand, 24 April 1942. (05:08) Brooklyn, NY. (Sun, Mercury, Saturn, Uranus in Taurus).

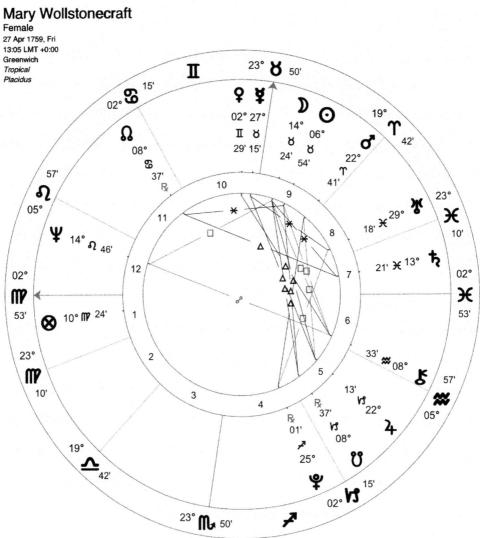

Mary Wollstonecraft

Female
27 Apr 1759, Fri
13:05 LMT +0:00
Greenwich
Tropical
Placidus

Mary Wollstonecraft: feminist writer
27 April 1759. (13:05) London

Mary was a writer, traveller and radical feminist pre-Feminism. As befits a Sun, Moon, Mercury and Midheaven in Taurus, she devoted her life to the struggle for women's equality, love and nature. She learnt early how precarious life could be if the 'head of the household' was feckless. Her father was a violent drunkard who squandered the family's wealth and was physically violent towards Mary's mother.

Mary left home to become self-supporting, first as a lady's companion for two women but could not abide either of them, then she started a school with a friend in Newington Green, a radical area of London. When it failed, Mary was encouraged to write for a living by the publisher, Johnson.

Her Sun, Moon, Mercury and Midheaven in Taurus, show her work ethic and need to be financially stable, and Mercury conjunct the MC shows a career in writing, with her words reaching a wide audience, lasting through time, also providing her with an income. Her dynamic, ground-breaking Mars in Aries gives her the courage to break new ground, while her Venus in Gemini suggests her love is expressed through words.

Mary wrote novels critical of patriarchal marriage and its effects on women: In *Mary: A Fiction* (1788) a woman is forced into a loveless marriage from economic necessity. *Maria: or The Wrongs of Woman* (1798 published posthumously) was considered her most radical feminist work; a woman is imprisoned in an insane asylum by her husband.

Mary wrote reviews and translated French and German books. She moved in radical circles, meeting Thomas Paine, author of *Rights of Man* (1791) and Radical Philosopher, William Godwin. Mary wrote the political pamphlet, *A Vindication of the Rights of Men* in later that year in response to Edmund Burke's critical *Reflections on the Revolution in France* (1790). It was a great success and the second edition published on 18 December named Mary as the author.

In her most famous book, *A Vindication of the Rights of Women* (1792), Mary argued that men did not treat women as human beings, but as pets or lapdogs, and that girls should receive a rational education. She believed this would benefit everyone; educated girls become rational mothers and would therefore raise the standard of the whole community.

Love was important to Mary, but her romantic life was complicated. She fell in love with the married artist Fuseli and suggested that they should live in a *ménage à trois* (very Venus in Gemini). His wife was appalled and Fuseli broke off the liaison.

Wounded, Mary travelled to Paris in December 1792, living there through the violent French Revolution. She witnessed dramatic events, "… Death and misery, in every shape of terrour, … the most extraordinary event that has ever been recorded."[27]

Unable to leave Paris, Mary's life was in danger. (In 1793 France and England were at war). she fell in love with an American chancer, Imlay, who registered her as his wife in the American embassy. This gave her some protection; the French and Americans were allies. Mary became pregnant during a freezing winter; food supplies were scarce in Paris and people were starving, so they retreated to Le Havre where Mary gave birth to her first child, Fanny, in 1794.

During this pregnancy, Mary wrote *An Historical and Moral View of the Origin and Progress of the French Revolution*, (published in December 1794). Imlay was often absent so Mary wrote to support herself yet, despite his lack of financial support, she was determined to make the relationship work. She returned to London in April 1795, tried to reconcile with Imlay, he refused and Mary attempted suicide by poisoning; Imlay saved her.

In a final attempt to win Imlay back, Mary, Fanny and a maid travelled to Sweden, Norway and Denmark on business for him. She spent three months exploring these countries and wrote the influential and, what is considered her best, book. *Letters Written in Sweden, Norway, and Denmark*, (1796) which cover topics from sociological reflections on Scandinavia and its peoples, to philosophical questions regarding identity, and political topics such as prison reform, land rights, and divorce laws.

In *Letters* Mary attacked Burke for placing higher value on the sublime (masculinity, terror, awe and strength) over the beautiful (femininity, passivity, delicacy, and weakness) in his *A Philosophical Enquiry into the Origin of Our Ideas of the Sublime and Beautiful (1757)*. Instead, Mary gives the sublime to sterility and the beautiful to fertility. For her, the beautiful is connected to mothers. Mary believed women were the beautiful, being both virtuous and useful. Using nature as a metaphor, Mary describes a spiritual experience on encountering a waterfall,

> "The impetuous dashing of the rebounding torrent from the dark cavities which mocked the exploring eye, produced an equal activity in my mind: my thoughts darted from earth to heaven, and I asked myself why I was chained to life and its misery? Still, the tumultuous emotions this sublime object excited were pleasurable; and, viewing it, my soul rose, with renewed dignity, above its cares—grasping at immortality."[28]

The book was such a success that Mary was able to pay off her debts. Realising her relationship with Imlay was over, she again attempted suicide, jumping into the River Thames, but was rescued by a passer-by.

When she recovered, Mary reconnected with her old radical circle, including William Godwin. Theirs was a happy, if short-lived, relationship; they lived in adjacent buildings so each could retain their independence and wrote letters to each other. It seems Mary had found her soul mate and, when Mary became pregnant again, they married. This caused public censure, revealing that she had not previously been married, although she had referred to herself as Mrs Imlay. Sadly, Mary died eleven days after giving birth to Mary (later Shelley) on 30.8.1797 (see Virgo). Godwin wrote a posthumous biography, incautiously detailing her love affairs. This caused public outrage and destroyed Mary's legacy. Feminists rediscovered her work in the twentieth century and her reputation was restored.

Other activists:
Florence Nightingale 12 May 1820. (14:00) Florence, Italy. (Sun and Moon in Taurus).
Nannie Helen Burroughs: feminist-activist, businesswoman 2 May 1879. (No time) Charlottesville Va. (Sun, Neptune and Pluto in Taurus).

Notes

1. Dione Διωνη was a Titan (pre-Olympic goddess) Hesiod, Theogony: 353. Dione may have once been an important goddess, especially as her name is the female form of Zeus, Δια. Hesiod names her at the beginning of his *Theogony* (17) with other important deities. The *Homeric Hymn to Apollo* (93) names her as 'one of the principal goddesses' present at the birth of Apollo. She was worshipped at Dodona in Epeirus, reputedly the oldest Greek oracle and at Naia where she had a cult along with Zeus Naios. Or she was daughter of either Oceanus or Tethys the sea nymph-so she represents earth and water. March, Jenny. 2002. *Dictionary of Classical Mythology*, Cassell, London. p.153.
    Euripides writes in *Helen* 1098:
    'Kypris, [Aphrodite] daughter of Dione, do not destroy me utterly. You have maltreated me enough before now, [1100] handing over my name, though not my body, to barbarians. Let me die, if you want to kill me, in my native land. Why are you so insatiable for mischief, practising arts of love, deceits, and treacherous schemes, and magic spells that bring bloodshed on families? [1105] If you were only moderate, in other ways you are by nature the sweetest of gods for men; I don't deny it.
    Homer, Iliad 5.370 'and now bright Aphrodite fell at the knees of her mother, Dione, Lattimore, Richmond. 2011. *The Iliad*. University of Chicago Press, Chicago.
2. Cythera was the most important centre for Cretan trade with the Peloponnese, it may be speculated her worship entered Greece via trading routes. The Cretan goddess is shown blowing a triton-shell, seashells decorated the floor of her palace sanctuary at Knossus. Graves, 2001, p.50.
3. Graves, 2001, p.49 says she is the same wide-ruling (pandemos) goddess who rose from Chaos and danced on the sea and was worshipped in Syria and Palestine as Ishtar or Ashtaroth.
4. Graves, (1955) p.50.
5. http://www.perseus.tufts.edu/hopper/text?doc=Perseus%3Atext%3A1999.01.0137%3Ahymn%3D5 accessed 16.7.2020.
6. See Max Dashu, https://www.suppressedhistories.net/Gallery/crete/crete.html Accessed 10-6-2020.
7. Quoted by Athenaeus *The Learned Banquet*. (2nd C CE).
8. Discovered as an inscription on a 3rd c BCE potsherd. Lombardo, Stanley. (trans.) 2016. *Sappho: complete poems and fragments*. Hackett, Indianapolis/Cambridge. p.4.
9. Willetts, R.F. 1962. *Cretan Cults and Festivals*. Routledge and Kean Paul, London. p.285.

10. (see: Gottner-Abendroth, H. (1982) Krause, M.T. (trans.) (1991) *The Dancing Goddess: Principles of a Matriarchal Aesthetic*. Boston. Beacon Press. For a discussion of dance pp.31–75).

11. http://www.perseus.tufts.edu/hopper/text?doc=Perseus%3Atext%3A1999.01.0133%3Abook%3D18%3Acard%3D590 accessed 2.9.2020.

12. https://www.encyclopedia.com/humanities/culture-magazines/dance-prehistoric-greece accessed 2.9.2020.

13. https://www.sacred-texts.com/cla/usappho/sph51.htm Accessed 21.12.2020.

14. http://www.perseus.tufts.edu/hopper/text?doc=Perseus%3Atext%3A1999.01.0137%3Ahymn%3D2 accessed 10.6.2020. (tans. Mine).

15. See www.suppressedhistories.net.

16. For a detailed discussion of the Four Elements see, Brooke, Elisabeth. 2019. *As Above So Below: Traditional Western Herbal Medicine*. Aeon Books, London.

17. http://www.ellafitzgerald.com/about/quotes accessed 3.3.2021.

18. https://lovequotes.symphonyoflove.net/ella-fitzgerald-love-quotes-and-sayings.html accessed 3.3.2021.

19. http://www.ellafitzgerald.com/about/quotes accessed 3.3.2021.

20. Holden, Stephen. 16th June 1996. Obituary. *'Ella Fitzgerald, the Voice of Jazz, Dies at 79*. The New York Times. https://www.nytimes.com/1996/06/16/nyregion/ella-fitzgerald-the-voice-of-jazz-dies-at-79.html?pagewanted=all Accessed 4.3.2021.

21. http://www.ellafitzgerald.com/about/quotes accessed 3.3.2021.

22. Holden, Stephen. 16th June 1996. Obituary. *'Ella Fitzgerald, the Voice of Jazz, Dies at 79*. The New York Times. https://www.nytimes.com/1996/06/16/nyregion/ella-fitzgerald-the-voice-of-jazz-dies-at-79.html?pagewanted=all Accessed 4.3.2021.

23. http://www.ellafitzgerald.com/about/quotes accessed 3.3.2021.

24. http://www.ellafitzgerald.com/about/quotes accessed 3.3.2021.

25. https://lovequotes.symphonyoflove.net/ella-fitzgerald-love-quotes-and-sayings.html accessed 3.3.2021.

26. http://www.ellafitzgerald.com/about/quotes accessed 3.3.2021.

27. Furniss, Tom. "Mary Wollstonecraft's French Revolution". *The Cambridge Companion to Mary Wollstonecraft*. Ed. Claudia L. Johnson. Cambridge: Cambridge University Press, 2002. p.67.

28. Wollstonecraft, Mary and Godwin, William. *A Short Residence in Sweden, Norway and Denmark* and *Memoirs of the Author of 'The Rights of Woman'*. Ed. Richard Holmes. 1987. Penguin Books, London. pp.152–3.

Gemini: Iris

Bees buzz in the Spring sunlight as a light rain begins to fall, they take shelter under green leaves and the rainbow spreads from sky to earth a linking bridge from the goddess to you.

She walks down the seven coloured bridge, colours sparkling and vibrant and teaches of the seven natures, the magic numbers of life, the seven planets, seven energy centres, the seven notes of the scale. Red for blood and life and root and earth. Orange for pleasure and sexuality and all the abundance. Yellow for self-love, self-acceptance and self-worth. Green for the heart which connects lower and higher energies, for universal love and joy and peace. Turquoise for loving speech and expression, for truth and music. Indigo for clear seeing the unseen, clairvoyance and visions. Violet for messages from the Goddess and divine communication. All these gifts the Goddess brings to you, to share around the world as you fly between Spirit and Earth and the Underworld your gifts bring solace and wisdom and joy and speech to all.

Iris (Ἶρις) was the daughter of the Titan Thaumas (wonder) and Oceanid Electra, so she was born from the union of the sky and the water. Iris was the personification of the rainbow and more generally of the relationship between heaven and earth, gods and humankind, which the rainbow represents. Iris was shown with wings, dressed in thin silk which, in sunlight, has the colours of the rainbow. She is sometimes said to be the wife of Zephyrus (the West wind) and mother of Eros, but again these may have been her original attributes, controlling or personifying the winds and sending messages of love.[1] (Fig. 17)

31

Fig. 17 Iris, pot 525 BCE.

> "Then Iris wrapped herself in her cloak of a thousand colours and painted the sky with the arc of the rainbow."[2]

Iris the rainbow is Hera's messenger, wearing her cloak of many colours she helps Zeus to flood the earth by sucking up moisture and making the clouds thick.[3]

The name Iris comes from (Ιρις) Greek for rainbow, and also Eris (Ερις: quarrel, debate and zeal) or *eirew* (ειρεω), from the verb, "to say." If so, the name Iris means speaker, or perhaps mouthpiece, while eiren (ειρηνη) is the old Ionic word for peace.

Iris was the link between gods and men and between the gods themselves when they were quarrelling, as both messenger and mediator. Iris appears in the *Iliad* but not in the *Odyssey*, where Hermes has replaced her.

There are two images of Iris: Rainbows portend storms or war,

> "The shimmering rainbow, a portent and sign of war, or of a wintry storm." Homer, *Iliad* 17:547–50.

Iris also brings messages. Zeus sends her to Poseidon, to convince him to withdraw.

> "Go on your way now, swift Iris, to the lord Poseidon, give him this message … and swift-footed Iris did not disobey him …" (*Iliad* 15:158,168)

Iris is known for her speed, "… as those times when out of the clouds the snow or hail whirls cold beneath the blast of the north wind born in the bright air, so rapidly [went] winged Iris the swift one, in her eagerness." (*Iliad* 15:170–2)

Her epithets were mostly those of speed: "Wind-footed," "swift-footed," "storm-footed." She was also frequently called "golden-winged."

Iris has a persuasive manner, "Then in turn, swift footed Iris answered him [Poseidon] … will you change a little? The hearts of the great can be changed." (*Iliad* 15:203)

Poseidon replies, "Now this, divine Iris, is a word properly spoken. It is a fine thing when a messenger is conscious of justice." (*Iliad* 15:206–7). Poseidon is convinced by Iris.

Iris is also the psychopomp who eases the passage of the dying. Virgil, in *The Aeneid* describes how Iris eases the suffering of broken hearted Dido when she is abandoned by Aeneus.

> "So then, dewy Iris flew down from heaven with saffron plumes, trailing thousands of multicoloured hues facing against the sun. She stood by Dido's head, [whispering]
>
> 'This I was ordered to do, to carry a sacrifice to Dis [Hades] and so I unbind your body.'
>
> So it happened, with her right hand Iris cut Dido's hair, then all the warmth melted away from her and Dido's life departed into the wind." *Aeneid*: 4:700–5

By cutting her hair as sacrifice to Hades, Iris releases the ties that bind Dido to the human realm and she is carried off, away from her suffering, by the winds. It is a beautiful image of the gentle touch of Gemini, the air sign, who allows the winds to carry the dead to peace.

Iris not only brings release from suffering for the blameless, but punishment to the wicked. In *The Madness of Heracles*, Iris appears with Lyssa (madness) to punish Heracles who has offended Hera.

> "Fear not, old men, as you see Lyssa born of Nyx (Night), for I am Iris, handmaiden of the gods. We come to do no harm to your city, we join forces against the body of one man only. Hera wills it to fix upon him [Heracles] fresh blood guilt by killing his children, and I wish the same. Unwed maiden of Black Night (Νύξ), your heart hard, lay your hands upon him so he might suffer. Send madness upon that man and child slaughter, show him tumult and send out frenzy (the leaping of the feet), drive him to be murderous, so that when he carries his own beautiful children on Acheron's ferry, massacred by him, he will understand this rage of Hera's and mine." (Euripides: 815–874)

While Iris is compassionate, she is also merciless in her punishment, when Nyx tries to dissuade her. Iris is unyielding and sarcastic, she dismisses any objection and reminds Lyssa what her job is and pulls rank; she and Hera will have their revenge, "Don't you rebuke the machinations of Hera!" Furthermore, "It was not to be moderate that the wife of Zeus sent you here!"[4] Lyssa has a job to do and that is to drive people mad; she may not question her orders. Heracles' crime is that he is the son of Zeus by another woman (ostensibly). Iris is the messenger of Hera and speaks her truth.

Heracles 'taming pathless wilds and raging sea,' offended Hera and Gaia who liked their 'pathless wilds' untamed; these were places where nymphs and maenads danced ecstatically. The twelve Labours of Heracles involved the killing or capturing of ancient symbols of the goddess (see Historical Background). The Nimean Lion, the Lernean Hydra, the Cerynian Hind, the Erymanthian Boar, cleaning the Augean Stables, the Stymphalian Birds, the Cretan Bull, the Horses of Diomedes, the girdle of Amazon Queen Hippolyte, the Cattle of Geryon, the Golden Apples of the Hesperides, the hound Cerebus. Hera is revenged. In a frenzied attack Heracles slaughters his wife and children and then is returned to sanity to suffer the enormity of his actions.

Iris not only brings punishment to mankind, but to the gods also.

> "When strife and feuds among the immortals are stirred up and one who lives in a house on Olympus should lie, Zeus then calls Iris to bring her golden jug, which contains that which is sworn upon, the famous cold water which pours down from high, steep, rocks. Far under the wide earth, a branch of Oceanus flows through black night from the sacred river and is divided into ten parts. These nine silver swirling streams wind around the earth and the wide back of the sea and fall into the brine, while the tenth flows out from a rock, bringing great misery to the gods."
> (Hesiod *Theogony* 775–798)

Iris then, is more than a handmaid who serves the gods. Iris brings the sacred waters from the tenth silver stream for swearing a sacred oath in her golden jug. The water is poured from the jug and an oath is sworn. (Fig. 18) It is the 'famous cold water' which comes from the high rocks. The punishment for lying on oath is exile for a year, unfed or watered, lying on a couch unattended. Afterwards, for another nine years the wrongdoer is banished from the assemblies and feasts of the gods.

Iris is one of the few gods who can enter Hades and return, so she has the sacred duty to carry the waters of the Styx (her mother was after all an Oceanid) back up to Olympus and the pour the liquid and bear witness to the oath.

Although Iris appears lightweight and ornamental, she has power and reach. She can be vengeful and implacable and demands the truth and recompense from wrongdoers. She does not enact the punishment herself; she brings Lyssa (madness) or the water for the oath and stands back for other gods to exact the penalty.

Iris is a messenger both compassionate (Dido) and vengeful (Heracles). She has an airy neutrality which states the facts, shines light on wrongdoing and steps back. As psychopomp, Iris releases suffering Dido to the winds.

Fig. 18 Iris and Hera, pot 480 BCE.

As an air sign, mutable Iris is wide ranging, unpredictable, changeable unbounded. She speaks to the gods and also mortals, she connects the upper world with the lower world, the world of humans and gods of the upper and underworld.

Air signs do not much like physicality, they like the wide airy open spaces of the mind. They need stimulus for their minds and love to chatter and like Iris are connectors, networkers, who move quickly between worlds. It is not unusual for them to have many separate spheres of friends in their lives, who represent different interests, they are kept apart and would be surprised if they met each other, they are so different.

Iris connects but is not affected by whatever she meets. She can be in the underworld or with the gods and is equally at ease in either world. She can enter and leave the underworld at liberty, unlike anyone else, and registers and reports but experiences slide off her shiny carapace. She is more about collecting experiences and less about experiencing them. For this reason Geminis can be called superficial, but really, they are interested in everything, especially bright and shiny things and people.

Iris is the servant and also the shapeshifter.[5] Inconstant but flexible, able to fit into many situations, she may suffer from being all things to all people. Iris can be the servant following others rather than taking a stand. Many politicians and journalists are Gemini, slippery and changeable, often with a flexible relationship to the truth. Gemini follows Taurus, she brings us messages about how to conserve the riches of the earth.

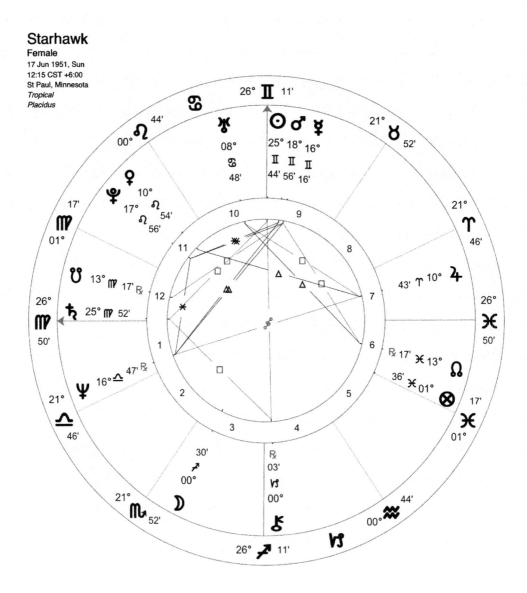

Starhawk

Female
17 Jun 1951, Sun
12:15 CST +6:00
St Paul, Minnesota
Tropical
Placidus

Starhawk: witch, activist
17 June 1951. (12:15) St. Paul Min

Author, activist, witch. Starhawk is a worshipper of the Goddess and a powerful voice in the movement of ecofeminism. Starhawk lives in San Francisco, where she works with Reclaiming, a tradition of Witchcraft that she co-founded in the late 1970s. She is internationally known as a trainer in nonviolence and direct action, and as an activist within the peace movement, women's movement, environmental movement, and anti-globalization movement. She travels and teaches widely in North America, Europe, and the Middle East, giving lectures and workshops. Iris as messenger and speaker.

Starhawk has Sun, Mercury and Mars in Gemini, conjunct her Midheaven, so her work is as a messenger to bring the teachings of the Goddess to many people.

> "The heritage, the culture, the knowledge of the ancient priestesses, healers, poets, singers, and seers were nearly lost, but a seed survived the flames that will blossom in a new age into thousands of flowers. The long sleep of Mother Goddess is ended. May She awaken in each of our hearts."[6]

Like Iris, Starhawk understands the darkness is part of who we are and must be integrated with compassion,

> "The depths of our own beings are not all sunlit; to see clearly, we must be willing to dive into the dark, inner abyss and acknowledge the creatures we may find there."[7]

Like Iris, the Witch knows the sunny uplands, the darkest places and values and preserves our natural world, all of which are a part of the Goddess' body and our own,

> "In the Craft, we do not believe in the Goddess—we connect with her; through the moon, the stars, the ocean, the earth, through trees, animals, through other human beings, through ourselves. She is here. She is within us all."[8]

This is the mystical union with the divine, discussed in the introduction.

Like Iris, Starhawk understands the sacred art of dying, this is her prayer to set the spirit free.

> "May the wind carry her spirit gently. May the Fire release her soul, May the Water cleanse her, may the Earth receive her, May the Goddess take her in her arms and guide her to rebirth."[9]

Starhawk's best known book is the *Spiral Dance* (see Melissae/Mercury).

"Energy moves in cycles, circles, spirals, vortexes, whirls, pulsations, waves, and rhythms—rarely if ever in simple straight lines."[10] *The Earth Path.*

Starhawk writes on integrity and keeping your word, (not making false oaths).

"To a person who practices honesty and keeps commitments, 'As I will, so mote it be' is not just a pretty phrase; it is a statement of fact." *The Spiral Dance.*[11]

Other activists:

Rachel Carson, *The Silent Spring.* 27 May 1907. (02:00) Springfield Pennsylvania (Sun, Mercury, Pluto in Gemini)

Marianna Mazzucato, *Rethinking Capitalism: Economics and Policy for Sustainable and Inclusive Growth.* 16 June 1968. (no time). Rome, Italy. (Sun, Mercury, Venus, Mars, in Gemini)

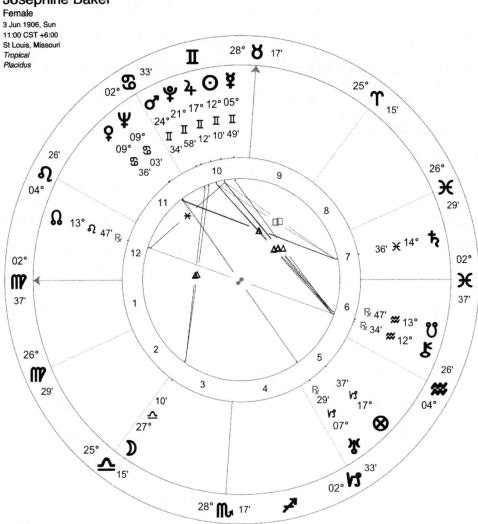

Josephine Baker
Female
3 Jun 1906, Sun
11:00 CST +6:00
St Louis, Missouri
Tropical
Placidus

Josephine Baker: spreading the message
3 June 1906. (11:00) St. Louis MO

"Surely the day will come when colour means nothing more than skin tone, when religion is seen uniquely as a way to speak one's soul; when birthplace has the weight of the throw of a dice and all men are born free, when understanding breeds love and brotherhood."[12]

Josephine had Mercury, Sun, Jupiter, Pluto and Mars in Gemini in her tenth house. Her words, her message was powerful and transformative. Her Libra Moon gave her dancing and beauty, while Venus Neptune in Cancer gave a softness and warmth as well as creativity and glamour.

Josephine was born into poverty and experienced homelessness as a child in East St Louis. Aged eight, she started work as a live-in domestic, for white families, and was treated harshly. She witnessed the horror of July, 1917, when whites rioted for two days, burning black homes, slaughtering, disembowelling and lynching. Six thousand blacks were driven from the city.[13]

At fifteen she moved to Harlem to pursue a dancing career and made friends with people from the Black Harlem Renaissance. In 1925, offered the chance to tour with a dance troupe in France, Josephine excitedly left America.

"One day I realized I was living in a country where I was afraid to be Black. It was only a country for White people. Not Black. So I left. I had been suffocating in the United States ... A lot of us left, not because we wanted to leave, but because we couldn't stand it anymore ... I felt liberated in Paris."[14]

Air needs space to breathe, and freedom to think. Paris, home to intellectuals, writers, and Jazz musicians welcomed her, and she became a sensation with her dance performance *Dance Sauvage* in 1925 dressed in a skirt made of artificial bananas, and *La Revue Negré*, dancing the Charleston on top of a drum dressed in ostrich feathers. Later she performed with her pet cheetah 'Chiquita' who wore a diamond collar.

"Since I personified the savage on the stage, I tried to be as civilized as possible in daily life."[15]

The French press was enthusiastic, describing her as, "Nefertiti and the Queen of Sheba and Cleopatra."[16]

Josephine brought the message of a creative, positive, ebullient, regal and historical Black woman to Paris. Like Iris, she brought sparkling beauty with her message.

Ernest Hemingway called her, "The most sensational woman anyone ever saw or ever will."[17] The author spent hours talking with her in Paris bars, and Picasso painted and drew her.

Being mutable, Iris makes an excellent spy, able to be all things to all people and slips between worlds effortlessly. When war broke out in September 1939, Josephine was recruited by the French Intelligence *Deuxieme Bureau* to spy on France's enemies. Performing her cabaret in embassies and nightclubs gave her the opportunity to listen to the talk among the enemy: Italians, Japanese and Germans, and report back. Like Iris, she was the messenger bringing secrets from the dark side.

When the Germans invaded France, Josephine left Paris to live on her estate in the Dordogne where she sheltered Free French volunteers and provided them with fake visas (Iris' opaque relationship with the truth), and organised entertainment for the Free French fighters. In recognition of her war work, Josephine was awarded the *Croix de Guerre* and the *Rosette de la Resistance* and the *Chevalier de le Legion d'honneur* by the leader of the Free French, Charles de Gaulle (Jupiter Pluto in the tenth house, fame, recognition).

In 1951 Josephine was invited back to America, but when she arrived in New York with her husband Jo, they were refused reservations at thirty-six hotels because she was Black. Speaking of the experience, Jo wrote,

> "Josephine left Paris rich, adored, famous throughout Europe. But in New York, in spite of the publicity that preceded her arrival, she was received as an uppity colored girl."[18]

Furious, Josephine wrote articles about racism in American. She gave a talk at Fisk University, a Black College in Nashville entitled, 'France, North Africa and the Equality of the Races in France.' In 1951 she exposed the Stork Club Manhattan when they refused to serve her. Josephine said,

> "I have walked into the palaces of kings and queens and into the houses of presidents. And much more. But I could not walk into a hotel in America and get a cup of coffee, and that made me mad. And when I get mad, you know that I open my big mouth. And then look out, 'cause when Josephine opens her mouth, they hear it all over the world ... "[19]

Josephine refused to perform for segregated audiences in the United States, although one Miami club eventually agreed to her demands; it was a sold-out run which she followed with a national tour. Although she received threatening phone calls from people claiming to be from the KKK, she said publicly that she was not afraid. Rave reviews and enthusiastic audiences accompanied her everywhere, climaxed by a parade in front of 100,000 people in Harlem after she was named NAACP's 'Woman of the Year' with Sunday, 20 May 1951 declared 'Josephine Baker Day.'

Josephine began adopting children, forming a family she called *The Rainbow Tribe*. She wanted to prove that, "Children of different ethnicities and religions could still be brothers." She adopted two girls and ten boys from, France, Morocco, Korea, Japan,

Columbia, Finland, Israel, Algeria, Ivory Coast, and Venezuela. They all lived together in her huge *Chateau Demilandes* in the Dordogne. She brought up her children in different religions as part of her experiment; of two children from Algeria one was raised as Muslim, and the other Catholic.

Josephine remained a huge celebrity in France. More than 20,000 people crowded the streets of Paris to watch her funeral procession, she was honoured by a twenty-one gun salute. *Place Joséphine Baker* in Montparnasse, Paris was dedicated in her honour.

As Iris, the messenger, she passed the torch on to the next generation.

> "I am not a young woman now, friends. My life is behind me. There is not too much fire burning inside me. And before it goes out, I want you to use what is left to light that fire in you."[20]

Other voices of resistance:
Harriet Beecher Stowe:14 June 1811. (11:00) Litchfield Conn. (Sun, Fortuna, Jupiter, Midheaven and Mercury in Gemini) author of *Uncle Tom's Cabin*.
Anne Frank, 12 June 1929. (06:30) Frankfurt. (Sun, Mercury in Gemini.) Diarist.

Notes

1. Grimal, 1987: 237.
2. Ovid, *Metamorphoses* book 11:587–590.
3. Ovid, *Metamorphoses* book 1:269–70.
4. http://www.perseus.tufts.edu/hopper/text?doc=Perseus%3Atext%3A1999.01.0101%3Acard%3D822
5. https://www.goddess-guide.com/iris.html accessed 21.9.2020.
6. https://www.goodreads.com/author/quotes/6376.Starhawk accessed 6.1.2021.
7. From the *Spiral Dance* https://www.goodreads.com/author/quotes/6376.Starhawk accessed 6.1.2021.
8. https://www.goodreads.com/author/quotes/6376.Starhawk?page=1 accessed 7.1.2021.
9. Starhawk, *City of Refuge*. https://www.goodreads.com/author/quotes/6376.Starhawk accessed 6.1.2021.
10. Starhawk. *The Earth Path: Grounding Your Spirit in the Rhythms of Nature*. https://www.goodreads.com/author/quotes/6376.Starhawk accessed 6.1.2021.
11. https://www.goodreads.com/author/quotes/6376.Starhawk?page=1 accessed 6.1.2021.
12. www. https://www.cmgww.com/stars/baker/ accessed 12.3.2021.
13. Murari, Tim. 26.8.1974. *Josephine Baker*. The Guardian newspaper. https://www.theguardian.com/stage/2015/aug/26/josephine-baker-interview-1974 accessed 13.3.2021.
14. www. https://www.cmgww.com/stars/baker/ accessed 12.3.2021.
15. www. https://www.cmgww.com/stars/baker/ accessed 12.3.2021.
16. Murari, Tim. 26.8.1974. *Josephine Baker*. The Guardian newspaper. https://www.theguardian.com/stage/2015/aug/26/josephine-baker-interview-1974 accessed 13.3.2021.
17. https://web.archive.org/web/20131017051325/http://www.cmgww.com/stars/baker/about/quotes2.html accessed 13.3.2021.

18. https://web.archive.org/web/20131017051325/http://www.cmgww.com/stars/baker/about/quotes2.html accessed 13.3.2021.

19. https://www.blackpast.org/african-american-history/speeches-african-american-history/1963-josephine-baker-speech-march-washington/ accessed 13.3.2021.

20. https://www.blackpast.org/african-american-history/speeches-african-american-history/1963-josephine-baker-speech-march-washington/ accessed 13.3.2021.

Cancer: Hestia

You sit on a beach at dusk, the wide blue sea glitters in front of you. It darkens to indigo as the first stars appear in the sky, the area is heavy with the scent of salt and sea.

You build a fire, picking up driftwood and enclose it with stones and watch the heat rise, the flames glow and the embers glimmer.

A fat, full Moon rises slowly on the horizon, lighting a golden pathway across the ocean. As night falls you place a pot on the hot stones and heat water for tea. Friends arrive, walking quietly from all directions. They approach you smiling, hands extended in friendship. You welcome them, they greet one another and they settle around the fire. One offers cake, another wine, a third fruit. There is a pleasant, soothing hum of conversation and you sit bathed in their warmth, their love, their friendship, as the Moon glows high in the sky above you, sending down blessing and love.

Hestia, one of the original goddesses, was the daughter of Rhea and Kronos. Because of a prophecy that one of his sons would oust him, Kronos swallowed all his children. Hestia was the eldest and the first to be swallowed and was the last to be disgorged, so she represents the beginning and the end.

"Hestia, in all the mighty houses of the immortal gods and men come, an everlasting sanctuary you claim as your own, the most ancient office you have, glorious your privilege and highly prized your honour. For without you, none of the solemn feasts of mortals begins, but a first and last libation of honey sweet wine is poured to Hestia." *Homeric Hymn 27*

Hestia is goddess of the hearth, and especially the sacred flame of the hearth, which warms members of the household and feeds them. She presided over the cooking of bread and the preparation of the family meal. She was the goddess of domestic life and gave blessings of health and happiness in the home. She was said to live in the innermost part of the home.[1] Hestia was the goddess who invented building houses. The hearth was also the altar of the house, where sacrifices to the domestic gods were made. In temples sacrifices were first made to Hestia.[2] The cooking of the communal feast of sacrificial meat was her task and the first meat was sacred to her.

Solemn oaths were sworn to Hestia goddess of the hearth in the home, and the hearth itself was the place of sacred asylum where suppliants invoked the protection of the inhabitants of the house. A town or city was seen as an extension of the family, so it too had a sacred hearth and flame which brought citizens to communal worship and represented harmony and concord within the community. The *prytaneion* (πρυτανειον) was the public building sacred to Hestia and a perpetual fire was kept alight there. It was where public officials, *pyrtanes* of each tribe (φυλη) met to discuss city business. There they ate communal meals, entertained foreign ambassadors and citizens who had served the state well, and the children of soldiers who had been killed in battle had a place at the table.[3] Breaking bread was a sacred act between people.

In the *prytaneion* Hestia had her sanctuary the *thalamus* (θαλαμος) or women's place with her statue and the sacred hearth. The *pyrtanes* sacrificed to her when they took up their office and swore an oath to serve the city honestly. This place, like the hearth of the home was where suppliants could call on the goddess to protect them; it was the place of asylum (ασυλον) in every town.

When a colony was sent out, the emigrants took the fire which was to burn on the hearth of their new home from that of the mother town. If ever the fire of Hestia's hearth went out, it could not be lit again with ordinary fire, but was set either by fire produced by friction, or by glass drawing fire from the sun.

There were few temples of Hestia in Greece, as in reality every *prytaneum* was a sanctuary of the goddess. A part of the sacrifices of any divinity, were offered to her. Hestia's offerings were, water, oil, wine, first fruits and a yearling calf.[4]

Hestia was depicted in Athenian vase painting as a modestly veiled woman sometimes holding a flowered branch (perhaps a chaste-tree, Vitex agnus castus[5]). In classical sculpture she was also veiled, with a kettle as her attribute. (Fig. 19)

Hestia is immune to the whiles of Aphrodite; passion does not interest her:

> "Nor yet does the pure maiden Hestia love Aphrodite's works. She was the first-born child of wily Kronos and youngest too, by will of Zeus who holds the aegis, a queenly maid whom both Poseidon and Apollo sought to wed. But she was wholly unwilling, nay, stubbornly refused; and touching the head of father, Zeus[6] who holds the aegis, she, that fair goddess, swore a great oath which has in truth been fulfilled, that she would be a maiden all her days. So, Zeus the Father gave her a high honour

Fig. 19 Hestia, pot, 5thC BCE.

instead of marriage, and she has her place in the midst of the house and has the richest portion. In all the temples of the gods she has a share of honour, and among all mortal men she is chief of the goddesses."[7] *Homeric Hymn to Aphrodite,* 5: 21–30

Hestia refused to marry. 'Marriage' of the gods is part of the Patriarchal takeover. While she declined to 'marry' either Apollo or Poseidon, Hestia was worshipped at Delphi and Olympus alongside them.

"Oh Hestia, who tends the divine shrine of far-shooting Apollo with the Most Holy Pythia, always rich anointing oil drips from your locks (tresses). Come to this house; enter in sympathetic support, along with Zeus, the wise counsellor. Grant as a well a pleasing grace to my song." *Homeric Hymn to Hestia* (24)[8]

Hestia never takes part in disputes or wars, nor does she take sides, she protects her own. For Hestia, the home and community is all. She is not interested in powerplays or worldly ambition, she wishes to keep the hearth warm and her tribe safe. This is her whole focus. she is the centre and the first in ritual, because without Hestia there is no safe place. She reminds us of the importance of family. Her family may be her tribe, not her biological relatives. Those she draws around her, who she picks up when they fall, who she keeps a watchful eye on because they are part of her. She feels deeply and can be clannish and prickly when she feels under stress and incurious about the world outside her circle, but she keeps her folks safe.

There was a rite called *amphidromia* where a baby was carried around the hearth a few days after birth, signifying the formal acceptance into the family. When a woman married in Classical times, she left her father's hearth and went to the hearth of her husband, representing woman as the fire which burns at the centre of the household.[9]

As goddess of the Hearth, Hestia represented the continuity, safety, and nourishment that both the family and the state were obliged to provide for its members. *Xenia* was the name for this sacred bond of friendship between people. Families and individuals swore a sacred oath to protect, shelter and defend those bound by the ties of *xenia*. Breaking the oath of *xenia* was a great taboo. Travellers would stay in the houses of *xenia*, they would intermarry and protect one another. In the *Iliad*, fighters on opposite sides of the war, who were bound by the code of *xenia*, would not fight one another, instead they acknowledged each other and stepped aside, so as not to break the sacred bond of friendship.[10]

Cancer protects her family, which may be a family of blood relatives, or a family of friends and she shelters them from outside threats. Often accused of being clannish, Hestia does not easily welcome newcomers into her tribe, nor does she forgive those who disrespect her family. Her kitchen is the centre of home, not the food as much as the emotional warmth and comfort. She draws people in and keeps them close.

Like Hestia, Cancer will not engage in battles and finds any brutish behaviour offensive and terrifying. She will hide and not fight. She will back down and favour abdication and withdrawal rather than meet with aggressors. Emotional calm is important to her, to the extent of causing bad feeling in others if she is feeling unsettled. But don't be mistaken, Hestia uses the soft power of water to get what she needs. Seemingly shy and passive, she moves slowly and cautiously, she wears down obstacles as she smiles very sweetly.

Although she is goddess of the hearth, Hestia is not necessarily a mother figure. Children may be more rambunctious and confronting that she can cope with. Hestia craves comfort and peace, so that she feels safe and nurtured. She loves the familiar and holds on to people. Kindness is the quality of water, and Hestia is kind, modest and changeable. As goddess of the hearth in every private house Hestia is the gentlest, most upright and most charitable of the Olympians.[11]

Dionysus, having established his worship throughout the world ascended to Olympus and was given a seat at the right hand of Zeus as one of the Great Ones. Hestia resigned her seat in his favour, doubtless glad to escape the Olympians. She knew she could always rely on a quiet welcome in any Greek city she wished to visit, as she is worshipped in every temple.[12] Hestia preferred to stay at home in Delphi and she plays no part in Greek myths. With the patriarchal take over perhaps Hestia was given no choice or couldn't bear the bickering and retreated with dignity.

Maggie Lena Walker

Female
15 Jul 1864, Fri
00:00 LMT +5:09:50
Richmond, Virginia
Tropical
Placidus

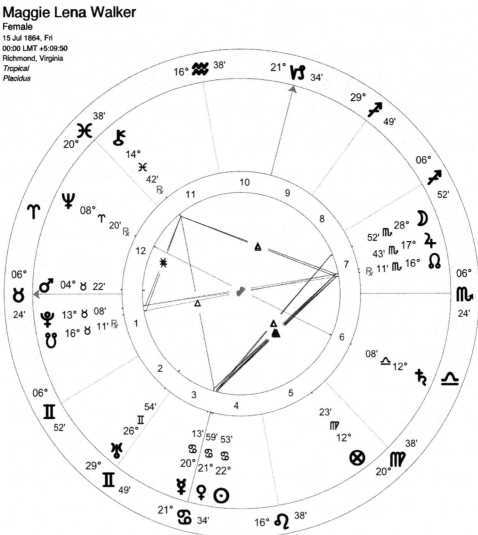

Maggie Lena Walker: Caring for my people
15 July 1864. (No time) Richmond VA

Maggie Lena Walker was born two years and two months after the end of the American Civil War in Richmond, Virginia. Her parents had been enslaved. She was an African American businesswoman, activist and teacher, and the first African-American woman to charter a bank and serve as its president in the US.[13]

Maggie has her Sun, Mercury and Venus conjunct in Cancer, showing her life's work was to care for her people and protect them, financially and politically. Her Jupiter (and possibly her Moon, depending on her time of birth) are in money savvy Scorpio, the ideal placing for a banker. Her Mars in Taurus did not take risks, preferred slow and steady growth, no doubt aided by her warm, non-threatening, kind persona (Venus in Cancer).

> "Walker's warm and engaging personality was part of the reason she proved to be
> a successful fundraiser; she also was skilled at navigating across racial and gender
> lines to accomplish her aims."[14]

Aged fourteen, Maggie joined the local council of the Independent Order of St. Luke, an African American fraternal organisation. Established in 1867 in Baltimore, it gave support and help to the sick, was a burial society, promoted self-sufficiency, and financial advancement for African Americans. Maggie rose to positions of increasing responsibility in the Order, until she was elected Right Worthy Grand Secretary in 1899. She held the post until she died. Through astute financial planning, she led the Order to financial security.[15]

> "Through her guidance of the Independent Order of St. Luke, Walker demonstrated
> that African American men and women could be leaders in business, politics, and
> education during a time when society insisted on the contrary."[16]

Maggie opened a women's community insurance company.[17] Encouraged by its success, she opened the St. Luke Penny Savings Bank in 1903 and served as the bank's first president, which she remained until 1929. The boards had several other women board members. Later she agreed to serve as chairman of the board of directors when the bank merged with two other Richmond banks to become The Consolidated Bank and Trust Company, an African-American owned institution. The bank offered loans and mortgages to black residents of Richmond, Virginia who could not raise loans from white-owned banks.[18]

By 1924 the bank spread to other areas in Virginia and had over 50,000 members. It survived the banking crash of the Great Depression, when many banks failed, and it remains a bank in Richmond today.[19] Until 2009, the bank was the oldest continually

51

African American-operated bank in the United States.[20] Maggie's life's work was to raise up her people.

> "Let us put our money together; let us use our money; let us put our money out as usury among ourselves and reap the benefit ourselves."[21]

Maggie founded the *St. Luke Herald* in 1902 to carry news of the Order of St. Luke to local branches and to help with its educational work. It became one of the largest black fraternal orders having over 100,000 members in twenty-four states. It was unique not only by its size, but because it was run by a woman, and most of the members were women.[22] By 1929 it was the leading African American newspaper in Richmond.[23]

Although gentle in demeanour, through her newspaper Maggie campaigned for the rights of Black people. In 1904 the paper called Richmond residents to boycott Virginia Passenger and Power Company streetcars who insisted on segregated seating. This boycott was so successful the company was declared bankrupt two months later.

The Order under Maggie also purchased and built properties to secure the financial stability of the bank and the Order, including St Luke's house, built using African American builders and architects, and now a listed building.[24] Hestia was known as the goddess who ruled house building; it is fitting that Maggie understood the importance of property ownership for the longevity of her projects.

In 1905, Maggie opened the St. Luke Emporium, a department store that offered African American women opportunities for work and gave the Black community access to cheaper goods. The Emporium allowed Black customers to shop with dignity—not forced to enter the store through a side door, they could try on clothing before buying, and could eat at the cafeterias. The mannequins were brown skinned and only Black women were employed as saleswomen.

Maggie also campaigned for votes for women, arguing that equal pay for their work would not become reality until, "Women force Capital to hear them at the ballot box."[25] When the Nineteenth Amendment (giving women the right to vote) was ratified in August 1920, Maggie and Ora Brown Stokes led a massive voter registration campaign which helped almost 2,500 local African American women to register. Sometimes, African American women segregated in city hall's crowded basement, were turned away after queuing all day. Ora Brown organised a phone tree which alerted the best time to register.[26]

Maggie served on the board of trustees for National Association of Coloured Women (NACW) and the Virginia Industrial School for Girls. She was an organiser. She was elected vice president of the local National Association for the Advancement of Coloured People (NAACP), was a member of the national NAACP board, and a member of the Virginia Interracial Commission.[27]

Her husband was accidentally killed in 1915. Luckily, her bank work made her financially comfortable. Her house was gradually enlarged, allowing her sons and their wives to live with her, as well as her mother and her household staff. This small community had Maggie at its centre like Hestia, the heart of the household. The house is now a museum owned by the National Park Service.[28]

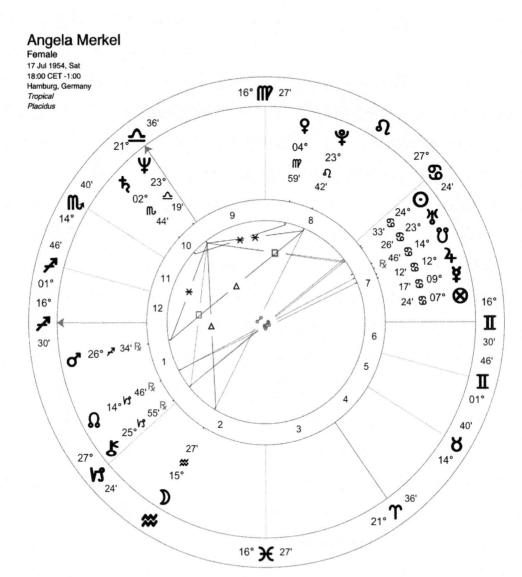

Angela Merkel

Female

17 Jul 1954, Sat
18:00 CET -1:00
Hamburg, Germany
Tropical
Placidus

Angela Merkel: Compassionate politician
17 July 1954. (18:00) Hamburg

Angela has Venus, Jupiter, Sun and Uranus in Cancer showing her motivation and life's work, caring for her people. Her Sagittarian Ascendant and Mars in Sagittarius gives her a cheerful, optimistic character.

> "I have a relatively sunny spirit, and I always had the expectation that my path through life would be relatively sunny, no matter what happened. I have never allowed myself to be bitter."[29]

Angela grew up in Communist East Germany. Her father a pastor, ran a home for disabled people; kindness was instilled in her from an early age.

> "To grow up in the neighbourhood of handicapped people was an important experience for me. I learned back then to treat them in a very normal way."[30]

East Germany was a deeply paranoid police state; people were recruited or blackmailed into spying on each other. Angela took a risk averse position to survive. Self-protection is central to a Cancerian.

> "I decided that if the system became too terrible, I would have to try to escape. But if it wasn't too bad then I wouldn't lead my life in opposition to the system, because I was scared of the damage that would do to me."[31]
>
> "The state has to assist and must not constrict. In this spirit it has to be the gardener and not the fence. We should be confident that the people want to get [socially] involved and want to assume responsibility." Süddeutsche Zeitung (sueddeutsche.de) May 20, 2006[32]

Merkel gained a PhD in Quantum chemistry, and uses her scientific rigour (Moon in Aquarius) to approach problems and make decisions.

> "Before you contradict her, you would think twice—she has the authority of somebody who knows that she's right,"[33]

Even when Angela reached a decision, she would sit with it until it felt like the time to act. She once told a story from her childhood of standing on a diving board for the full hour of a swimming lesson until, at the bell, she finally jumped.[34]

Germans call the Chancellor Mutti, or Mother. First used by competitors in her party as an insult, the name stuck; the public responded to her as their mother figure so she grew to like the nickname. Family is important to her. After the fall of the Berlin Wall in 1989.

> "She stayed not out of loyalty to the state but because she had her network there, her family."[35]

Angela entered politics, a token woman, an 'Eastie,' patronised by the macho men in Kohl's Christian Democratic party. Once in government, with her assistant Beate Baumann, the two women took on the male politicians. They targeted their enemies but did not publicly celebrate their victories. In 1996, during negotiations over a nuclear-waste law, Gerhard Schröder, two years away from becoming Chancellor, called her performance as environment minister 'pitiful.' In an interview with Herlinde Koelbl that year, Merkel said, "I will put him in the corner, just like he did with me. I still need time, but one day the time will come for this, and I am already looking forward." It took nine years but she succeeded.[36]

Angela later took down Kohl following a corruption scandal. Kohl later remarked, "I brought my killer … I put the snake on my arm."[37] She has Saturn in Scorpio in the tenth house of career and government, never forgetting a slight, taking time to deliver a deadly revenge.

> "If you cross her, you end up dead. There's nothing cushy about her. There's a whole list of alpha males who thought they would get her out of the way, and they're all now in other walks of life." Former US Ambassador to Germany John Kornblum.[38]

Her tactics are careful and non-aggressive; her signature plodding pace so tries the patience of Germans they created a verb: *Merkeling*.[39]

> "Careful: unpretentiousness can be a weapon! … One of the secrets of the success of Angela Merkel is that she knows how to deal with vain men. She knows you shoot a mountain cock best when it's courting a hen. Angela Merkel is a patient hunter of courting mountain cocks. With the patience of an angel, she waits for her moment."[40]

Hestia dislikes confrontation and was happy to leave Olympus when brash Dionysus came. Angela's attack method is classic Cancer territory; take away someone's foundation and they crumble. Cancer is protective, but when she withdraws that protection her adversaries fall. Cancerians feel things deeply and the quotation above shows they are often underestimated. However, Angela shows they can have great ambition and still be modest; they will never forget a slight and sitting by the riverbank watching the bodies of your enemies' float by, is their excellent strategy for success.

Shy and awkward, Cancer dislikes being in the limelight.

"She's very difficult to know, and that is a reason for her success ... It seems she is not from this world. Psychologically, she gives everybody the feeling of, 'I will take care of you.'"[41]

Her close knit inner circle (family) consists of just six or seven key aides, two of whom have been with her throughout her political career. She lives in a humble flat with her partner and does the shopping on a Friday accompanied by her security men. Privately, Angela is warm and funny, "I think most of the time I've spent with her she is smiling," says Robert Kimmitt, a former ambassador who has known her since 1991.[42]

In summer 2015 over a million refugees, mainly from Syria, claimed asylum in Germany, after Hungary closed its borders. Warned it would be a disaster for the country, Angela demonstrated compassionate leadership, "We can handle this." Safety, home, freedom from repression and non-violence are all characteristic of her fifteen year career as Chancellor of Germany, when she was arguably the most powerful woman in the world.

Other social activists:
Malala Yousafzai activist and campaigner 2 July 1997. (08:15) Mingora Pakistan. Sun in Cancer.

Notes

1. Homeric Hymn 30. Callimachus, Hymn in Del 325, Cer 129.
2. Homeric Hymn 31/32.
3. Liddell & Scott (1941) p.613.
4. https://www.theoi.com/Ouranios/Hestia.html accessed 20.8.2020.
5. Vitex is an anaphrodisiac. See, Brooke, Elisabeth. 2018. *A Woman's Book of Herbs,* Aeon Press, London. p.164.
6. An example of supplication.
7. http://www.perseus.tufts.edu/hopper/text?doc=Perseus%3Atext%3A1999.01.0137%3Ahymn%3D5 accessed 20.6.2020.
8. http://www.perseus.tufts.edu/hopper/text?doc=Perseus%3atext%3a1999.01.0137%3ahymn%3d24 accessed 20.6.2020. (trans. mine).
9. Blundell, Sue. 1995. *Women in Ancient Greece.* British Museum Press. London. p.32.
10. Supplication involved taking the knee and holding a man's beard or putting a hand on their thigh. This indicated you were putting yourself under divine protection-your life in their hands literally, the gods punished severely those who did not respect the rights of suppliants. This is similar to the rights of sanctuary in the European Christian traditions-where churches were deemed sacrosanct and inviolate.
11. Graves 2011: pp.74–76.
12. Graves, 2011: p.106.
13. https://www.nps.gov/mawa/learn/historyculture/maggie-lena-walker.htm accessed 21.9.202.
14. National Register of Historic Places. https://www.dhr.virginia.gov/wp-content/uploads/2018/04/127-0352_StLukeBuildingUpdate_2018_NRHP_FINAL.pdf. p.12 accessed 2.1.2021.

15. https://edu.lva.virginia.gov/changemakers/items/show/104 accessed 2.1.2021.
16. Legacy, Maggie L. Walker National Historic Site, National Park Service. https://www.nps.gov/museum/exhibits/Maggie_Walker/legacy.html. accessed 20.12.2020.
17. Norword, Arlisha, N. *Maggie Lena Walker 1864-1934.* 2017. National Women's History Museum. https://www.womenshistory.org/education-resources/biographies/maggie-lena-walker accessed 2.1.2021.
18. https://www.biography.com/scholar/maggie-lena-walker accessed 15.8.2020.
19. Norword, Arlisha, N. *Maggie Lena Walker 1864-1934.* 2017. National Women's History Museum. https://www.womenshistory.org/education-resources/biographies/maggie-lena-walker accessed 2.1.2021.
20. https://www.nps.gov/mawa/learn/historyculture/maggie-lena-walker.htm accessed 2.1.2021.
21. https://www.nps.gov/mawa/learn/historyculture/maggie-lena-walker.htm accessed 2.1.2021.
22. National Register of Historic Places https://www.dhr.virginia.gov/wp-content/uploads/2018/04/127-0352_StLukeBuildingUpdate_2018_NRHP_FINAL.pdf. p.7. accessed 2.1.2021.
23. National Register of Historic Places https://www.dhr.virginia.gov/wp-content/uploads/2018/04/127-0352_StLukeBuildingUpdate_2018_NRHP_FINAL.pdf. p.12. accessed 2.1.2021.
24. National Register of Historic Places https://www.dhr.virginia.gov/wp-content/uploads/2018/04/127-0352_StLukeBuildingUpdate_2018_NRHP_FINAL.pdf. p.16. has details of the properties built and purchased by the Order.
25. https://edu.lva.virginia.gov/changemakers/items/show/104 accessed 2.1.2021
26. Ora Brown Stokes," *Virginia Changemakers,* https://edu.lva.virginia.gov/changemakers/items/show/384 accessed January 2, 2021.
27. https://www.nps.gov/mawa/learn/historyculture/maggie-lena-walker.htm. accessed 2.1.2021.
28. https://www.nps.gov/mawa/learn/historyculture/maggie-lena-walker.htm. accessed 20.12.2020.
29. Packer, George. 24.11.2014. *The Quiet German: The astonishing rise of Angela Merkel, the most powerful woman in the world.* New Yorker Magazine. https://www.newyorker.com/magazine/2014/12/01/quiet-german accessed 13.3.2021.
30. Packer, George. 24.11.2014. *The Quiet German: The astonishing rise of Angela Merkel, the most powerful woman in the world.* New Yorker Magazine. https://www.newyorker.com/magazine/2014/12/01/quiet-german accessed 13.3.2021.
31. Packer, George. 24.11.2014. *The Quiet German: The astonishing rise of Angela Merkel, the most powerful woman in the world.* New Yorker Magazine. https://www.newyorker.com/magazine/2014/12/01/quiet-german accessed 13.3.2021.
32. https://en.wikiquote.org/wiki/Angela_Merkel accessed 15.3.2021.
33. Packer, George. 24.11.2014. *The Quiet German: The astonishing rise of Angela Merkel, the most powerful woman in the world.* New Yorker Magazine. https://www.newyorker.com/magazine/2014/12/01/quiet-german accessed 13.3.2021.
34. Packer, George. 24.11.2014. *The Quiet German: The astonishing rise of Angela Merkel, the most powerful woman in the world.* New Yorker Magazine. https://www.newyorker.com/magazine/2014/12/01/quiet-german accessed 13.3.2021.

35. Packer, George. 24.11.2014. *The Quiet German: The astonishing rise of Angela Merkel, the most powerful woman in the world.* New Yorker Magazine. https://www.newyorker.com/magazine/2014/12/01/quiet-german accessed 13.3.2021.
36. Vick, Karl. Shuster, Simon. 2015. *Chancellor of the Free World.* Time magazine. https://time.com/time-person-of-the-year-2015-angela-merkel/ accessed 15.3.2021.
37. Packer, George. 24.11.2014. *The Quiet German: The astonishing rise of Angela Merkel, the most powerful woman in the world.* New Yorker Magazine. https://www.newyorker.com/magazine/2014/12/01/quiet-german accessed 13.3.2021.
38. Packer, George. 24.11.2014. *The Quiet German: The astonishing rise of Angela Merkel, the most powerful woman in the world.* New Yorker Magazine. https://www.newyorker.com/magazine/2014/12/01/quiet-german accessed 13.3.2021.
39. Vick, Karl. Shuster, Simon. 2015. *Chancellor of the Free World.* Time magazine. https://time.com/time-person-of-the-year-2015-angela-merkel/ accessed 15.3.2021.
40. Packer, George. 24.11.2014. *The Quiet German: The astonishing rise of Angela Merkel, the most powerful woman in the world.* New Yorker Magazine. https://www.newyorker.com/magazine/2014/12/01/quiet-german accessed 13.3.2021.
41. Packer, George. 24.11.2014. *The Quiet German: The astonishing rise of Angela Merkel, the most powerful woman in the world.* New Yorker Magazine. https://www.newyorker.com/magazine/2014/12/01/quiet-german accessed 13.3.2021.
42. Vick, Karl. Shuster, Simon. 2015. *Chancellor of the Free World.* Time magazine. https://time.com/time-person-of-the-year-2015-angela-merkel/ accessed 15.3.2021.

Leo: Hera

You stand tall, the Sun at midday behind you, shining in a cloudless blue sky. Your hair is outlined like a corona, sparkling, dazzling, electric. You are with your people, they are waiting for your words of inspiration, excited for you to show them the way, for you have the vision. They crowd around, radiating in your warmth as you raise your hands and begin to speak.

Bringing into the present the wisdom of the ancestors, you beguile them with stories, they laugh and are inspired, they celebrate their unity, they adore you as leader, children come, they tumble around laughing.

You stay in the centre surrounded by your tribe, complete, awesome, radiant.

Hera was the daughter of Cronos and Rhea. She was born on the island of Samos or perhaps Argos, and was raised in Arcadia by Temenus, son of Pelasgus. The seasons (Horae) were her nurses. Other traditions have her raised at the ends of the world by Oceanus and Tethys, who Rhea entrusted with her with while Zeus was struggling with the Titans. Hera was always grateful to them and when they argued she tried to be the peacemaker.[1]

"Hera with the golden throne, born of Rhea, Queen of the Immortals, bearing a distinguished eminent nature. Sister and wife of Zeus. All the Blessed ones from high Olympus stand in awe of her, as does Zeus who delights in thunder." *Homeric Hymn to Hera*[2]

The name Hera (ἥρα) means pleasure and happiness[3] but may also be derived from the word for hero (ἥρω) which might be traced back to the Linear B words meaning 'of the year' or 'of the season', itself reminiscent of the ancient Greek word (ὥρα) or season. This Mycenaean word is believed to be related to the older Proto Indo-European for the word lady or mistress. The evolution from mistress of the seasons to hero/protectress may represent the changing nature of Hera from the Kretan to the Classical era.[4]

The oldest and most important Greek temples were dedicated to Hera. The island of Samos, believed by some to be her birthplace, was a centre for worship of the goddess as far back as the Mycenaean period in the mid-2nd millennium BCE, a major cult centre was created there from the 8th century BCE. Excavations on Samos have revealed votive offerings, many of them late 8th and 7th centuries BCE, show that Hera at Samos was not merely a local Greek goddess of the Aegean. Figures of gods and suppliants and other offerings from Armenia, Babylon, Iran, Assyria and Egypt have been found. This shows the power and reverence the goddess commanded. Her temple complex was a site for pilgrimage throughout the great empires of the Middle East.[5]

The Argive temple situated between Argos and Mycenae had a massive gold and ivory statue of Hera on her throne, reputedly made by the great sculptor Polycleitus. On her crown were shown the Graces and the Horae (Ωραε seasons); in one hand she held the pomegranate and in the other a sceptre, with a cuckoo on top. The great fifth and sixth century temples in Paestum built for Hera, show the importance of her cult in *Magna Graeca* (Italy). Her favourite places were Argos, and Mycenae.[6] Hera had the earliest temple built at Olympia (650–600 BCE). Hera's seated cult figure was older than the warrior figure of Zeus that accompanied it. Tiryns was another major cult centre to the goddess during the 7th century BCE.

Hera was an ancient Pelasgian[7] goddess whose land was invaded by the immigrant Achaeans (Hellenes who came from the valley of the Danube). Zeus was their wrathful, warlike god. As we have seen (Historical Background), the story of the Olympians is one of conquest, rape and landgrab. Originally a supreme goddess in her own right, Hera is 'married' to Zeus and their relationship is one of constant discord. She is ridiculed as the nagging wife, the shrew, the consort who stays despite a constant stream of insults to her distinguished, eminent nature. Hera is the template for the long-suffering Greek wife, who has power only by default through her husband, the ultimate patriarch and misogynist.

In Homer Hera is reduced to a nagging shrew of a wife, a parodic, vengeful character, who submits to his superior will. I am guessing those who travelled from as far away as Iran to worship her and who built the massive temples for her cult, would not have seen her in this way.

By Classical times Hera's previous power and prestige has gone, and we are left with a pantomime trophy wife, who should put up and shut up. She is given reverence only as a symbol of the devoted spouse, not in her own right. Jane Harrison speaks of the, "Ceaseless, turbulent hostility between Zeus and Hera," who he cannot even beat into submission.[8]

Hera is not subject to Zeus and is never subdued by the upstart sky god (Graves, 2011:55). Zeus never entirely trusted Hera, although he sometimes accepted her advice. Her powers curtailed, Hera used subterfuge to get what she wanted, sometimes borrowing Aphrodite's girdle so Zeus would be distracted by lust. When Zeus' pride and petulance became intolerable, he was tied up by Hera, Poseidon, Apollo and the other Olympians, except Hestia. Thetis the nymph organised his release. Hera was the ringleader and Zeus suspended her from the sky with a golden handcuff on each wrist and an anvil fastened to her ankles.[9] Graves suggests that the fights between Zeus and Hera represent the barbarous Dorian age when women were deprived of all their magical power, except that of prophecy, and became regarded as chattels (2011:54).

Harrison also suggests these arguments are not conjugal jealousy, but 'racial rivalry.' Hera whose name may been from Yar-a-the Spirit of the year,[10] who brings fruits in their season (1927, 18–19). Hesiod changed Hera to be subservient to Zeus; she who had previously been the inspirer becomes the temptress; she who made all things becomes their slave. Hera is left only with her physical beauty, like a slave with tricks (Harrison, 1927, 285).

Hera had an oracle at Pagae. The only gift 'left to her by Zeus' was the gift of prophecy. Hera's cult image had horns, a cow goddess, as did Astarte, Io, Isis or Hathor. Both Athene's chief priestess at Athens and Hera's at Argos were members of the Lion clan, into which they adopted sacred kings. A gold ring found at Tiryns shows four lion men making a libation to a seated goddess, who may be Hera, the bird perching behind her throne may be a cuckoo.[11] (Fig. 20)

Hera's twins Ares and Eris were conceived when Hera touched the Hawthorn blossom (which is associated with miraculous conception in European myth) and its 'sister' thorn, the Blackthorn, which is associated with strife (Eris) (Graves, 2011:51).

Fig. 20 Solar Goddess or Priestess or Queen with Lions, signet ring, Tiryns, 14thC BCE.

Hera is shown with a sceptre and crown; her royal bird was the peacock, with its many-seeing eyes.

Graves, (2011:187) claims the Olympic games, the *Heraia*, were originally a foot race, run by girls, for the privilege of becoming the priestess of the Moon Goddess Hera (Pausanius v.16.2). It is believed this was an annual event held in the month Parthenios, which means of the maiden [Gr παρθενειος]. The festival began with the presentation to Hera of a new *peplos* (robe) after which races were held in the Olympic stadium. The competitors wore short tunics, exposing their right shoulder and breast. The track was five sixths of the length of the Olympic track and the prizes were olive crowns (or headdresses) and some of the meat of the cow sacrificed to Hera.[12] When Zeus married Hera, i.e. when a new form of sacred marriage was introduced by the Achaeans, a second foot race was instituted for young men to be the consort of the priestess. (Fig. 21)

Zeus found Hera in Knossos where he unsuccessfully courted her, she was not interested and perhaps revolted by his warlike, arrogant manner. Zeus disguised himself as a cuckoo and she took him up and held him, whereupon he transformed himself back into a god and raped her, claiming her body as his, her shrine as his, her land as his. Myth has it, Hera was forced to marry Zeus through shame.[13] Perhaps this is better explained as patriarchy overcoming matriarchy through trickery, violence, rape, and social shaming. Rape is less a sexual act and more an expression of domination through humiliation; under patriarchy, women do not even

Fig. 21 Zeus and Hera, Temple of Hera, Sicily, 5thC BCE.

have agency over their own bodies, they are owned, invaded, and imprisoned and degraded by men.

Hera's forced marriage to Zeus may represent how Krete and Mycenae were overthrown by the Hellenes. Graves (2011:51) suggests that Zeus' trickery in becoming a lost cuckoo echoes how the Hellenes arrived in Krete as fugitives, bedraggled and helpless. Zeus took Hera's sceptre which was surmounted with the cuckoo. Gold leaf figurines of a naked Argive goddess holding cuckoos have been found at Mycenae and cuckoos perch on a gold-leaf model temple from the same site. On the Kretan sarcophagus from *Hagia Triada* a cuckoo perches on a *Labyris* (double axe). Perhaps the Kretans took pity on these refugees and they were given employment in the royal or temple guard. The warlike Hellenes subsequently seized the kingdom, in the same way Zeus seized Hera. It is known that Knossos was sacked in 1700 BCE and 1400 BCE, Mycenae in 1300 BCE.

The oldest tradition places the wedding of Hera and Zeus in the Garden of the Hesperides, which was a mystical symbol of fertility, in the heart of an eternal spring.[14] All the gods brought gifts to the wedding; Gaia (Mother Earth) gave Hera a tree with golden apples which she found to be so beautiful she planted them in her garden on the shores of the Ocean.[15] It was later guarded by the Hesperides in Hera's orchard on Mount Atlas. Other traditions say they were married in on the summit of Mount Ida in Phrygia or in Euboea where they landed when they came from Crete.[16] Festivals celebrating this 'first marriage' took place all over Greece (getting the message across). A statue of the goddess was dressed in the costume of a young bride and carried in procession through the city to a shrine where a marital bed had been made ready.[17]

Their wedding night took place on Samos and lasted 300 years;[18] the honeymoon lasted thirty years. It is suggested it took 300 years for the Hellenes to force monogamy (patriarchy) on Hera's people. Previously there had been no 'marriage' in the sense of owning and controlling women, but women and men took lovers as they wished, and children were a communal responsibility.

As the 'first lady' Hera's 'job' was to police wives and husbands. As such, myths of her vengefulness and jealousy are legion. She attacked her husband's 'mistresses' (or the women he raped) and their progeny. She tried to prevent Leto giving birth to Apollo and Artemis by distracting her daughter Eilithyia who was midwife to the gods. She persecuted Io and also Heracles and Dionysus sons of Zeus. She destroyed Heracles (see Gemini-Iris).

In this extract we see outraged Hera in action:

"At once then came the soulful eyed Queen, Hera. With the flat of her hand she struck the earth and uttered this command: 'Hear me now, heavenly Gaia and wide Ouranos, both the Titans and the gods living under the earth in great Tartarus, from whence both gods and men come. Listen one and all, give me a child without Zeus, no less in strength than him, but may he be better, as great as roving-eyed Zeus, son of Kronos.'

Immediately she spoke, pounding the earth with her great hands; then life-giving Gaia began to move and seeing this, Hera was delighted down to her soul, for she intended to accomplish this." *The Homeric Hymn to Apollo*[19] 333–342)

Zeus had offended Hera by giving birth to Athene through his head, side stepping her 'role' as mother and child bearer. So, Hera asks the earth itself, Gaia, to give her a child parthenogenically. She calls on all the gods, the Olympians, and the Titans, (pre-Olympians). By pounding on the earth with her hands, the earth is impregnated. Hera then retreats with dignity to her temples,

"From this time then, for an entire year not once did she go to the bed of Zeus the wise counsel nor once to her richly wrought throne, which formerly she sat on, giving counsel to him with her shrewd judgement: instead, she waited in her temples where many sacrificed to her, soulful-eyed Hera delighted in these offerings." (*Homeric Hymn to Apollo* 343–348)

Hera gives birth.

"So then, when the months and the days came to an end and as the year passed and the seasons went around, the goddess gave birth to one neither of the gods nor of mankind, Typhoon (Typhoeus), both wondrous and calamitous, the bane of mankind. At once, soulful eyed Queen Hera took it and presented it to the female dragon (at Delphi) giving evil (trouble) to evil (trouble), and she (the she-dragon) welcomed it into her home." (349–354)

So, Hera gave birth parthenogenically to an evil being, neither mortal nor immortal and she gave it to the 'evil' female dragon. What are we to make of this? This hymn is rich in symbolism. The goddess, without the god, is mother to monsters? The dark earth needs the light masculine principle to banish its darkness/wickedness/evil doings? Any child who is not born of the union of male and female is a monster?

The myth of Apollo slaying the female dragon is usually read as the light-principle overcoming the darkness, the sophisticated over the primitive, mind over instinct. Remembering that Hera was the greater goddess, to whom massive temple shrines were erected, the myth seems again to show the violent overthrow of an earth goddess to a solar one. This 'monster' was conceived parthenogenically by Hera, furious about Zeus' creation of Athena. Her revenge is deep and deadly, she withdraws from his bed and his life and stays in her temples, receiving offerings. Gaia, the earth does her bidding and something non-human is born, which hunts men and kills them. The monster is the hideous, the shadow side of Leo/Hera who, when her dignity is assaulted, is vicious and vengeful. The dragon is of course a female figure, chthonic (of the deep earth) who represents our instincts and our fears. The bright shining Apollo rejects the earth, the shadow, the powerful female archetype; patriarchy has no need for it. They only wish the powerless, risible feminine, which they control through violence and neuter with ridicule.

To my mind this is such a Leonine story. How dare he! How dare he! Her wounded pride is terrible to behold. And her vengeance deadly. For those who know any strong Leonine women, it will come as no surprise that Hera is their goddess, not because she was wife of Zeus but because she was a great, powerful goddess in her own right, long before he came along. She fights, she suffers assaults on her dignity badly and will not be crushed, silenced or dismissed. All very Leonine. Leo can be as sweet as honey, as long as she is queen bee, but vicious and unrelenting in her punishment of those who do not value her, respect her and (ahem) worship her. The warmth and light and welcome of a Leo woman is a glory to behold; but remember the dragon; this lady has fangs.

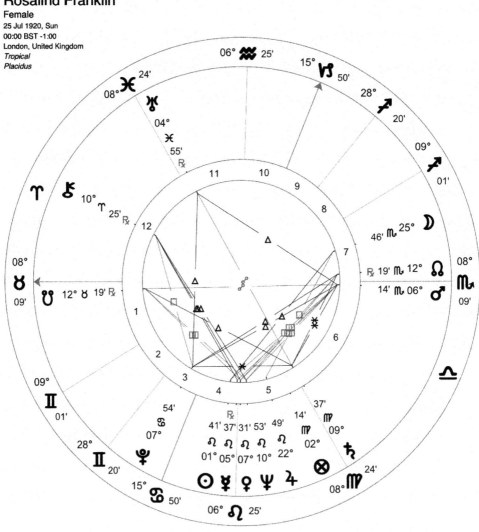

Rosalind Franklin

Female
25 Jul 1920, Sun
00:00 BST -1:00
London, United Kingdom
Tropical
Placidus

Rosalind Franklin: Brilliance
25 July 1920 (no time) London

"I considered her a genius, and I don't use that word lightly."[20]
J. D. Bernal, head of physics, Birkbeck, University of London.

Rosalind was an English chemist and X-ray crystallographer who made contributions to the understanding of the molecular structures of DNA (deoxyribonucleic acid), RNA (ribonucleic acid), viruses, coal, and graphite. Although her works on coal and viruses were appreciated in her lifetime, her contributions to the discovery of the structure of DNA were largely recognised posthumously.

Rosalind has a brilliant Sun, Mercury, Neptune, Venus and Jupiter in Leo. Her Moon may be in Sagittarius or late Scorpio as we do not have her birth time.

After years of study and research at Cambridge and the British Coal Utilisation Research Association (BCURA), Rosalind earned her PhD in 1945. She became an accomplished X-ray crystallographer working as a *chercheur* (post-doctoral researcher) under Jacques Mering at the *Laboratoire Central des Services Chimiques de l'Etat* from 1947, and in 1951 moved to King's College London studying X-ray diffraction which would eventually reveal the double helix of DNA.[21]

Regrettably, there was bad feeling between her and the other researcher, Wilkins. Rosalind understood she would be independent (and shine as a true Leo) whereas Wilkins expected she would work with him, perhaps as his assistant, (painful for a Leo to be so undervalued).[22]

Cobb, (2015) suggests a personality clash, "Wilkins was quiet and hated arguments; Franklin was forceful and thrived on intellectual debate."[23] It could have been professional rivalry, simple misogyny, or anti-Semitism.

Rosalind's friend Norma Sutherland recalled her as forceful and uncompromising, "Her manner was brusque and at times confrontational—she aroused quite a lot of hostility among the people she talked to, and she seemed quite insensitive to this."[24] This may have been because Rosalind refused to be the docile, subservient woman expected in the 1950s and she was not interested in pandering to the male ego, just like Hera.

Leo can be both the imperious queen and the super supportive leader. It has been argued that Rosalind was 'difficult' but, being such a strong Leo type,

> "Expecting the high standards from others that she constantly demanded of herself, she prompted dislike as well as deep loyalty from colleagues."[25]

Rosalind had five planets in Leo (a Stellium), Sun, Mercury, Venus, Neptune and Jupiter. She was a star and some of her more insecure male colleagues did everything they could to diminish her brilliance. She may also have had Leo pride which reacts negatively when disrespected.

"Franklin's surviving letters confirm the testimony of friends and family that she was a person of intense feelings and intelligence who was committed to scientific research but also fully enjoyed leisure activities—sports, sewing, travelling, entertaining."[26]

Rosalind's preliminary work was pivotal to Watson and Crick discovering the helical structure of the DNA molecule. Photograph 51 taken by Rosalind and R. G. Gosling showed the clearest picture of DNA. Watson says of this, "My mouth fell open and my pulse began to race."[27] He pressed Wilkins for an interpretation of the measurements but Watson didn't know how to interpret a diffraction photo, other than that an "X" meant helix. Watson and Crick were not chemists and made mistakes in the structure.

Rosalind's precise observations from her X-ray crystallography revealed the exact chemical structure of DNA, not Photograph 51. Her data in a 1952 Medical Research Council report inspired Watson and Crick to alter the proposed structure of their model in 1953.[28]

Rosalind's calculations were included in a brief informal report in 1953 passed on to Watson and Crick who did not ask anyone at King's for permission to use Franklin's data, something she was particularly sensitive about. (Leo expects to be given her due and publicly recognised).

Professor Patricia Fara, President of the British Society for the History of Science (2016–18), Clare College, University of Cambridge wrote,

"This notoriously unpleasant and complex chain of events was mired in personal misunderstandings, resentments and ambitions, but also reflected contrasting approaches to scientific research. Whereas Franklin adhered to a methodological ideology, Crick and Watson built models as exploratory tools, without waiting until all the data had been compiled. Indeed, in their first brief announcement in *Nature*, Crick and Watson supplied no supporting experimental evidence other than Gosling and Franklin's photograph 51."[29]

(Notice the order in which the names are listed).

Maddox suggested they did not cite Rosalind's work because Watson and Crick would have had to say where the unpublished material had come from.[30] He writes, "Such acknowledgement as they gave her was very muted and always coupled with the name of Wilkins,"[31] who was not involved in Rosalind's research but had access to her findings.

Established at Birkbeck, Rosalind lead pioneering work on the molecular structures of viruses. After her death in 1958, her team member Aaron Klug continued her research, winning the Nobel Prize in Chemistry in 1982.

Rosalind died aged 37, of ovarian cancer; it has been suggested that her intensive work with X rays may have been a contributory factor.[32] Hera also shows courage, in the face of terrible circumstances.

"Her (Rosalind's) devotion to research showed itself at its finest in the last months of her life. Although stricken with an illness which she knew would be fatal, she continued to work right up to the end."[33]

Other scientists:
Alice Ball, 24 July 1892. (No time) Seattle, Washington State (Sun, Moon, Mercury in Leo).

Jacqueline Kennedy Onassis

Female
28 Jul 1929, Sun
14:30 EDT +4:00
East Patchogue, New York
Tropical
Placidus

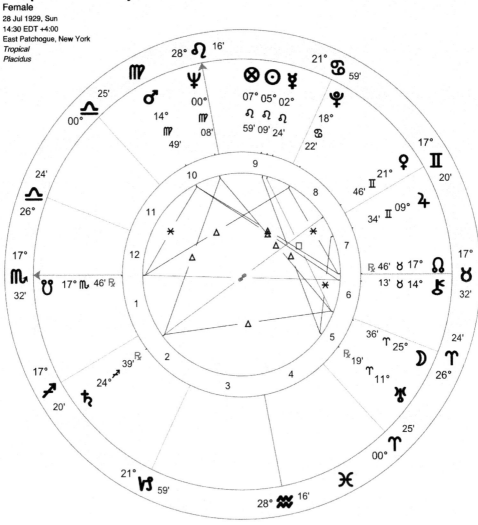

Jacqueline Kennedy Onassis: Queen consort
28 July 1929. (14:30) Southampton New York

Another heroic Leo was Jacqueline Kennedy Onassis. She had a Sun, Mercury conjunction in Leo in the ninth house and a Leo MC. Jacqueline epitomises the wounded consort of powerful men. She was the consummate partner; beautiful, stylish, intelligent, she supported her husband who was a visionary, but also a sick man, and who had affairs throughout their marriage which must have pained her, although theirs was a love match,

> "Now, I think that I should have known that he was magic all along. I did know it—but I should have guessed that it would be too much to ask to grow old with him and see our children grow up together. So now, he is a legend when he would have preferred to be a man."[34]
>
> "Don't let it be forgot, that once there was a spot, for one brief, shining moment that was known as Camelot. There'll be great presidents again ... but there will never be another Camelot."[35]

In her senior class yearbook, Jacqueline was acknowledged for, "Her wit, her accomplishment as a horsewoman, and her unwillingness to become a housewife."[36]

She won a twelve-month junior editorship at *Vogue* magazine; she had been selected over several hundred other women nationwide. The position entailed working for six months in the magazine's New York City office and spending the remaining six months in Paris. On her first day of work, the editor pointed out she was too old for this role; she was twenty-two, and should instead be thinking of marriage. Humiliated, she left after one day.[37]

Jaqueline subsequently worked for the *Washington Times Herald* and covered the coronation of Elizabeth II in London. She met politician John Kennedy through mutual friends. He proposed but, as she was working overseas, she took a month to accept.

Their wedding was the biggest social event of the season with 700 guests and a reception for 1200 people. Leo loves a party and wealth, luxury and extravagance. She campaigned for Kennedy during the Senate elections and the 'Jackie effect' was soon noticed,

> "The size of the crowd was twice as big" when she appeared with her husband, she was "always cheerful and obliging" although she was shy and not a natural campaigner.[38]

This demonstrates the brilliance of Leo the queen. Her intelligence was clear, she had, "Tremendous awareness, an all-seeing eye and a ruthless judgment."[39]

Kennedy was elected President in 1960. Although Jacqueline was pregnant and did not campaign with him, her style was the subject of media scrutiny. As First

Lady she undertook renovation of the White House reflecting its historic character. Jacqueline was the first Presidential wife to hire a press secretary, she kept her child away from the press, and became a fashion trendsetter with her classic pill box hats and Chanel suits.

Jacqueline helped Kennedy's international standing and often she was the focus of media attention. On one Paris visit Jacqueline, who spoke fluent French, delighted the crowds. President Kennedy joked,

> "I am the man who accompanied Jacqueline Kennedy to Paris—and I have enjoyed it!"[40]

In early 1963 her third child was born prematurely and died. Falling into depression, Jacqueline went to recuperate on her friend Aristotle's yacht. She was criticised for this. In November she accompanied Kennedy on a tour of Texas. He was shot and killed in a motorcade, as she sat beside him.

> "[I] saw in the President's car a bundle of pink, just like a drift of blossoms, lying in the back seat. It was Mrs Kennedy lying over the President's body."[41]

Images of his blood on her pink Channel suit, which she refused to change, shocked the world. Jacqueline said to the Vice President's Johnson's wife, let them "see what they have done to Jack."[42]

She continued to wear the blood-stained pink suit as she boarded Air Force One and stood next to Johnson when he took the oath of office as president. Her Scorpio Ascendant would not baulk at such a bloody display.

Her Leonine dignity and courage were lauded. Despite her fear of the crowds, and the reminders of Kennedy's death, she paid homage to another great man, by attended the funeral of Martin Luther King Jr in April 1968, but when her close confidant and Kennedy's brother Robert, was assassinated in June 1968 she feared for her children's safety.

> "If they're killing Kennedys, then my children are targets ... I want to get out of this country."[43]

Jacqueline married her old friend Onassis in Greece in October 1968 on Scorpios his private island. Onassis' vast wealth gave her the privacy and protection she needed for herself and her children. When Onassis died in 1975, she returned to New York, and for the remainder of her life worked in publishing as an editor, her first love (Sun, Mercury in the ninth house).

Although Jacqueline was the ultimate consort, tragic queen, son John F. Kennedy, Jr. said she died majestically,

"Surrounded by her friends and her family and her books, and the people and the things that she loved … She did it in her very own way, and on her own terms, and we all feel lucky for that."[44]

See also Princess Margaret of England (an unhappy Sun Leo) 21 August 1930. (21:22) Forfar, Scotland.

Notes

1. Grimal, 1987, p.192.
2. http://www.perseus.tufts.edu/hopper/text?doc=Perseus%3Atext%3A1999.01.0137%3Ahymn%3D12 accessed 23.6.2020.
3. Liddell and Scott, p.308.
4. https://mythopedia.com/greek-mythology/gods/hera/ accessed 9.1.2021.
5. https://www.ancient.eu/Hera/ accessed 27.6.2020.
6. March, 2002, p.193.
7. There is a great deal of dispute who and where the Pelasgians lived, Herodotus lists an area by common consent they inhabited most of Greece around the Aegean and some of the islands.
8. Jane Harrison *Myths of Greece and Rome* (1927) p.18.
9. Graves, 2011, p.55.
10. The etymology of Hera's name is subject to much debate.
11. Others suggest it depicts Demeter and the bird is an eagle see: Papathanassiou, Kyriakos. (undated). https://www.academia.edu/4389733/ON_THE_FAMOUS_MYCENAEAN_SIGNET_RING_CMS_I_179_OF_THE_TIRYNS_TREASURE?email_work_card=title accessed 3.7.2020.
12. Blundell, Sue. 1995. *Women in Ancient Greece.* British Museum Press, London. p.33.
13. Graves, 2011:50 *passim.*
14. Grimal, 1987, p.192.
15. A sacred king sacrificed to Hera whose body was safely under the earth and whose soul had gone to enjoy her paradise at the back of the North Wind. His golden Apples, in Greek and Celtic myth, were passports to paradise. Graves, 2011, p.52.
16. Grimal, 1987, p.192.
17. Grimal, 1987, p.193.
18. Graves, 2011, p.52.
19. https://www.perseus.tufts.edu/hopper/text?doc=Perseus%3Atext%3A1999.01.0137%3Ahymn%3D3 accessed 30.6.2020.
20. Tyson, Peter. *Defending Franklin's Legacy.* NOVA April 2003 https://www.pbs.org/wgbh/nova/photo51/elkin.html
21. Cobb, Matthew. June 23rd 2015. *Sexism in Science: did Watson and Crick really steal Rosalind Franklin's data?* Guardian Newspaper https://www.theguardian.com/science/2015/jun/23/sexism-in-science-did-watson-and-crick-really-steal-rosalind-franklins-data accessed 10.1.2021.

22. Lee, Jane, J. May 19th 2013. *6 Women Scientists who were snubbed due to sexism.* National Geographic https://www.nationalgeographic.com/news/2013/5/130519-women-scientists-overlooked-dna-history-science/ accessed 11.1.2021.

23. Cobb, Matthew. June 23rd 2015. *Sexism in Science: did Watson and Crick really steal Rosalind Franklin's data?* Guardian Newspaper https://www.theguardian.com/science/2015/jun/23/sexism-in-science-did-watson-and-crick-really-steal-rosalind-franklins-data accessed 10.1.2021.

24. Cobb, Matthew. June 23rd 2015. *Sexism in Science: did Watson and Crick really steal Rosalind Franklin's data?* Guardian Newspaper https://www.theguardian.com/science/2015/jun/23/sexism-in-science-did-watson-and-crick-really-steal-rosalind-franklins-data accessed 10.1.2021.

25. Fara, Patricia. The Rosalind Franklin Institute https://www.rfi.ac.uk/about/rosalind-franklin/ accessed 11.1.2021.

26. Fara, Patricia. The Rosalind Franklin Institute https://www.rfi.ac.uk/about/rosalind-franklin/ accessed 11.1.2021.

27. Cobb, Matthew. June 23rd 2015. *Sexism in Science: did Watson and Crick really steal Rosalind Franklin's data?* Guardian Newspaper https://www.theguardian.com/science/2015/jun/23/sexism-in-science-did-watson-and-crick-really-steal-rosalind-franklins-data accessed 10.1.2021.

28. Tyson, Peter. *Defending Franklin's Legacy.* NOVA April 2003 https://www.pbs.org/wgbh/nova/photo51/elki-glossary.html#bern

29. Fara, Patricia. The Rosalind Franklin Institute https://www.rfi.ac.uk/about/rosalind-franklin/ accessed 11.1.2021.

30. Maddox, Brenda. 2003. *Rosalind Franklin: The Dark Lady of DNA.* London: Harper Collins. p.207.

31. Maddox, Brenda. 2003. *Rosalind Franklin: The Dark Lady of DNA.* London: Harper Collins. pp.316–7.

32. Tyson, Peter. *Defending Franklin's Legacy.* NOVA April 2003 https://www.pbs.org/wgbh/nova/photo51/elkin.html accessed 11.01.2021.

33. Bernal, John Desmond https://www.azquotes.com/quote/997587 accessed 12.01.2021.

34. Quoted from article written by Jacqueline Kennedy for *Look* Magazine (17 November 1964) JFK memorial issue.

35. White, Theodore, H. *An Epilogue.* Life Magazine, Dec 6, 1963, pp. 158–159. https://books.google.co.uk/books?id=T1IEAAAAMBAJ&pg=PA158&redir_esc=y#v=onepage&q&f=false accessed 12.1.2021

36. Spoto, Donald. (2000). *Jacqueline Bouvier Kennedy Onassis: A Life.* St. Martin's Press, p.57.

37. Leaming, Barbara. (2014). *Jacqueline Bouvier Kennedy Onassis: The Untold Story.* Macmillan, London. pp.19–21.

38. Spoto, pp.142–144.

39. Schlesinger, Arthur M., Jr. (2002) [1965]. *A Thousand Days: John F. Kennedy in the White House.* Mariner Books. New York. p.17.

40. Blair, W. Grainger (June 3, 1961). *"Just an Escort, Kennedy Jokes As Wife's Charm Enchants Paris; First Lady Wins Bouquets From Press—She Also Has Brief Chance to Visit Museum and Admire Manet".* The New York Times accessed 12.1.2021.

41. Lady Bird Johnson. *Selections from Lady Bird's Diary on the assassination: November 22, 1963. Portrait of a First Lady* https://www.pbs.org/ladybird/epicenter/epicenter_doc_diary.html accessed 12.1.2021.

42. Lady Bird Johnson. *Selections from Lady Bird's Diary on the assassination: November 22, 1963. Portrait of a First Lady* https://www.pbs.org/ladybird/epicenter/epicenter_doc_diary.html accessed 12.1.2021.

43. Seelye, Katherine (July 19, 1999). *"John F. Kennedy Jr., Heir to a Formidable Dynasty"*. The New York Times.

44. https://www.youtube.com/watch?v=XvqOCSRH4-E accessed 12.1.2021.

Virgo: Demeter

It is a warm summer's day. You are standing at the edge of a ripe cornfield. The sky is bright blue. There is a soft breeze and the golden corn sways gently in the wind. You watch the ripe crops, ready for harvest and you are content.

As your feet are planted firmly on the ground, you feel the whole of life buzzing beneath them, the warm, rich earth, the moist green grass, the insects hurrying about, keeping life going. You feel your body working effortlessly as you stand there, inner and outer in perfect harmony.

Now you rest at the edge of the harvested field, the crop has been cut down and stored for the winter, the dark earth is revealed. Harvest, the cycle of life, sow, growth, harvest, rest.

As night falls you follow a torch lit procession around the fields as women sing a dirge, older women, Crones, lead them, their faces marked with the passage of time. They lead you through the darkness to an altar in a grove of trees.

Here they speak of the reaping, the barrenness, the relentless cycle of birth and death. They teach the Mysteries. Torches are lit and as food is shared the Sun rises and together you welcome in another day, new and reborn. You do not forget the darkness but you welcome the light, old and young, mother, maiden and crone. You are life, past, present and future.

Demeter was the grain Mother of settled agriculture, unlike Gaia who was the Earth mother of hunter gatherers. Demeter originated from Krete her name comes from deai-δηαι-barley/grains, or de-δη earth, meter μητηρ, mother.[1] Demeter had male companions, maybe lovers or apprentices. Another name for her is 'she who bears fruits' (καρφορος-husks, chaff, that which is dry). Agriculture was magically dependent on women. Its success connected with fertility and childbearing.[2]

"Lovely haired Demeter, august goddess... Aloof Demeter of the Golden Sword,
Giver of the Fruits of the Earth." *Homeric Hymn to Demeter,* (1–5)[3]

Demeter is the grief of the mother, both the biological mother and the grain mother.
(Fig. 22) There is a long Homeric *Hymn to Demeter* which describes her experience of
losing her child with vivid and heart-breaking intensity. When she hears Persephone's
voice calling out for help, (for the story of Persephone see Taurus and Scorpio).

"A sharp pain seized her heart, and she ripped apart with her lovely hands, the
headdress covering her lose flowing immortal hair. She threw off her dark cloak
from both shoulders and set off like a huge bird of prey. Across dry land and watery
oceans, she searched for her [Kore/Persephone]." (40–44)[4]

Demeter shows the pain and passion of motherhood. In a gesture of mourning she rips
apart her head covering and releases her wild hair. Women's hair is one of their super-
powers, unbinding and uncovering hair throws down a gauntlet to patriarchy, which
loves to cover up, or even shave hair off, it is so dangerous. Her hair free, Demeter is
transformed into a bird of prey with huge wings. She soars over earth and sea, searching for her daughter. Extraordinary imagery, of a powerful primaeval force, a solitary
journey, gliding and hovering as these raptors do. And she is alone, without help. No
one will tell her anything. Still she continues, a heartbroken mother seeking her child.

"For nine[5] days afterwards Queen Deo roamed the earth, holding in her hands
flaming pine torches.[6] Grief struck, she took neither ambrosia nor sweet nectar, nor
did she bathe her body with water." (47–50)

Fig. 22 Demeter/Goddess, fresco, Mycenaean 1300 BCE.

Demeter searches for nine days.[7] She wanders across the earth with lighted torches, fasting and filthy. This is the mask of mourning, no comfort, no sustenance just deep immersion in feeling and with hope that her daughter will be found, and all will return to normal. But of course, after tragedy there is no return, there is a new normal, going back cannot happen whatever the privations and sacrifices made. It is done. The grief is concocted within her, gathering in her heart as grief does. It will eventually give birth to a new reality, but not yet. The magical number nine may also represent the human gestation period.

> "But when on the tenth day, she came upon the light of dawn. Hecate came to her, holding a torch in her hands and bearing a message for her." (*Homeric Hymn to Demeter* 51–52)

Here, Hekate is not the feared goddess of witchcraft she becomes under patriarchy,[8] but a crone, an elder who was in her cave and heard Persephone's cries for help. She comes from her seclusion, or perhaps meditation, and completes the triad of Mother: Demeter, Maiden: Kore and Crone: Hekate, the sacred trinity of the Goddess. They may also represent body: Kore, emotions: Demeter and mind: Hecate. Once Hekate arrives, Demeter realises focused action needs to be taken, her emotional outpouring will not solve their problem. Hekate speaks,

> "Queen Demeter, you who bring on the fruits in their season, bestowing splendid gifts. Which of the gods of the heavens and mortal men, kidnapped Persephone and put your beloved soul in mourning? For her voice was heard, but I did not see with my eyes who it was." (54–57)

The Crone Hekate knows a violence has been done to the child, Crones are traditionally the wise women, seers and wisdom keepers. Crones watch and gather wisdom and they are on hand to help mothers and maidens. Together they go to Helios, who travels over the earth in his chariot and sees everything that happens there. He tells them,

> "Queen Demeter, lovely haired daughter of Rhea, as you will see, I stand in great awe of you and take pity for your mourning for your daughter of the slim ankles. None other of the immortals has the blame, only Zeus the cloud gatherer. For he gave this nubile wife to Hades, his own brother who asked for her. And he carried her off to the murky, dark underworld with his horses, while she shouted loudly." (75–81)

Here we have the violent insertion of patriarchy into the world of goddesses. Zeus gifts his sister's child to his brother who asked for her. Women and girls have no agency, they are property to be bartered and gifted. Rape, abduction, and violence are normalised and, as Helios explains, this is no bad thing,

"But goddess, stop your loud weeping, there is no need to hold on to your great anger in vain in this way." (82–83)

Despite his 'awe' of her, Demeter's feelings are trivialised, and she is told to be quiet and let go of her anger. Helios continues,

"It is not shameful for your daughter to marry immortal Hades, ruler over many. He is your brother and from the same family, both an honour. He gained his portion, a third part of the first division of spoils he obtained by lot,[9] to be king of the multitude he lives with." (84–87)

So, rape and violence are less important than family honour and power. Whatever the details of her 'marriage' Demeter should be grateful her daughter is now married to a king. Demeter is not consoled or persuaded. She is raging.

"But the terrible pain and more anguish came into her heart, raging, then she turned her back on the son of Kronos surrounded by black clouds and on the assembly of gods and high Olympus and she went to the cities and the rich fields of men disguising her body for a long time." (90–94)

Demeter turns away from her Olympian family, there is no help for her there. She arrives at Eleusis (a sacred place, the name means, 'fragrant with incense') and sits beside the *well of the maiden* under the shade of an olive tree. Again, it is women who rescue Demeter and offer her refuge and succour. The King's four daughters whose names suggest their natures, *Kallidike* (beautiful justice), *Kleisidike* (the key to justice) *Demo* (the people) and *Kallithoe* (beautiful sacrifices) arrive at the well to draw water (wells are liminal spaces where women gather and network, but also where danger exists, women are often kidnapped at the well).[10]

Demeter explains how she came to be in Eleusis.

"I came on the wide vastness of the sea from Krete, unwillingly, by force, against my will, through fate the male pirates took me away. And when the nimble ship put in at *Thorikus*, there the women in a crowd and the men too, went on land and were preparing a meal at the stern of the ship. But for me, my spirit did not wish for this delicious meal, so secretly I hurried away and fled that black land and the arrogant sailors. For not having been bought, they could not sell me into slavery nor enjoy my honour. In this way I came here wandering. But I do not know what this land is nor who lives here." (123–134)

Demeter recounts arriving on mainland Greece. Eleusis is a Mycenaean city about seventeen kilometres from Athens. It is possible this episode describes the invasion of Krete[11] by Hellenes and the capture of its women for slavery. Rites like those in Eleusis were performed in Krete, open to all. Burkett claims that classical myths have a 'historical dimension'[12] because the people listening to them would need to recognise and relate to the story[13] so perhaps this is history she is recounting. Demeter is taken on as a nurse to Demophoon son of the king. She says she will protect the child,

> "I will willingly take charge of this son of yours, as you bid me. I will nurture him. I trust he will not be harmed nor attacked by mischiefs of his nurse nor from bewitching spells. For I know a powerful antidote for evil, the best of charms and excellent safeguards against witchery or magical roots." (226–230)

Unlike Zeus who blasts humans with his thunderbolts, Demeter takes roots from the earth and prepares potions to protect. To thank them she decides to make the child an Immortal by burning away his human nature in the fire each night and anointing him with ambrosia during the day. But to no avail, the child's mother discovers them and screams, breaking the spell. Demeter furious reveals herself as goddess.

> "So spoke the magnificent goddess and she changed her form, discarding the old woman. Her beauty spread out around and a lovely fragrance emanated from her perfumed robes. From the divine body of the goddess a glowing light was cast far and wide. Her golden locks tumbled down on her shoulders." (276–279)

From the darkness of mourning comes light. Demeter is still a goddess. Like a shock to the system, she remembers who she is.

> "Behold I am Demeter, who is the greatest and much honoured and who brings advantage and who makes delight for both men and gods!" (268–70)

And she finds her power again. Another Virgoan trait, they can seem humble and ordinary, like a nanny, but beneath they shine out with beauty and radiance. These are good lessons for Virgo, who too easily takes a back seat and a modest role, because she is wounded or denied. But she is the bright goddess, full of lustre and perfume.

The women wait through the night with the goddess (one could speculate what transpired, perhaps an initiation). In the morning, the men are summoned, Demeter instructs them,

> "Come now and made ready a great temple for me and an altar and below it the whole country, beneath the city with a high, steep wall on a hill above the place of the beautiful dances (the well of the Kallichorus[14])." (270–274)

The temple is built above the city of Eleusis as instructed, and Demeter goes there.

> "… Golden Demeter sat down there, far away from all the blessed gods, she waited with longing, diminished, for her richly dressed daughter. And she made a dread year on all the nourishing earth and for mankind truly terrible. The earth did not

send up any seedlings, hidden by richly dressed Demeter. Many were the ploughs and oxen dragged on to the earth in vain, and much bright barley fell on to the earth to no avail. For now, she would wholly destroy the race of articulate mankind from hard famine, she deprived the Olympians of the glorious honour of offerings and having sacrifices and gifts." (303–12)

Demeter has remembered where her power lies; shouting, pleading, wandering are futile, she withdraws and waits (and perhaps meditates). Despite his bluster and dramatics, Zeus and the other gods cannot survive when Demeter blights the land. Men will no longer sacrifice to the gods and they will all die. By non-action, Demeter's power is devastating. She shows her hand without words, and soon enough even Zeus himself is begging her to stop her blight. She will not. Until her daughter is returned to her, Demeter is adamant, the famine will continue. Zeus capitulates.

This is the power of Virgo. She does not confront but shows rather than telling. Domestic life is devalued until labour is withdrawn and then everyone realises that life grinds to a halt without her daily rituals; bread is not baked, nor clothes washed, nor children fed, life is blighted. It takes a lot for Virgo to stop, but when she does it is devastating. I am writing this during the 'lock down' in the UK following the corona virus in 2020–1. When everything stopped, we all saw who were the important people that made our life possible; supermarket workers, delivery drivers, healthcare professionals, teachers, transport workers, the quiet people behind the scenes who ordinarily we did not notice, suddenly we became incredibly grateful for their work, carrying on quietly in those fearful times. This is Virgo, like the bees who pollinate our crops, we will not notice them until they have gone, and nothing grows, and we starve (see Mercury the Melissae).

In thanks to the people of Eleusis, Demeter teaches them her Mysteries.

"And I myself will demonstrate these mysteries, so when you are performing them purely, you may appease my heart." (274)

Virgo the sign of ritual, the grain, fertility and barrenness, magic and dance, music and meditation. All these were incorporated in Demeter's Mysteries. The *Eleusinian Mysteries* were open to all, men, women, citizens and slaves and concerned the descent and ascent of Persephone. The *Thesmophoria* for women citizens only related to the mourning of Demeter. (see Appendix 3 for details)

Negatively, ritual can express itself as compulsions such as obsessive-compulsive disorder (OCD) for which Virgo is known, but harness that ritualistic nature to the positive and you get people who embody and integrate ritual in their daily lives. The classic example is Yoga, particularly Ashtanga Yoga where the practitioner repeats the same sequence six days a week, a moving meditation. This is a very Virgoan activity, using the physical body (earth) ritual (Virgo) to reach a meditative state (and maybe even enlightenment) through discipline and surrender. Kino is the female face of yoga.

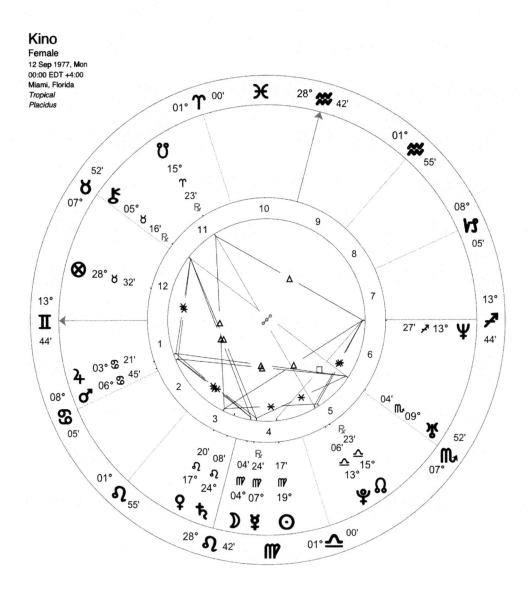

Kino
Female
12 Sep 1977, Mon
00:00 EDT +4:00
Miami, Florida
Tropical
Placidus

Kino MacGregor: Yoga practitioner
12 September 1977. (no time) Miami FL

"When you come to the yoga mat, you are starting on a journey that will turn you into a totally new person, if you let it. In order to be re-invented, you have to acknowledge that—despite all you know—you really don't know anything."[15]

Kino has Mercury Moon and Sun in Virgo which show her dedication, attention to fine detail, and spiritual questing, Mars Jupiter in Cancer show her caring for her tribe of yogi, exemplified by her large network of followers and her non-judgemental, warm style of communicating. Venus Saturn in Leo will show her need to perform (Leo) and the downside of fame (Saturn). She has received much criticism for her style of dress, her way of teaching, but as a true Virgo she has studied the practice in depth with an ancient lineage of yoga.

Kino became the youngest certified Ashtanga yoga teacher when she was twenty-nine (this is the time of the Saturn return see Transits). Kino has practised yoga for the past twenty years. She follows the lineage of Vamana Rishi and the Ashtanga method of K. Pattabhi Jois of Mysore India.

"Yoga and the awakening of the spiritual path are a full-fledged revolution of the mind. It is about deep and permanent healing of the core of your being and a restoration to your true nature, that is love."[16]

MacGregor's Instagram account where she shares her yoga practice, teachings, yoga challenges and inspirational writing and photos of her Ashtanga Yoga practice has 1.1 million followers as of January 2019.

"We have the freedom to choose how we react, even when it feels like we can't control it. But that lack of control is just a habit that's set up shop in our minds. In yoga, we call this samsara. *Samsaras* are habitual reactions influenced by moments that happened in the past."[17]

MacGregor's YouTube channel created in 2011 has 738,000 subscribers and over 140 million views. MacGregor is currently practicing Fifth Series (Advanced Series C) within the Ashtanga Yoga method. With Sun, Moon and Mercury in hardworking, detail orientated Virgo, Kino emphasises there is no quick fix.

"Stillness is the mind's unrealized potential, the promised land of consciousness just on the other side of the river of thoughts. To get there, like everything else in yoga, you have to practice."[18]

Kino has written about her own mental health issues and uses Vipassana meditation and increasingly shares meditation techniques with her followers.

> "The steps that spiritual growth traces are more circular, winding, twisting, meandering. Inner learning takes time and patience for the lessons to steep deeply into the folds of your soul There is no fast track for the unravelling of years or potentially lifetimes of old patterning."[19]

Like many serious yoga practitioners, Kino steers away from spiritual competitiveness, instead counselling a down to earth (Virgo) approach to enlightenment,

> "No matter if your awakening happens today, tomorrow, or in a thousand years, it will all be exactly the same. What matters is that you are here, now, and have the potential to put in the work, to take a few steps further on the path, and to live a life with just a bit more happiness, peace and joy. Perhaps that in and of itself could be considered living life fully awake, with your spiritual eyes wide open."[20]

MacGregor has written five books including a memoir, *Sacred Fire: My Journey into Ashtanga Yoga* (2012). In 2013, she published *The Power of Ashtanga Yoga*; a comprehensive view of the practice and her personal insights and guidance. Her latest book, *Get Your Yoga On*, (2020), is aimed at widening the appeal of yoga to all ages, peoples, body types and levels of fitness.

> "The traditional practice of yoga is about waking up your potential to live in alignment, harmony and connection with this powerful, grand energy that is the Source of all life. Obviously, this state of wakefulness is not just about standing on your head or putting your leg behind your head. The yogic state is a 24-hours a day, 7 days a week, 365 days a year commitment to elevate, evolve and awaken. This is a sadhana."[21]

Kino runs the OMstars online channel to bring yoga to the world and make it accessible to everyone. It presents a variety of yoga methods, the philosophical background to yoga, pranayama and chanting and a diverse range of teachers.

> "Liberation only happens when it happens for all. Liberation for one is not liberation at all."[22]

Mary Shelley
Female
30 Aug 1797, Wed
23:20 LMT +0:00
Greenwich
Tropical
Placidus

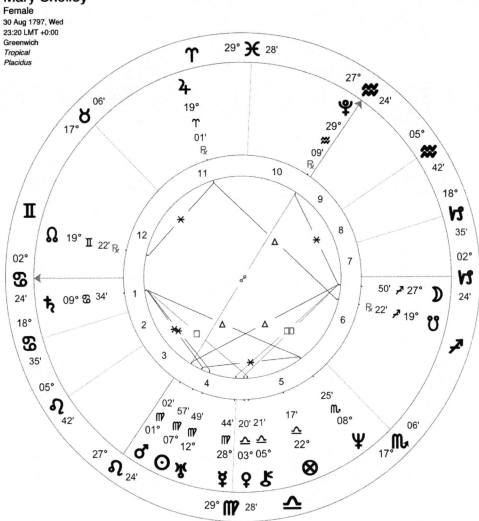

Mary Shelley: Writer, futurist
30-08-1797. 23h20 London

Mary Shelley has Mars, Sun, Uranus, and Mercury in Virgo.

Mary was the daughter of feminist philosopher, Mary Wollstonecraft (see Taurus), and political philosopher William Godwin, who raised her. He described her, aged fifteen, as,

> "Singularly bold, somewhat imperious, and active of mind. Her desire of knowledge is great, and her perseverance in everything she undertakes almost invincible."[23]

Mary had the sharp Virgo mind and the persistence and hard work of an earth sign. Uranus conjunct the Sun gives a brilliance as well as an eccentricity and wilfulness. Uranus was newly discovered, (1781) and is associated with the discovery of electricity as well as revolution. The cluster of planets in her fourth house suggests her life's work was looking for her 'tribe', her people. Her Moon in Sagittarius shows a love of philosophy and the need for freedom, it is a wandering, questioning Moon. Virgo loves the natural world and understands the importance of solitude in nature to feel her feet on the ground and orientate herself.

> "It was beneath the trees of the grounds belonging to our house, or on the bleak sides of the woodless mountains near, that my true compositions, the airy flights of my imagination, were born and fostered."[24]

The intelligentsia of her time was interested in chemistry and what we now call physics; two of the most noted natural philosophers among her contemporaries were Giovanni Aldini, who made many public attempts at human reanimation through bio-electric Galvanism in London[25] and Johann Konrad Dippel, who claimed to have substances which prolonged life. There was much debate how to identify the dead, and many people were miraculously brought back to life especially after drowning.

Mary's most famous book was *Frankenstein*. The original subtitle of the book was *The Modern Prometheus* which refers to the Greek myth of the Titan Prometheus who created humankind in the image of the gods, so Zeus could breathe on them and animate them. Prometheus taught man to hunt, stole fire from the gods and gave it to mankind. Fire meant man was able to cook flesh and eat it. Mary was a radical vegetarian and considered meat-eating had a brutalising effect on people.

Victor Frankenstein resembles Prometheus, who created a man using new technology to re-animate a corpse.

Mary eloped with the poet Shelley when she was sixteen and for the next few years travelled in Europe with him and other friends, including the poet Byron. Mary wrote that they discussed these issues,

"I was a devout but nearly silent listener. Perhaps a corpse would be re-animated; galvanism had given token of such things: perhaps the component parts of a creature might be manufactured, brought together, and endued with vital warmth. Night waned upon this talk, and even the witching hour had gone by before we retired to rest. When I placed my head on my pillow, I did not sleep, nor could I be said to think. My imagination, unbidden, possessed and guided me, gifting the successive images that arose in my mind with a vividness far beyond the usual bounds of reverie. I saw—with shut eyes, but acute mental vision,—I saw the pale student of unhallowed arts kneeling beside the thing he had put together. I saw the hideous phantasm of a man stretched out, and then, on the working of some powerful engine, show signs of life, and stir with an uneasy, half vital motion."[26]

This typical Uranian flash of brilliance is like a waking vision. Mary's description of bringing the creature to life reminds us of Demeter, re-animating or burning off the human portion of Demophoon.

"He grew up in the women's room[27] and he grew like a god, eating neither grains nor breastfeeding his mother's milk. For by day, beautiful-crowned Demeter anointed him with ambrosia as if he were born a god and blew sweetness over him as she held him to her breasts. While at night she hid him in the heart of the fire, like a brand, in secret from his loving parents, for whom it was a marvel how he grew, his precocious development, for face to face he resembled one of the gods. And she might have made him both un-ageing and immortal, if richly dressed Metanoia (his mother) had not foolishly one night looked in from her fragrant bedroom and seen." (*Homeric Hymn to Demeter* 235–245)

Demeter intends to confer immortality on the child, the greatest gift she can give, but humans interfere where they should not; Frankenstein meddles with the natural order of things and creates a monster.

"Frightful must it be; for supremely frightful would be the effect of any human endeavour to mock the stupendous mechanism of the Creator of the world."[28]

Mary Shelley experienced much death in her life; her mother died days after giving birth to her, Shelley died in a boating accident, and three of her four children died in childhood. No stranger to loss and despair, like Demeter, Mary experienced the dark, lonely halls of grief,

"Solitude was my only consolation - deep, dark, deathlike solitude."[29]

Raised as a free thinking woman and a feminist, Mary Shelley lived life on her own terms, financially supporting marginalised women, and having a literary career.

Her experiments with an open marriage with Shelley brought her heartache, the public and private censure of her lifestyle and 'morals,' and she had to fight to retain custody of her surviving son after Shelley's death.

Mary wrote throughout her life; she published novels, travel journals, a volume of her mother's letters, and edited her husband Percy Bysshe Shelley's poetry. In *Falkner*, (1837) she argues that when female values of solidarity, cooperation and compassion supersede violent and destructive masculinity, men will be liberated to express their kindness, and generosity.

Her biographical sketches for *Lardner's Cabinet Cyclopedia* (1829–46) demonstrated her radical beliefs. She criticised patriarchal institutions such as primogeniture and wrote of the value of domesticity, romance, family, sympathy and benevolence which she believed would improve society. The huge print run of these books, 40,000 per volume, gave her radical politics a wide audience. Her travelogues[30] also gave a platform for her political arguments against war, the monarchy, slavery and the class system. But it is *Frankenstein* she is remembered for.

Virgo is found in many writers, the famous Agatha Christie, Jeanette Winterson, Edith Sitwell, A.S. Byatt. Mary Shelley, who wrote Frankenstein, illustrates that Virgo need for order and service as well as debating the nature of good and evil and transforming the dead, making life out of death.

Notes

1. Liddell and Scott, *Greek English Lexicon,* (1944) Clarendon Press, Oxford p.157.
2. Harrison *Prologemena* p.273, 271.
3. http://www.perseus.tufts.edu/hopper/text?doc=Perseus%3Atext%3A1999.01.0137%3Ahymn%3D2 accessed 5.7.2020.
4. http://www.perseus.tufts.edu/hopper/text?doc=Perseus%3atext%3a1999.01.0137%3ahymn%3d2 accessed 21.6.2020.
5. Hera is the Greek word for nine, see note ccxvi blow.
6. Torches are used in the Eleusian rites see Appendix 2.
7. The Pythagoreans (c6th C BCE) believed nine was a sacred number, it was the number of the seven planets plus earth and what they called Central Fire, the tenth planet, Counter Earth, was so secret it was perpetually hidden by the Sun. Perhaps Central Fire was Uranus and Counter Earth was Pluto?
8. The root of the word is Greek, pater-father (πατηρ) and rule-arche (αρχη) the rule of the fathers.
9. After the patriarchal takeover, the world was divided between the three brothers, Zeus the sky, Poseidon the sea and Hades the underworld.
10. Foley, p.41 Water is associated with virginity, initiation and marriage. Water for weddings was drawn from special wells. Water is the home of sybils, water sprites and the various female monsters that 'heroes' kill (see Pythia and Sun) Water is used for divination and in the performed secret rites at Eleusis, these four sisters may have been the first priestesses of the Mysteries. Wells could be dangerous places, women could be abducted or assaulted there, both drawing water from a well and carrying water used in the cults of Demeter and Persephone. Water collecting is usually work

for young women, hence their surprise at finding Demeter/Crone there. Demeter may have sat by the well Kallichoros (καλλιχορος-well of the beautiful dancers) which is a part of the ritual, a sacred olive grew beside it (olive again).

11. Graves, 2011, pp.95–6.
12. Burkett, Walter. *Greek Religion*. 1985. Harvard University Press, Cambridge MA. in Morford, 2015, p.14.
13. See also Morford, 2015, p.76 discusses Calimachus' first *Hymn to Zeus* which places Zeus not in Crete but Greece, reflecting the arrival of the Hellenes in Crete around 2000 BCE bringing Zeus with them. This is an attempt to link both the geography and geology of the gods of both cultures. Zeus from the Indo-Europeans and Rhea from the Near East.
14. Kalli-beautiful καλλι, chorus: women dancers, singers, musicians χορος.
15. Instagram post, 4 Jan 2021. https://www.instagram.com/kinoyoga/ accessed 13.1.2021.
16. Instagram post 1.12.2020. https://www.instagram.com/kinoyoga/ accessed 13.1.2021.
17. Instagram, 4.12.2001. https://www.instagram.com/kinoyoga/ accessed 13.1.2021.
18. Kino. *Yoga is Stillness*. (undated) https://www.kinoyoga.com/challenge-day-27-yoga-is-stillness/ accessed 13.1.2021.
19. Kino, 8.9.2020. *Planting the seeds of awakening*. Blogpost https://www.kinoyoga.com/blog-media/ accessed 13.1.2021.
20. Kino *Awakening* 18.1.2020. Blogpost. https://www.kinoyoga.com/blog-media/ accessed 13.1.2021.
21. Kino, *Practice, Abhyasa, Sadhana*. Blogpost (undated) https://www.kinoyoga.com/blog-media/page/5/ accessed 13.1.2021.
22. Kino, Instagram post 25.10.2020. https://www.instagram.com/p/CGxgN2cnR_g/ accessed 14.1.2021.
23. Sunstein, Emily W. *Mary Shelley: Romance and Reality*. 1991. Baltimore: Johns Hopkins University Press. p.58.
24. Spark, Muriel. *Mary Shelley*. London: Cardinal, 1987. p.17.
25. *Ruston, Sharon (25 November 2015). "The Science of Life and Death in Mary Shelley's Frankenstein". The Public Domain Review*. https://publicdomainreview.org/essay/the-science-of-life-and-death-in-mary-shelleys-frankenstein. *Accessed 9.7.2020.*
26. *Ruston, Sharon (25 November 2015). "The Science of Life and Death in Mary Shelley's Frankenstein". The Public Domain Review*. https://publicdomainreview.org/essay/the-science-of-life-and-death-in-mary-shelleys-frankenstein. *Accessed 9.7.2020. (unreferenced).*
27. It is interesting that the word for women's room megaron (μεγαρον) is the same word for sanctuary, shrine and the pits sacred to Demeter and Persephone into which piglets were thrown in the festival of Thesmorphoria.
28. Quoted in Spark, Muriel. *Mary Shelley*. London: Cardinal, 1987. p.157, from Mary Shelley's introduction to the 1831 edition of Frankenstein.
29. https://www.goodreads.com/author/quotes/11139.Mary_Wollstonecraft_Shelley accessed 14.1.2021.
30. *History of a Six Weeks' Tour* (1817), *Rambles in Germany and Italy in 1840, 1842, and 1843* (1844).

Libra: Aphrodite Urania

Bright light, you stand as the sunlight shimmers, catching the dew on a spider's web. The world begins a brand new day. All around you is beauty, fresh green leaves, the warm summer's breeze of an early morning, the scent of flowers waking up on another gorgeous day. The whole wide vista from the tor you are standing on gives you a panorama of beauty.

You see women talking, laughing, sharing stories and you join them laughing, speaking their truths over the cauldron of the mind.

You begin the dance, someone takes up the flute, another the drum; as the song calls out, your beautiful clothes rustle in the breeze, a myriad of colours; magenta, turquoise, azure blue, crimson, violet, indigo, forest green, sun yellow, midnight blue, rose pink, scarlet, burnt umber, fiery orange. You become a swirling ribbon of colour and light.

You become one as they dance faster and faster, spinning, laughing, singing, flashing colour and sound. Your feet leave the earth and you fly, rippling through the warm air. You soar and glide and are weightless. Together you are beauty and you are one brilliant ribbon of colour, light and sound and laughter.

Aphrodite Urania is the airy Aphrodite, the goddess of the air sign Libra. She embodies the Libran worship of beauty and sees its connection with goodness.

> "For the beautiful only becomes so when seen,
> While the good will always become beautiful."

Sappho 50[1]

Although we do not have her birth details, Sappho is an ideal Aphrodite Urania. She was born on Lesbos around 630 BCE and lived in the city of Mytilene, which was a byword for luxurious living. Her work shows both Greek and Eastern Lydian influences (Lesbos was less than a day's travel from the capital of Lydia). Plato called her the Tenth Muse. She was celebrated by the Ancient Greeks as one of their finest poets, along with Homer. Sappho's image is found on vases and coins throughout history. The Roman poets Horace and Catullus, who read all her work, praised her style and brilliance. Few of Sappho's poems survive, reportedly, there were nine volumes of them.[2] Lines of her poetry were often quoted by later authors discussing her lyric poetry and style. Fragments have been recently discovered discarded as rubbish in the Egyptian desert at Oxyrhynchus. Sappho wrote a type of lyric poetry which is named after her. Her writing is sparse but deeply evocative of love, desire and heartbreak,

"Honestly, I wish I were dead.
When she left me she wept
Profusely and told me,
'Oh how we suffered in all this.'"

(Frag. 94[3])

Sappho's poetry was sung accompanied by the lyre.

"Come, divine lyre shell,
Become sweet music."

(118[4])

Aphrodite Urania loves the arts, especially music and poetry. (Fig. 23) Sappho is believed to have instructed the young women of the city in poetry, and possibly taught members of the female chorus who sang, danced and played the drums and pipes at wedding celebrations and rituals. Sappho mentions the Musicians House (Μοισοπολων) in one of her poems; this may have been a gathering place for the performance and study of music. Sappho may have been a *Thiasos* (θιασος) a person singing and dancing in honour of the goddess.[5] *Thiasai* existed in Sparta and elsewhere in Greece. Here, Sappho writes of the marriage celebrations of Hektor and Andromache.

'The sweet melody of the double flute and
The clatter of the sistras
and the maidens high-voiced sang sacred songs
and the wondrous music reached the heavens,
and everywhere in the streets mixing bowls and cups
with myrrh and cassia and frankincense combined ... [making incense]
and the older women with their chorus sang."

(44[6])

Fig. 23 Sappho, vase, 5thC BCE.

Sappho's poems are full of luxury and beauty,

> "With delicious scarlet clothes,
> Golden bracelets
> Beautiful multicoloured jewels, ivory
> And untold silver engraved chalices."

(44)

Sappho's poetry mirrors the *Homeric Hymn to Aphrodite;*

> "The golden crowned Horae[7] received her gladly and they wrapped immortal robes around her and on her divine head they placed a beautiful, exquisitely made, golden diadem, and in her pierced ears she was adorned with both copper and golden ornaments. And around her soft throat and her silver shining breast, the Horae arranged golden necklaces and fillets of gold which they themselves wore, so they could go to the enchanting dances of the gods in the palace of their father. And when they had put around her body all these adornments, they lead her to the immortals, who, seeing her kindly greeted her, they welcomed her with their hands and each one prayed to carry her home to be his wedded wife. They were spellbound by the gorgeous form of the violet crowned Kythereia." *Homeric Hymn to Aphrodite.* 6:1–18[8]

In the patriarchal myth Aphrodite Urania was not born from a woman but from the foam which came from the genitals of Uranus when Zeus cut them off and threw them in the sea. She was the goddess of Cyprus (Kypria) and the pre-patriarchal myth has her rise from the sea, birthed by the waves, no male genitalia involved. She ritually renews her virginity (natural purity—not sexual abstinence) in Paphos, Cyprus, as do Hera and Athena.[9]

It is believed Aphrodite originated in Syria or Palestine; she shares attributes in common with Ishtar and Astarte and entered Greece via Cyprus. When she was assimilated into the Hellenic myths she was 'married' to Hephaestus. Hephaestus' net, with which he traps Aphrodite, was originally hers as a sea goddess and was used in her rituals in Cyprus.[10]

Aphrodite's temple in Knossos had seashells embedded on the floor, and an image of her blowing the triton (conch) shell has been found on a gemstone from the Idean cave in Krete with a sea-anemone lying beside her altar; the sea urchin and cuttle fish were sacred to her.

Aphrodite Urania embodies, beauty, luxury, and adornment. Here is Aphrodite preparing to seduce,

> "She wore a shimmering robe brighter than a flashing flame encrusted with beautiful golden embroidery and it shone like the full moon upon her soft breasts, a marvel to see. And she fastened on twisted bracelets and glittering earrings shaped like

flowers and beautiful necklaces around her soft throat." *Homeric Hymn to Aphrodite.* (5: 86–92)[11]

This fragment from Sappho embodies the Libran Aphrodite: cerebral, a worshipper of all that is beautiful and poetic.

> "For I myself adore luxury, to me love possesses the magnificence and beauty of the sun." Sappho 76.[12]

Aphrodite Urania is refined and thoughtful; being airy she is articulate as well as a worshipper and victim of the pain of romantic love.

> "Once again, leg-trembling Love shakes me with her sweet-bitter lance." 130[13]

Sappho adores nature, but it is a more cerebral appreciation than Aphrodite Pandemos (Taurus). Sappho describes the Garden of the Nymphs, who are the attendants of Aphrodite, along with the Horae:

> "And by the cool stream, as a breeze whispers through the branches, sleep drifts down from quivering leaves, among the roses." 2[14]

She understands the power of the Moon,

> "The stars about the beautiful moon hide their shining selves whenever she is most full and beams her silvery light upon the earth." (34)[15]

She also describes ritual,

> "The moon rose full, and around the altar, assembled the women." 154[16]

Sappho as a mentor to young women, writes evocatively on her deep friendships, and perhaps love affairs, with women.

> "There was no holy shrine
> Where we were absent,
> No grove,
> No dance
> No sound."
>
> (94)

In one fragment she refers to her 'beautiful women' (the kalai, καλλαι) who may have been members of her coterie, or women she was mentoring. Sappho has a Libran waspishness over poor style, and jealousy of another's attention wandering.

"What peasant, wearing fashions from the farm
captivates you with her charm?
She does not even know that
A raised hem shows her ankles."

(57)

The power Aphrodite did have, was to cause people and gods alike to fall in hopelessly in love. She did have a wicked and sometimes cruel sense of humour, but then love can be cruel too.

"Like a hurricane smashing an oak tree, high on a mountainside. Love shattered my mind." (47)[17]

This is a powerful, economic description of the devastation love can bring to the cerebral mind. Sappho likens it to an elemental force that even a mighty oak tree cannot withstand.

Libra is the first of the six signs of the collective. The first six signs, Aries-Virgo are about developing as an individual, the next six deal with our relationships with others; close relationships, work, politics anything that brings us into relationship with other people. Libra, ruled by Aphrodite Urania, teaches how we lovingly (or not) relate to the other. In personal relationships and in the world around us. It is no surprise then that many politicians are found in this sign. With love (or their version of it) they try to bring harmony and balance to the world.

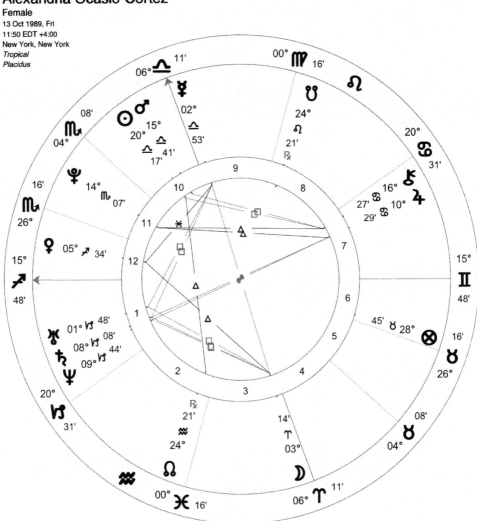

Alexandria Ocasio-Cortez

Female
13 Oct 1989, Fri
11:50 EDT +4:00
New York, New York
Tropical
Placidus

Alexandria Ocasio-Cortez: Politician
13 October 1989. (11:50) New York

"True love is radical because it requires us to see ourselves in all people. Otherwise, it isn't love. Love is revolutionary because it has us treat ALL people as we would ourselves—not because we are charitable, but because we are one. That is love's radical conclusion." Twitter post: 25 December 2018

Alexandria Ocasio-Cortez or AOC as she is known as, is an American politician, activist, and community organiser. A member of the Democratic Party, she has been the U.S. Representative for New York's 14th congressional district since 3 January 2019. On election, she became the youngest woman to serve in Congress at twenty-nine (see Transits) She is a member of the Democratic Socialists of America. She has a degree in International Relations and Economics from Boston University. Before running for Congress, AOC was a community organiser working in the Bronx, and educational director for the 2017 Northeast Collegiate World Series for the National Hispanic Institute. Active on social media (as you would expect an air sign) she has over nine million followers. She has a razor sharp mind and has no fear of speaking truth to power and tackling contentious issues with decorum.

On race,

"Black folks are descendants of slaves that were imported, quote-unquote by slave owners, to the United States for the explicit purpose of cultivating crops. And it was predicated on white supremacy and racial superiority, but we have to understand that white supremacy exists for a reason, and it exists for very specific cultural and economic reasons. And LBJ talked about this—like, if you can convince a poor white man that he's superior to a black man, he'll empty his pockets for you.

And so it's not just economic reasons why racism exists but there are economic reasons why racism is perpetuated and incentivized. More of that's housing, income, et cetera. And like I said on Monday with Ta-Nehisi, until America tells the truth about itself we're never going to heal.

And this—it's like this thing that as a culture we hide ... it's like this big wound with a big ugly scab on it, and it's just going to stay this itchy thing that we keep going back to until we just deal with it."[18]

On corruption in politics,

"What we are seeing now is a ruling class of corporations and a very small elite that have captured government. The Koch brothers own every Republican in the Senate. They own 'em. They don't cast a vote unless their sugar daddies tell 'em what to do. But seventy percent of Americans believe in Medicare for all. Ninety percent of Americans believe we need to get money out of politics. Eighty-something [percent] believe that climate change is a real, systemic and urgent problem. Sixty-seven percent of Americans believe that immigrants are a positive force in the United States of America. I believe that I'm fighting for the American consensus."[19]

On consensus,

"There is so much fear and hate. We must negate it with active, courageous love."[20]

On honesty,

"Give people the respect of your honest opinion, and always meet them where they're at."[21]

On misogyny, following Republican Senator Yoho, calling her a "Fucking bitch,' and that she was, "Out of her freakin mind," (a common accusation against women; that they are mad),many women would have hidden with shame. Instead, AOC called him out in the media and created a huge news story. Typically of the bully, when confronted, the senator both offered a public apology and denied saying the words. Her dignified take down of him went viral.

"This issue is not about one incident. It is cultural. It is a culture of lack of impunity, of accepting of violence and violent language against women, and an entire structure of power that supports that."[22]

On environmental politics,

"The age difference between myself (29) + oldest House members is 60yrs. For better or worse, young people will live in the world Congress leaves behind. That's why I focus on our future: addressing climate change & runaway income inequality, ending school-to-prison pipelines, etc." (Twitter: 23 December 2018)

AOC with three planets, including her midheaven, in Libra, shows the fierce, cerebral warrior that she is. Her work in Congress, especially her grilling of big business and speaking truth to power is legendary. She refused to be cowed by Congress and the old power structures. When derided for having been a waitress, she replied that most Americans would respect her for being hard working. Implacable, fearless (that warrior Aries moon) deceptively charming, Libra/Sagittarius lulls her political opponents into false confidence and then she forensically eviscerates them.

Air signs are great idea-people, they have vision and are extremely persuasive, combined with love, they have a vision for the betterment of humanity. And of course, they are articulate and have razor sharp minds.

Other politicians:

Eleanor Roosevelt (11 October 1884. (11:00) New York) Mercury, conjunct the MC, Sun, North Node in Libra).

Margaret Thatcher, the first woman Prime Minister of the UK, had Sun, Mars and Mercury in Libra (13 October 1925. (09:00) Grantham).

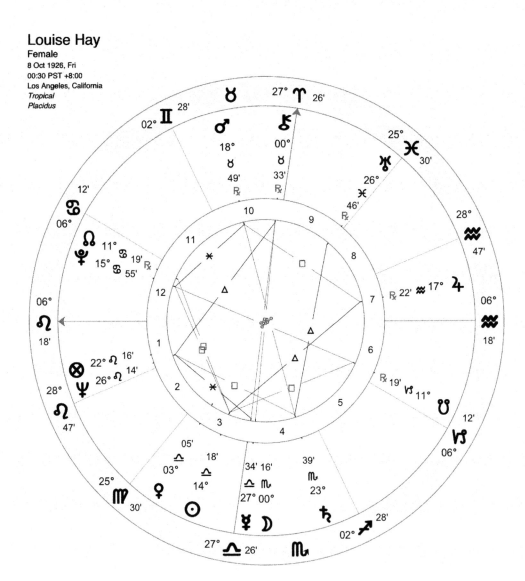

Louise Hay

Female
8 Oct 1926, Fri
00:30 PST +8:00
Los Angeles, California
Tropical
Placidus

Louise Hay: Healing with love
8 October 1926. (00:30) Los Angeles, CA

"When we really love ourselves, everything in our life works."[23]

Louise Hay may be credited with beginning the positive psychology movement of the 1970s. Born to a poor mother, Louise was raped by a neighbour when she was five. She dropped out of high school age fifteen and gave birth to her only child who was adopted on her sixteenth birthday. She moved to New York, married and began work as a model, and was fairly successful. After fourteen years of marriage her husband left her for another woman. She began studying at the Church of Religious Science (Ernest Holmes) and became a practitioner teaching positive affirmations to heal physical illness.

> "When people come to me with a problem…there is only one thing I ever work on, and that is LOVING THE SELF."[24]

In 1976 she wrote a pamphlet *Heal Your Body* which matched up emotional conflicts and physical illnesses and gave affirmations to heal them. It was published as a book in 1984.

> "I listen with love to my body's messages."[25]

In 1977/8 she was diagnosed with cervical cancer which Louise believed was trauma from her rape and she healed herself using alternative therapies, emotional release and forgiveness.

> "Deep at the center of my being, there is an infinite well of love."[26]

Louise was asked to help people suffering from AIDS and began the *Hay Rides* which looked at the emotional causes of the disease. Soon she was running groups of hundreds of people which brought her into the media spotlight.

> "It seems to me that everyone on this planet whom I know or have worked with is suffering from self-hatred and guilt to one degree or another. The more self-hatred and guilt we have, the less our lives work. The less self-hatred and guilt we have, the better our lives work, on all levels."[27]

In the same week in March 1988, she appeared on the Oprah Winfrey Show and the Paul Donahue Show (see Transits). Her book became a best seller and has sold more than fifty million copies to date.

"In the infinity of life where I am, all is perfect, whole and complete."[28]

Louise started Hay House publishing house which publishes many of the big names in the personal development movement, like Deepak Chopra and Wayne Dyer.

Louise also started the Hay Foundation in 1986; it supports organisations that supply food, shelter, counselling, hospice care and money to those in need.

"We are all one."[29]

Louise has Sun, Venus and Mercury in Libra in the third and fourth (Mercury) houses. Venus Urania is the intellectual Venus so it is no surprise that Louise talked, wrote and affirmed of how we all need to love ourselves. She believed that all life's problems, illness, poverty, relationship issues, work problems came from self-hatred and the lack of forgiveness of others. Louise believed love is the key to all healing. Affirmations were key to her work, using words in a repetitive manner to change your thought patterns, and your life.

"If we are willing to do the mental work, almost anything can be healed."[30]

Notes

1. Galen (c 160CE) quotes these lines in *Exhortation to Learning*. 'It is better therefore, knowing as we do that youthful beauty is like the flowers of spring, its allurement lasting but a short time, to agree with the Lesbian poetess, and to believe Solon when he points out the same.' https://www.sacred-texts.com/cla/usappho/sph99.htm accessed 2.6.2020.
2. Aristophanes of Byzantium, head librarian at the library of Alexandria, co-edited the nine book collection with Aristarchus of Samothrace circa, 257–180 BCE. Poochigian, Aaron (trans.) Sapho. (2015) *Sung with Love: poems and fragments*. Penguin Books, London. p.viii.
3. From a 6thc CE parchment see Lombardo, Stanley. (trans.) 2016. *Sappho Complete Poems and Fragments*. Hackette, Cambridge.p.38.
4. https://www.sacred-texts.com/cla/usappho/sph43.htm accessed 2.6.2020.
5. Liddell and Scott, p.319.
6. 3rd c CE [Oxyrhynchus 1232 & 2076] Lombardo, 2016, p.23.
7. The Horae (the hours) were goddesses of the seasons, daughter of Zeus and Themis, sisters of the Fates. They were, Eunomia (good order), Dike (justice) and Eirene (peace). They open the cloud-gates on Olympus and with the Graces are companions of Aphrodite and dance with her in festivals and in Olympus. March, 2002, p.205.
8. http://www.perseus.tufts.edu/hopper/text?doc=Perseus%3Atext%3A1999.01.0138%3Ahymn%3D6
9. Harrison, p.311.
10. Graves, 2011, p.50, 71.

11. http://www.perseus.tufts.edu/hopper/text?doc=Perseus%3Atext%3A1999.01.0137%3Ahymn%3D5 accessed 17.7.2020.

12. https://www.sacred-texts.com/cla/usappho/sph77.htm accessed 2.5.2020. trans. mine.

13. https://www.sacred-texts.com/cla/usappho/sph39.htm accessed 2.5.2020. trans. mine.

14. Quoted by Hermogenes about A.D. 170. https://www.sacred-texts.com/cla/usappho/sph06.htm accessed 18.1.2021.

15. https://www.sacred-texts.com/cla/usappho/sph05.htm accessed 18.1.2021.

16. Hepaeiston quotes this https://www.sacred-texts.com/cla/usappho/sph51.htm Accessed 18.1.2021.

17. https://www.sacred-texts.com/cla/usappho/sph41.htm

18. The Intercept podcast. *Alexandria Ocasio Cortez on her first weeks in Washington.* 28th January 2019. https://theintercept.com/2019/01/28/alexandria-ocasio-cortez-podcast/ accessed 19.1.2021.

19. Morris, Alex. 27 February 2019. *Alexandria Ocasio Cortez wants the Country to think Big.* Rolling Stone Magazine. https://www.rollingstone.com/politics/politics-features/alexandria-ocasio-cortez-congress-interview-797214/ accessed 19.1.2021.

20. https://thesuccesselite.com/top-30-alexandria-ocasio-cortez-quotes-that-will-inspire-you-to-be-courageous/ accessed 19.1.2021.

21. https://thesuccesselite.com/top-30-alexandria-ocasio-cortez-quotes-that-will-inspire-you-to-be-courageous/ accessed 19.1.2021.

22. Taylor, Joanna, 24 July 2020. *7 Perfect points that AOC made in her scathing speech about sexism that everyone should read.* The Indy100 https://www.indy100.com/news/alexandria-ocasio-cortez-sexism-speech-9636011 accessed 19.1.2021.

23. Hay, Louise.1987. *You Can Heal Your Life.* Hay House, Carlsbad, CA, p. xiii.

24. Hay, 1987, p.8.

25. Hay 1987, p.123.

26. Hay, 1987, p.102.

27. https://www.thecoachingtoolscompany.com/23-favourite-quotes-from-louise-hay-wise-uplifting-and-inspiring/ accessed 3.4.2021.

28. Hay, 1987, p.111.

29. Hay, 1987, p.215.

30. https://www.thecoachingtoolscompany.com/23-favourite-quotes-from-louise-hay-wise-uplifting-and-inspiring/ accessed 3.4.2021.

Scorpio: Persephone

Darkness, a warm, close, deep, ancient darkness, not frightening, but safe like the womb, a primaeval gloom.

You walk through the torch-lit passages, the walls damp and musty littered with semi-precious stones which glitter, tempting, enticing you to follow.

You are far underground. Your sandalled feet tread softly on the earth, you bring your cloak tighter around you, the chill deepens, the further in you go.

You stop and listen, in the dark you hear crying and moaning. There is fear here, and pain. You carry a jar with healing waters and move towards the sounds.

You enter a room and they come to you, the broken ones and you anoint them as they approach, you hold up a mirror of wisdom and self-knowledge to wash away their pain by showing them the deepest secrets of their souls.

You know their pain, you feel it, your body vibrates, glows and hums with it.

They are at rest now, so you climb your throne and sit and survey your dark realm, blessed, replete with grace.

You take up a dark crown and hold it feeling its weight. Three pomegranate seeds appear in your hand. You understand if you eat the seeds, you can wear the crown and console those weeping. If you do not, you may join them.

You think of your mother, of childhood and innocence, of sunlight and flowers and laughter.

You remember the dead and their suffering and imagine joining them and shiver.

But if you take the crown, you can have both.

This is your choice, power in the darkness.

One foot in shadow, one in sunlight.

Persephone, Queen of the Underworld, is the dark sister of Kore the maiden goddess. Kore represents Joy and Hope; Persephone, is referred to as that 'dread goddess'.

In the myth, perhaps Persephone was tricked by Hades into swallowing a pomegranate seed, or perhaps he tempted her, or perhaps she chose to do so after spending some time in her new kingdom. Is it better to be a Queen than an eternal daughter? For Scorpio, the answer would always be a Queen.

Hades offered her to be,

"Mistress of everything which lives and moves." *Homeric Hymn* 2:331–3.

Blundell, (1995:41) suggests that, once Persephone has tasted the food of Hades, she is subject to the sacred bond of xenia (χενια) which means she has to stay loyal to her host.

Pomegranate is also a symbol of fertility and death (the blood red juice) or menstruation (so death and rebirth or fertility). (Fig. 24)

Scorpio is the female expression of Mars, she is a warrior but in a more subtle and indirect way, because this is Mars in a water sign, so she flows and ebbs and pools like water. It is also a fixed sign, and always with fixity, there is always the issue of getting stuck. When water gets stuck there is always a possibility of poisoning, corruption, and toxicity.

Her marriage with Hades is a barren one, there are no children. But Persephone has queenly duties and arbitrates over issues to do with the dead.

Hermes is sent down to Hades to bring Persephone back to her mother.

Fig. 24 Persephone rising, seal, Boeotia, 1550 BCE.

... "Straightaway, eager, he rushed down into the depths of the earth from the home of the gods. And he reached the king who was inside his palace lying on his bed with his shy [helpless], unwilling wife, yearning very much for her mother." *Homeric Hymn to Demeter* 340–344[1]

Hades agrees to let Persephone go, but he reminds her,

"Go, Persephone to your dark veiled mother. Kind in your heart with strength and spirit. Don't be very angry beyond what is reasonable for anything. For it is not shameful for you, one of the immortals, for me to be your husband, my own brother is your father, Zeus. And here, you will be Queen of everyone who lives and moves here. And you will bear the greatest honour among us immortals. And those who wrong you, for those who don't appease your power with sacrifices and offerings purely given, and perform fit and proper rituals, their punishment will be everlasting. Thus, he spoke, and a very thoughtful Persephone rejoiced and swiftly she leapt up with joy." (360–370)

Hades offers her a kingdom, formidable powers over both the living and the dead, and eternal punishment for those who do not honour her appropriately. Persephone was 'very thoughtful,'[2] perhaps weighing up what he has offered her. Then, Hades gave her a pomegranate seed to eat, secretly. So, there is the offer of power but also a trick. Demeter describes Hades as 'vile.' (395) Hades himself may understand this, and perhaps knowing the goddess he offers her something sweet, to seal her fate. Why Persephone did not notice is unclear, perhaps in her eagerness to leave she did not, but it seems unlikely. Maybe Persephone was humouring Hades, happy to be gone.

"But by stealth he gave to her a honey sweet pomegranate seed to eat. For his own sake, plotting that she might not stay with her fearsome, dark-veiled mother." (371–374)

It is the beauty of the flower that catches Persephone, and the sweetness of the Pomegranate which ambushes her again. Being Queen of Hades is a powerful role but not a sweet one; there is no light in Hades, no beautiful flowers. If she wants this power, Persephone will have to let go of beauty and sweetness. And here is a teaching for Scorpio; her power lies in the dark, hidden depths, which are unpalatable for many mortals to contemplate. Persephone reigns in the land of the dead, in the darkness. Scorpio knows this country well, they nearly always, in my experience suffer a life trauma when young which shapes and informs their lives thereafter. Scorpios lose their innocence early, they know the darkness, they often experience abuses of power or death of family members in childhood which teaches them that grief, pain and suffering are a part of life. To survive, Scorpio develops a hard shell and a resilience which can create cynicism and cruelty.

The fate of Persephone mirrors the experience of some young women in patriarchy who are married off, sometimes for money, to pay a debt, to lessen the economic burden on the household, often against the mother's wishes, taken from home to the home of strangers (sometimes overseas, never seeing her own family again) and in some cases raped by their husbands. It can be described as a death in some cases, of individual identity, or the more real risk of death in childbirth, or at the hands of her new in-laws.

When Persephone rises from Hades, she brings Spring growth but also death into the upper world. With life there is always death, with shadow always light. The Mysteries of Eleusis were believed to act out the rape of Persephone and her return. Celebrants would process from Athens to Eleusis, a fourteen mile journey along the Sacred Way. In the *telesterion* (the place of initiation) rituals took place which were open to men and women. The secrecy of the Mysteries was preserved and we can only guess what occurred. It is suggested that, as Persephone ascended from Hades, the *telesterion* would be flooded with light from torches, just as Hekate led Demeter in torchlight searching for her daughter.

Like Persephone and Hades, the true treasure of Scorpio lies deep underground, in the unconscious, in those areas of life that are taboo: power, sex, death and money. Scorpios, along with Capricorns, but for different reasons, often become fabulously wealthy. They understand that money is power, and sexy, and they love the competition, the chase of getting rich. For Scorpio it is not so much the money itself, but the dominance and control money brings, the risk taking and competition. Likewise, Scorpio's enchantment with sex, it is the conquest, the deep, exploration of her sexual nature which fascinates, cosy cuddles are not really on the menu here, or if they are present, it is a by-product rather than an aim.

Of course, in our post-classical world, the other realm of Hades is the unconscious, those things buried deep within in us which, if they are not made conscious, rule our lives like software silently running in the background. Psychotherapy was developed in the 1920s when Pluto the co-ruler of Scorpio was found; no coincidence I believe. Besides the worldly treasures, the real treasure of Scorpio lies in exploring the unconscious, with courage, as it is a fearful place, full of ghosts, compulsions, and illusions. Knowledge is power, the Scorpio who is able to explore these depths, gains a self-mastery, which cannot be shaken by external events.

Scorpio is the second sign of the collective, here we integrate the dark with the light and stand witness to our personal and collective shadow. Scorpios often make people feel uncomfortable, as if they have x-ray vision; they do. Some signs live in the future, like Aries and Aquarius, but Scorpio lives underground and sees all our games and powerplays, tracks our motives and weaknesses. They see, and with their sometimes jaded eye, they store up our secrets and resentments should they need to use them in some future time.

For this reason I think Persephone chose to take the pomegranate and tie herself to the dark lord, she understood that she could not enjoy the sunny uplands as Kore, the maiden, unless she too, descended and made peace with her dead.

There were two major festivals of Persephone, *Thesmorphoria* and the Mysteries of Eleusis. Both had underground elements to the rituals and the revelation of secrets in torchlight. Both of these *Mysteries* had an aspect of revelation, and both claimed they would make the after-life in Hades blissful. Sappho suggests what happens to those who are not initiates,

> "When you die, you will be unmourned and forever forgotten,
>   No one will miss you, for you have not gathered the roses of the Pierian Muses
> [to make a garland and dance]. Invisible even in the halls of Hades, you will wander among the dead a shade, a wraith." (55[3])

The fact that Persephone had eaten while in Hades was gleefully reported by Ascalaphus, the son of the underworld river god Acheron. As punishment either Demeter or Persephone, or perhaps both of them, turned him into an owl whose lonely hooting haunts the night.

Scorpio is the sister who will bring up the dark, the difficult the unpalatable truths. She is the visitor to the dark realms of the taboo, who brings messages from the underworld.

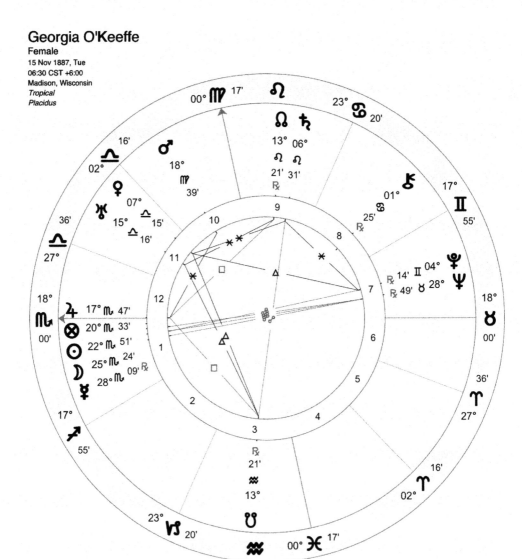

Georgia O'Keeffe
Female
15 Nov 1887, Tue
06:30 CST +6:00
Madison, Wisconsin
Tropical
Placidus

Georgia O'Keeffe: Artist
15 November 1887. (06:30) Sun Prairie WI

Georgia's first prize-winning painting was *Dead Rabbit with Copper pot* (1908). Forced to leave college when her father went bankrupt, she took a job as a commercial artist because she disliked the traditional painting she had been taught.

Her powerful Scorpio planets, a stellium of Jupiter, Ascendant, Sun and Moon, Mercury, all opposed her painterly Neptune in Taurus. She took nature (Taurus, Kore) and transformed it into something deeper, darker and more confronting. She discarded the traditional ways of painting, developing her own style, which, although she disputed it, brings a powerful female eroticism forefront in her work.

> "I decided to start anew, to strip away what I had been taught."[4]

After several years teaching art she had her first exhibition of a series of charcoal drawings at the Gallery 291, owned by Steiglitz in New York. He described her work as the,

> "Purest, finest, sincerest things that had entered *291* in a long while."[5]

He became her patron and lover which allowed her to paint full time. Experimenting with style, Georgia began painting flowers,

> "A flower is relatively small. Everyone has many associations with a flower—the idea of flowers. You put out your hand to touch the flower—lean forward to smell it—maybe touch it with your lips almost without thinking—or give it to someone to please them. Still—in a way—nobody sees a flower—really—it is so small—we haven't got time—and to see takes time, like to have a friend takes time ... So I said to myself—I'll paint what I see—what the flower is to me but I'll paint it big and they will be surprised into taking time to look at it ... "[6]

Georgia's circle in New York discussed Freud's and other works on sex and psychology, including Havelock Ellis' *Studies in the Psychology of Sex*, which claimed that art is inspired and driven by sexual energy. Stieglitz argued that Georgia's flowers are metaphorical studies of the vulva. Georgia demurred,

> "Well—I made you take time to look at what I saw and when you took time to really notice my flower, you hung all your own associations with flowers on my flower and you write about my flower as if I think and see what you think and see of the flower—and I don't."[7]

One of her more famous paintings, *Black Iris* (1926), reproduced on a massive scale the structure of the iris plant. It evokes the vagina with soft petals revealing a deep, sensual interior. It is both intimate and erotic, full of power, mystical and spiritual. The size of the painting and its subject matter caused a stir in the art world with its soft, gorgeous colours, which epitomised the woman who was both on display and hidden.

"There's something about black. You feel hidden away in it."[8]

Georgia first went to New Mexico in 1929 with a woman friend and thereafter spent part of every year there painting. She suffered breakdowns in the early 1930s and was admitted to hospital several times.

"I've been absolutely terrified every moment of my life—and I've never let it keep me from doing a single thing I wanted to do."[9]

Like Persephone, beguiled by flowers, once picked, they took her on an erotic journey into a deeper, darker place. Georgia admits to being terrified, but courageously moved forwards none the less (Scorpio is ruled by Mars) and her furies brought her to a place of inner torment (her breakdowns) and to a barren, foreign land (which of course was not barren but stripped down to the bare essentials as desert landscapes are), where she found solace in solitude, nature and her art. Scorpio, like Mars-ruled Aries needs seclusion to express themselves. She moved to New Mexico permanently in 1940. For her, the desert was,

"Such a beautiful, untouched lonely feeling place, such a fine part of what I call the Faraway."[10]

Georgia explored the dark places in her breakdowns and the barren places, in the desert, images of life, the flowers, death the skull paintings, and nature in microcosm and macrocosm. She broke boundaries and taboos, and always lived on her own terms.

"I'm glad I want everything in the world—good and bad—bitter and sweet—I want it all."[11]

Stieglitz, mentor, then husband, plucked her from obscurity and made her his queen; she became the bestselling female artist in the world. A Hades-like figure, he was said to be the reason for her depression and breakdowns when he took up with another young artist. Her painting, of the poisonous *Jimson*[12] *Weed/White Flower No 1* sold for $44,405,000 in 2014 more than three times the previous world auction record for any female artist.

It is interesting this is the flower painting which brought her the most accolades. The painting shows the plant as epic; the picture is almost entirely filled with Datura flowers that grow wild in the desert in New Mexico. Georgia painted Datura many times, fascinated by it; Datura flowers as the sun sets which evoked the darkness, "The coolness and sweetness of the evening."[13]

Datura is deadly, poisonous; Georgia cultivated it in her garden. Hallucinogenic, it is used for spiritual journeying, but also has been used in suicide and murder. It seems a suitable signature plant for someone with so much Scorpio in her chart; dicing with death, weaving beauty from deadly poisons.

> "I have lived on a razor's edge. So what if you fall off—I'd rather be doing something I really wanted to do. I'd walk it again."[14]

Other Scorpio artists:

Bjork: 21 November 1965. (07:50) Reykjavik Iceland. (Sun, Moon, Ascendant and Neptune in Scorpio)

Another part of Scorpio, burying deep into the mysteries of life, is shown in the chart of Marie Curie.

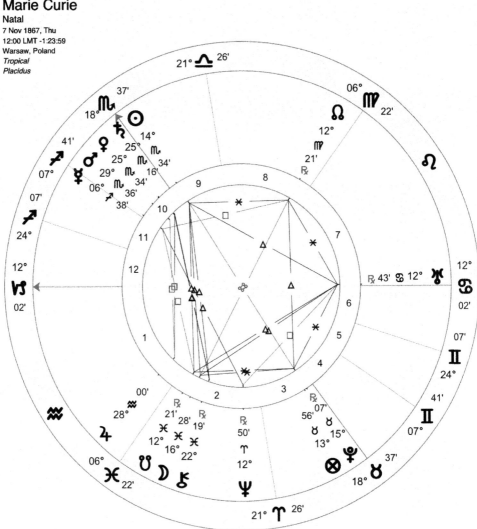

Marie Curie

Natal

7 Nov 1867, Thu
12:00 LMT -1:23:59
Warsaw, Poland
Tropical
Placidus

Marie Curie: Physicist
7 November 1867. (12:00) Warsaw Poland. (K 22 pisc)

"We must have perseverance and above all confidence in ourselves. We must believe that we are gifted for something and that this thing must be attained."[15]

Marie Curie was the first woman to receive a PhD in France, the first person to win two Nobel Prizes, the first female professor at the Sorbonne, and the first woman to be honoured at the Panthéon, Paris.

Marie has a fascinating chart, she has Sun, Saturn, Venus and Mars in Scorpio, a Grand Trine in water with the Moon in Pisces and Uranus in Cancer, Uranus is the planet of innovation and experiment, with Pluto the planet of radioactivity (discovered in 1930) making a Kite formation. Her Scorpio nature pushed her to discover scientific truths, notwithstanding being blocked and hindered by some male scientists, although helped and championed by others. Her compassionate, dreamy Pisces Moon impelled her to use her discoveries for the alleviation of suffering, both in the war and afterwards.

"Humanity also needs dreamers, for whom the disinterested development of an enterprise is so captivating that it becomes impossible for them to devote their care to their own material profit."[16]

She was the daughter of two teachers who sought to contribute to the Polish resistance movement through education, including mathematics and physics, which contributed to her decision to pursue science. She began by conducting chemistry and physics experiments with her father at an 'underground' Polish university in Warsaw.[17]

In 1891, Marie moved to Paris, enrolled at the Sorbonne to read physics and mathematics, and married Pierre Curie in 1895. Marie and Pierre worked together in his research space which Marie, as a woman, would not have received. His support was invaluable in male-dominated science.

A few years after marrying Pierre (after the birth of their first child, Irène), Marie began studying for a doctorate in the new field of radioactivity, a significant turning point in her career.

The Curies became research workers at the School of Chemistry and Physics in Paris and began their pioneering work into invisible rays given off by uranium, recently been discovered by Becquerel. In 1903, when Pierre Curie and Henri Becquerel were nominated for the Nobel Prize in Physics for their work on radioactivity, Swedish mathematician Gosta Mittag-Leffler, a fierce advocate of women in science, argued that Marie should also be considered alongside her husband. Eventually the 1903 Nobel Prize for Physics was awarded jointly to Marie and Pierre Curie and Henri Becquerel—the same year Marie obtained her PhD in Physics.

In April 1906, Pierre Curie was tragically killed in a road accident. A fortnight later, Curie was offered her late husband's position as an assistant lecturer at the Sorbonne. Two years later, she was made a full professor, the first female professor there.

Subsequently, British scientist Kelvin argued the Curies couple's findings about radium were inaccurate; that radium was instead a compound of lead and helium. To prove him wrong, Marie isolated pure radium by electrolyzing molten radium chloride; she was vindicated.

> "There are sadistic scientists who hurry to hunt down errors instead of establishing the truth."[18]

In 1911, although right-wing newspapers reported that Marie Curie had an affair with Paul Langevin, a Sorbonne colleague and former student of her husband's and the scientific discoveries were his, Marie disproved this slander by winning a second Nobel prize in Chemistry for the discovery of radium and polonium, awarded to her alone. She had isolated radium in 1902 (as radium chloride, its atomic weight 225.93).

> "First principle: never to let oneself be beaten down by persons or by events."[19]

The Sorbonne built the first radium institute with two laboratories; one for study of radioactivity under Marie Curie's direction, and the other for biological research into the treatment of cancer.[20]

> "A scientist in his laboratory is not a mere technician: he is also a child confronting natural phenomena that impress him as though they were fairy tales."[21]

When war broke out in 1914, Marie stopped her research to aid the war effort, and developed mobile x-ray machines or *Petits Curies*. A fearless Scorpio, in October 1914 She travelled to casualty clearing stations near the front line accompanied her daughter Irene, aged17. They x-rayed wounded men to locate fractures, bullets and shrapnel. As Director of the Red Cross Radiological Service, she raised funds in Paris for money, supplies and vehicles which could be converted. Marie had Sun, Saturn, Venus and Mars and Midheaven in Scorpio, with a compassionate Moon in Pisces.

> "You cannot hope to build a better world without improving the individuals. To that end each of us must work for his own improvement, and at the same time share a general responsibility for all humanity, our particular duty being to aid those to whom we think we can be most useful."[22]

After the war, she worked hard to raise money for her Radium Institute, but by 1920 she was experiencing health problems, probably due to exposure to radioactive materials. On July 4, 1934, Marie died of aplastic anaemia, a condition that occurs when bone marrow fails to produce new blood cells.

She was buried next to her husband in Sceaux, a commune in southern Paris, although in 1995, their remains were moved and interred in the Pantheon in Paris alongside France's greatest citizens. The Curies received another honour in 1944 when the 96th element on the periodic table of elements was discovered and named 'curium.'

> "I am one of those who think, like Nobel, that humanity will draw more good than evil from new discoveries."[23]

Arguably x-rays transformed medicine, particularly trauma medicine; radio therapy is still used today to treat malignancy.[24] Her Capricorn Ascendant gave her the persistence and determination and ambition to make the very best of herself and her gifts, gave her a natural authority and keen analytical skills.

Born on the same day eleven years later, Lise Meitner 7 November 1878 (17:25) Vienna Austria was the co-discover of nuclear fission, with Otto Hanh. Lise had Venus, Sun and Mercury in Scorpio, Mercury was opposite Pluto in Taurus. Although denied the Nobel prize, the element 109 *Meitnerium* was named in her honour.[25]

Notes

1. https://www.perseus.tufts.edu/hopper/text?doc=Perseus%3Atext%3A1999.01.0137 %3Ahymn%3D2 accessed 21.06.2020.
2. Another translation of περιφρων (perithrone) is artful, crafty. https://www.perseus. tufts.edu/hopper/morph?l=peri%2Ffrwn&la=greek&can=peri%2Ffrwn0&prior=de\ &d=Perseus:text:1999.01.0137:hymn=2&i=1#lexicon accessed 21.7.2020.
3. Plutarch also quotes this fragment, twice in fact, once as if written to a rich woman, and again when he says that the crown of roses was assigned to the Muses, for he remembers that Sappho had said these same words to some uneducated woman. [However, I think it refers to the uninitiated] https://www.sacred-texts.com/cla/usappho/ sph66.htm accessed 2.6.2020.
4. https://news.artnet.com/art-world/10-quotes-georgia-okeeffe-birthday-749411 accessed 25.1.2021.
5. *Biography.com Editors (April 27,2017). "Georgia O'Keeffe". Biography Channel. A&E Television Networks.* https://www.biography.com/artist/georgia-okeeffe. accessed 25.1.2021.
6. https://www.widewalls.ch/magazine/georgia-o-keeffe-flowers accessed 24.7.2020.
7. https://www.widewalls.ch/magazine/georgia-o-keeffe-flowers accessed 24.7.2020.
8. http://www.art-quotes.com/auth_search.php?authid=69#.YA6u01inzFg accessed 25.1.2021.
9. https://news.artnet.com/art-world/10-quotes-georgia-okeeffe-birthday-749411 accessed 25.1.2021.
10. *Tufts, Eleanor. National Museum of Women in the Arts; International Exhibitions Foundation (1987). American women artists, 1830–1930. International Exhibitions Foundation for the National Museum of Women in the Arts. p.83.*

11. http://www.art-quotes.com/auth_search.php?authid=69#.YA6u01inzFg accessed 25.1.2021.

12. Jimson Weed or Datura Stramonium, is a deadly poison and hallucinogenic plant which grows in the desert. Interestingly, Don Juan the Yaqui shaman called it *Yerba del Diabolo,* and said, 'She (Datura) is as powerful as the best of allies, but there is something I personally don't like about her. She distorts men. She gives them a taste of power too soon without fortifying their hearts and makes them domineering and unpredictable. She makes them weak in the middle of their great power.' https://www.angelfire.com/electronic/awakening101/carlos_datura.html accessed 25.1.2021.

13. https://www.widewalls.ch/magazine/georgia-o-keeffe-flowers accessed 24.7.2020.

14. http://www.art-quotes.com/auth_search.php?authid=69#.YA6u01inzFg accessed 25.1.2021.

15. https://www.goalcast.com/2018/02/23/14-inspiring-marie-curie-quotes/ accessed 29.1.2021.

16. https://www.mariecurie.org.uk/who/our-history/marie-curie-the-scientist accessed 30.1.2021.

17. https://www.sciencemuseum.org.uk/objects-and-stories/women-physics accessed 29.1.2021.

18. https://wearetechwomen.com/inspirational-quotes-marie-curie-physicist-chemist-pioneer-in-the-study-of-radiation/ accessed 30.1.2021.

19. https://www.goalcast.com/2018/02/23/14-inspiring-marie-curie-quotes/ accessed 29.1.2021.

20. https://www.mariecurie.org.uk/who/our-history/marie-curie-the-scientist accessed 30.1.2021.

21. https://wearetechwomen.com/inspirational-quotes-marie-curie-physicist-chemist-pioneer-in-the-study-of-radiation/ accessed 30.1.2021.

22. https://wearetechwomen.com/inspirational-quotes-marie-curie-physicist-chemist-pioneer-in-the-study-of-radiation/ accessed 30.1.2021.

23. https://www.goalcast.com/2018/02/23/14-inspiring-marie-curie-quotes/ accessed 29.1.2021.

24. Marie Curie allowed her name to be used to name a hospital in Hampstead. The Marie Curie charity works to support people with terminal illness. www.mariecurie.org.

25. https://www.sciencemuseum.org.uk/objects-and-stories/women-physics accessed 29.1.2021.

Sagittarius: Artemis

Out on the mountain you run between tall, ancient trees, your hounds race beside you panting, falcons dive and soar in the milky sky, eagles perch in the treetops, poised to swoop. Your soft kidskin boots pad softly, noiselessly on the rocky ground. You hunt at dawn when the prey is soft with sleep. You pull your bow and take your aim. The shot is true and you fell the beast and run on.

You are wild, long hair blows free in the wind, your short tunic gives you ease of movement, your dogs by your side as you dash like lightning through this ancient forest.

Behind, your sisters collect the kill for the feast tonight. Not one piece wasted from the animal sacrifice. You are one with them, you hunt as a pack, wild in these barren hills, you breathe in the freedom of the mountainside, the space, the emptiness. You live to run and hunt.

A woman labouring calls you. Your hounds form a circle around her. You lay down your bow and bring clear water from the stream, washing your hands and her face. You kneel before her and speak of the wildness, running like beasts, body and spirit in tandem, pure instinct. She kneels forward and her struggle begins. The dogs howl as she paces, their cries matching hers, your companions hold her as she retreats into her body, that wild place. You unbind her hair and she shakes it free as the infant crowns and new life comes. They sleep guarded by the hounds as you celebrate with dance and a gentle flute music. You dance for life, for freedom and for peace.

"I sing of Artemis of the golden bow, boisterous, august maiden, deer hunting, shooter of arrows, sister of Apollo of the golden sword. Delighting in the hunt, down the shady hills and the windy mountaintops, stretching out her golden bow, releasing whispering arrows. And the tops of lofty mountains tremble and the thick

125

woodland echoes with the terrible screams of wild beasts and the land shakes and
the fish-filled sea. She has a brave heart, and, on every side, she turns around and
kills the race of wild beasts. But when this hunter of wild beasts is satisfied and
her heart is cheered, releasing her well-worn bow, she comes to the great palace of
her beloved brother Phoebus Apollo in Delphi, that abundant place. Putting on the
beautiful dances of the Muses and the Graces. There, she hangs up her unstrung
bow and arrows and, beautifully dressed, she leads the dance. And they let soar
their divine voices, singing of Leto of the fine ankles, who gave birth to her children, the most excellent among the immortals both by their deeds and their will."
Homeric Hymn to Artemis 27.[1]

The origin of her name suggests Artemis was a pre-Hellenic goddess. It is believed
that a precursor of Artemis was worshipped in Krete as the goddess of mountains
and hunting, Called Britomartis in the east and Diktynna in the west of the island.[2] In
Mycenaean Greek, Artemis or *a-te-mi-to* /Artemitos/ (a genitive form) and *a-ti-mi-te*
/Artimitei/ (in the dative) has been found in Linear B at the place complex in Pylos.[3]
Other scholars suggest her name comes from *arktos* (αρκτος) which means bear.

Sanctuaries of Artemis were always in liminal spaces, often built by borders of
countries, usually in the wild countryside, the sea or mountainous areas. Building a
sanctuary was one was of marking a boundary line between communities. As many
rituals to Artemis were women only, it meant women had to rely on the goddess to
protect them. The location of her sanctuaries epitomised the wildness of the goddess
herself.

> "Artemis, lovely Artemis, so kind
>   To the ravening lions, tender helpless cubs, The suckling of young beasts that
> stalk the wilds." Aeschylus *Agamemnon* 141–3

A cult of the bear grew up around Artemis. The sanctuary of Artemis at Brauron
was active from at least the eighth century to the fourth century BCE. Pre-pubescent
and adolescent Athenian girls were sent there, a remote town by the sea, to serve
the Goddess for one year. During this time, the girls were known as *arktoi*, or little
she-bears.

A bear was in the habit of visiting the town of Brauron. The people of the town fed
it and in time it became tame. One day, a girl teased the bear, and, in some versions
of the myth, it killed her, while, in other versions, it clawed out her eyes. Either way,
the girl's brothers killed the bear, and Artemis, enraged, sent a plague to the town.
She demanded that young girls 'act the bear' before they married, in atonement for
the bear's death. The sanctuary was built to placate her. (Fig. 25)

The festival of Arketia was celebrated every four years. Ceramics found at the site
show young women, girl children to young adults running, dancing holding torches
and wreaths, sometimes with a palm tree, their hair loose. This ritual, which occurred

Fig. 25 Mistress of the Mountains, seal, Knossos, 1500 BCE.

before marriage, may have been young girls being purged of their animal nature before they became domesticated.[4] At some point during the ritual/initiation they wore saffron robes. Saffron from the crocus flower, has associations with love, desire and sex magic, as well as yielding a beautiful yellow dye. The Saffron harvest is pictures in Kretan art. In *Lysistrata* (351) Kleonike and Lysistrata swear to arouse their husbands by 'enticing in our saffron nighties.' It is possible that part of the ritual involved teaching the young women sexual secrets prior to their marriage. Or perhaps information around childbearing, and pregnancy. It was a 'last chance' for women and girls to run wild in the company of their peers, to dance, celebrate and perhaps be initiated by older women or priestesses of Artemis. In Thessaly girls performed a ritual where they played the part of fawns.[5]

Iphigeneia sacrificed by her father Agamemnon, is rescued by Artemis and a deer is substituted for her. Iphigeneia becomes priestess of Artemis at Brauron. Her function at the sanctuary is to accept baby clothes made by women who died in childbirth. It has been suggested that the giving away of these clothes was part of the mourning ritual for the dead mother.

"You, Iphigenia, must be key-holder for this goddess on the hallowed stairs of Brauron, to die and be buried there. They will dedicate clothes to you, finely-woven robes which women who have died in childbirth leave in their homes." *Iphigeneia in Taurus* (1462–7)

Artemis is the goddess women sacrificed to in childbirth and who was called upon to help labour, and the new-born would be presented to her at her temple and perform a ritual, *Pausotokeia*. (Blundell 1998:34)

> "I invoke, Artemis, mistress of the bow, the heavenly helpful guardian goddess of childbirth." *Hippolytus* (164–5)

Labour and childbirth are the closest women get to a pure animal state, when we encounter our pure physicality and understand that the body has its own wisdom, rhythms and threat. Patriarchal medicine has tried to tame nature, as another way of distancing women from their inner beast, but many women understand that control of labour and childbirth is women's wild territory and best left to them to manage.[6]

Kallisto a virgin follower of Artemis was raped by Zeus. She was turned into a bear by Artemis. She later became the constellation, the Great Bear. The myth of Iphigenia and Kallisto both show the dangers of being a woman; death by men and rape.[7] Herbs of the genus *Artemisia* especially Mugwort (*Artemisia vulgaris*) are used to help childbirth and delivery, Mugwort is also a magical, dreaming herb, for trance states.[8] The bow and arrow, hunting dogs, a quiver and hunting knives, the deer and the cypress tree are all sacred to Artemis.

Xenophon of Ephesos (2ndC CE) describes a fictional procession in honour of Artemis, which is doubtless based on actual practice.

> "A prodigy of loveliness surpassing all other maidens. Her eyes shining sometimes like a girl's and sometimes as severe as of a chaste goddess. Her dress was a frock of purple, her wrap was a fawn skin and a quiver hung down on her shoulders. She carried a bow and a javelin and dogs fled at her heels. Time and again when the Ephesans saw her in the sacred procession they bowed down as the very goddess."[9]

Freedom is the word for Artemis, when Zeus offers her cities, she declines saying she does not visit them much. Her home is in the wild mountaintops of Greece. She is described as a virgin goddess, but perhaps unmarried might be a better way to put it. She is not interested in domesticity, the legal and social restraints put on married women and mothers. She wishes to be free, and she wishes all beings to be free. She both hunts animals and protects their young. As a hunter she has a keen eye and a sharp point, she goes for the kill and from the beginning she is dedicated to the wild open spaces, an outside life where she has agency and control. (Fig. 26)

Artemis is one of the two goddesses, (see Hestia) who are immune to Aphrodite's whiles. She has no interest in the romantic love Aphrodite offers and prefers to have the wind in her hair as she explores the remote places. She does, however, know how to have fun. There is a Greek saying, "Where has Artemis not danced?"[10] Sagittarians are known for their love of music, dance, socialising and merriment.

Fig. 26 Artemis, vase, Etruscan, 6thC BCE.

Jane Goodall

Female
3 Apr 1934, Tue
23:30 UT +0:00
London, United Kingdom
Tropical
Placidus

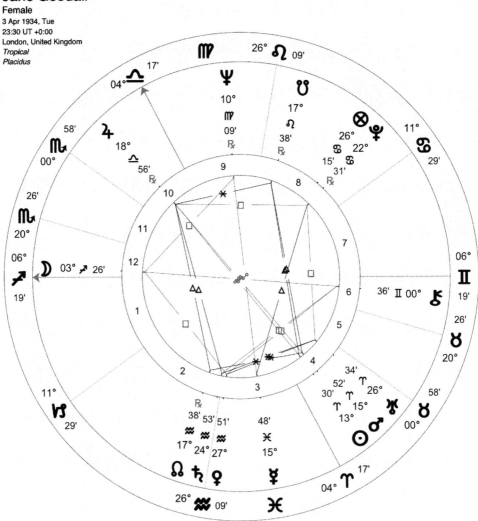

Jane Goodall: Animal protector
3 April 1934 (23:30) London

"I don't have any idea of who or what God is. But I do believe in some great spiritual power. I feel it particularly when I'm out in nature. It's just something that's bigger and stronger than what I am or what anybody is. I feel it. And it's enough for me."[11]

Jane Goodall is a primatologist, ethologist, and anthropologist, well-known for her sixty year study of chimpanzee social and family interactions in Gombe Stream National Park, Tanzania. She founded the Jane Goodall Institute[12] and the programme and has worked extensively on conservation and animal welfare issues. She served on the board of the Nonhuman Rights Project since its founding in 1996. In April 2002, she was named a UN Messenger of Peace and is an honorary member of the World Future Council.

Jane's research showed that behaviour which was believed to be uniquely human was shared by chimpanzees. They have strong mother and child and sibling bonds, show compassion, comfort others when mourning and will adopt orphan chimps.[13]

Although she has a strong Sun Mars conjunction in Aries, Jane has her Moon conjunct her Ascendant in Sagittarius showing the area of life she chose to express her unique skills. She is Aries the trail blazer, opening up the way for women to work in the field in primatology. For her first trip to Gombe, her mother had to accompany her; a single woman couldn't travel there alone. Her passion for animals is seen in her films; she also had the scientific discipline to report negatives: meat-eating and warmongering behaviour of the apes.

Goodall wrote in 1993:

"When, in the early 1960s, I brazenly used such words as 'childhood', 'adolescence', 'motivation', 'excitement', and 'mood' I was much criticised. Even worse was my crime of suggesting that chimpanzees had 'personalities'. I was ascribing human characteristics to nonhuman animals and was thus guilty of that worst of ethological sins -anthropomorphism."[14]

Jane named the chimps, instead of the customary numbering, helping her to develop close bonds with them, and she is believed to be the only human ever accepted into chimpanzee society.

Her influence has inspired several generations of women to enter the field of primatology. When she began her research in the 1950s it was a male-dominated discipline; today there are equal numbers of men and women. Jane earned her doctorate at Cambridge in ethnology in 1965 on the *Behaviour of free-living chimpanzees*, using data from her first five years at the Gombe Reserve. She became only one of eight people

131

to be awarded a PhD in this way despite having no undergraduate degree. Such 'rule breaking' is typical of an Aries Sun who feels no need to follow rules.

In 1977, Goodall established the Jane Goodall Institute (JGI), which supports the Gombe research, and campaigns to protect chimpanzees and their habitats.

> "When legendary scientist Jane Goodall first came to Tanzania more than 35 years ago to study the chimpanzees of Gombe National Park, the vast, flourishing forest teemed with apes. Today, the park is ravaged by logging, and home to only about 40 chimps, who live confined to a few protected square miles."[15]

JGI has nineteen offices around the world, and is celebrated for community-centred conservation and development programs in Africa. Roots and Shoots has worked with young people worldwide since 1991 when a group of sixteen local teenagers met with Goodall at her home in Dar es Salaam, Tanzania. They were concerned about pollution in the city, deforestation in the mountains, and the welfare of both wild and domestic animals. Jane attended their meetings but the group was run by the young people.. Her model for youth led activism, helped by resources and leaders from Roots and Leaves has now grown into a worldwide movement of over 10,000 groups in over one hundred countries.[16]

Sagittarius has a broad reach and often has overseas connections. Prior to the virus (2020) it was said Jane travelled over 300 days per year. She has campaigned about climate change, has met Greta Thunberg and campaigns against animal testing. She is a vegetarian and promotes the diet for ethical, environmental, and health reasons. In, *The Inner World of Farm Animals*, Goodall writes that farm animals are,

> "… Far more aware and intelligent than we ever imagined and, despite having been bred as domestic slaves,[17] they are individual beings in their own right. As such, they deserve our respect. And our help. Who will plead for them if we are silent?"[18]

Goodall has also said:

> "Thousands of people who say they 'love' animals sit down once or twice a day to enjoy the flesh of creatures who have been treated so with little respect and kindness just to make more meat."

Her easy going sanguine Sagittarius Moon and Ascendant gives her a warm, non-threatening personality and also a great sense of humour. Gary Larson drew a cartoon showing two chimpanzees grooming. One finds a blonde human hair on the other and inquires, "Conducting a little more 'research' with that Jane Goodall tramp?" The Jane Goodall Institute thought this was in bad taste and sought legal advice but, when Jane saw the cartoon, she loved it, had the cartoon printed on a tee shirt and sold it to raise funds for the Institute. She wrote a preface to Larson's *The Far Side Gallery 5*, giving her account of the incident. Jane praised Larson's cartoons, which often compare the behaviour of humans and animals.

Jane embodies the Artemisian love of animals, wild places, young people and connections across the globe, as well as a keen sense of humour and playfulness.

While Jane brought to the world's attention the plight of animals, Margaret Mead's life' work was looking at the human animal and its behaviour.

Margaret Mead

Female
16 Dec 1901, Mon
09:00 EST +5:00
Philadelphia
Tropical
Placidus

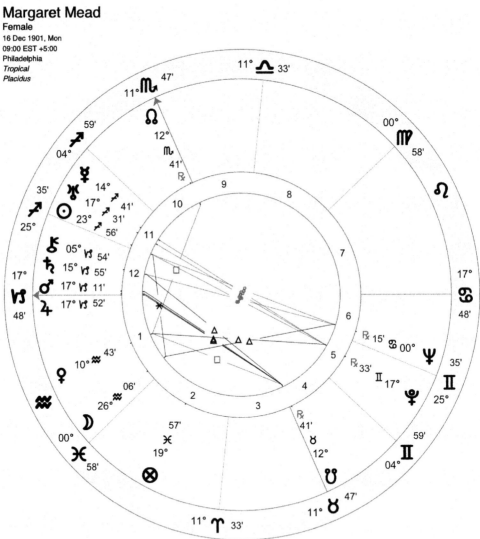

Margaret Mead: Anthropologist
16 December 1901. (09:00) Philadelphia PA

"Human nature is almost unbelievably malleable, responding accurately and contrastingly to contrasting cultural conditions."[19]

Margaret was a cultural anthropologist who became famous for her book, *Coming of Age in Samoa*, published in 1928. Brought up by a feminist, sociologist mother, Emily Fogg Mead,

"I think it was my grandmother who gave me my ease in being a woman. She was unquestionably feminine—small and dainty and pretty and wholly without masculine protest or feminist aggrievement. She had gone to college when this was a very unusual thing for a girl to do, she had a very firm grasp of anything she paid attention to, she had married and had a child, and she a career of her own. All this was true of my mother as well. But my mother was filled with passionate resentment about the condition of women, as perhaps my grandmother might have been had my grandfather lived and had she borne five children and had little opportunity to use her special gifts and training. As it was, the two women I knew best were mothers and had professional training. So I had no reason to doubt that brains were suitable for a woman. And as I had my father's kind of mind—which was also his mother's—I learned that the mind is not sex-typed."[20]

Margaret studied anthropology under Franz Boas and Ruth Benedict, graduating in 1923, and went to Samoa in 1925, to research Samoan adolescent girls. She found that the Samoans were open about sex, masturbation, death, childbirth and, as a consequence, teenage girls did not experience fear and complexes around these areas. Children were brought up communally and did not have the same focus for rebellion as American adolescents.

The book caused a storm by suggesting that American society was the cause of teenagers' unhappiness. Her colleagues trashed her book; anthropologist Edward Sapir, a jilted lover of Mead's, called it 'cheap and dull,' and her a 'loathsome bitch.'[21]

Margaret had Sun, Mercury and Uranus in Sagittarius in the eleventh house, showing her bold and innovative (Uranus) writing and research (Mercury) on the subject of groups and the collective (eleventh house). Her Saturn, Mars and Jupiter conjunct her Capricorn Ascendant gave her the gravitas (Saturn, Capricorn) the scientific skills (Saturn) and the love of philosophy (Jupiter) as well as the skills to negotiate academia and stand up for herself (Mars in Capricorn). Her Moon in Aquarius (the future) gave her insight into how a better world might organise itself to give equal opportunity to women (the Moon).

In 1926, Margaret became assistant curator at the American Museum of Natural History in New York and stayed in post until her retirement in 1964.

In 1929, she earned her PhD at Columbia University and began researching Native Americans in 1930, and then making many trips to New Guinea to study the tribes between 1931 and 1935. Margaret wrote twenty-four books and co-authored or edited eighteen more. Her hardworking Mars Jupiter and Saturn in Capricorn on her Ascendant mean diligence went with ambition. She was respected, and became a cultural commentator in the fifties, sixties and seventies on feminism, childrearing, sexuality, marriage and other cultural issues of that time.

> "Man's role is uncertain, undefined, and perhaps unnecessary. By a great effort man has hit upon a method of compensating himself for his basic inferiority. Equipped with various mysterious noise-making instruments, whose potency rests upon their actual form's being unknown to those who hear the sounds—that is, the women and children must never know that they are really bamboo flutes, or hollow logs, or bits of elliptic wood whirled on strings—they can get the male children away from the women, brand them as incomplete, and themselves turn boys into men. Women, it is true, make human beings, but only men can make men."[22]

Her relationships were unorthodox for the time (Moon in Aquarius). Margaret married three men and considered that she had made three good marriages, each giving a period of growth and producing good work. She also continued a long-term relationship with Ruth Benedict. Margaret believed that an individual's sexual orientation might evolve throughout life, and her close personal and professional relationship with anthropologist Rhoda Metraux lasted from 1955 until her death in 1978.

Margaret had a daughter, Mary, in 1939, despite having been told she was infertile, and applied her theories on child rearing, such as demand feeding, hands-on practices of child-rearing—revolutionary at the time (Moon in Aquarius). Mead's paediatrician, Benjamin Spock, subsequently incorporated Margaret's own practices and beliefs derived from her ethnological fieldwork, particularly breastfeeding on demand, into his writings.

> "She promoted breast-feeding when American paediatricians sought to abolish it and opened the minds of obstetricians about natural childbirth in an era when millions of babies were born heavily sedated. She helped change thinking about child-rearing, education, sex, menopause, ageing and race, based on her own and others' fieldwork in cultures once considered too exotic to be relevant."[23]

Margaret wrote that culture was as much responsible as biology for influencing human behaviour. Her adventurous Sun, Mercury and Uranus in the eleventh house of society made her a radical and provocative cultural commentator. She was a great supporter of liberal social reform. She believed personality characteristics were shaped by cultural conditioning rather than heredity.

"We must recognize that beneath the superficial classifications of sex and race the same potentialities exist, recurring generation after generation, only to perish because society has no place for them."[24]

After her death in 1978, some anthropologists tried to dismiss her original works, but Margaret remains the most celebrated anthropologist in the 20th century.

Her contention that culture rather than biology determines how people behave, that the sexes do not have biological determinism, was in part responsible for the social revolution of the sixties and seventies in feminism, the human potential movement and other countercultural trends of those years.

Mead's 1948 book *Male and Female* includes material not just on Samoa but on seven different traditional cultures she had studied directly. She used ethnographic data from these and other cultures to launch a frontal assault on the then-prevailing Western idea that every major aspect of gender-assigned roles stemmed from biological determinants and was therefore inevitable and unchangeable.

Again, we have the idea of freedom for men and women; men too, are brutalised by patriarchy. Margaret uncovered truths about humans that society found unpalatable and then revolutionary and finally have become normalised. Then and now, her theories annoy conservative thinkers (patriarchal followers of the father-god) who seek to control women, and her book remains a cause celebre in right wing circles.

Margaret follows Boaz's anti-Darwinian, progressive teachings, in a time when eugenics was seriously debated in scientific circles (pre 1939).

"Mead opposed genetic determinism, racism, sexism, militarism and stultifying religious morality. She was biased—and she was right."[25]

She advocated a tolerant, peaceful society, where biology did not determine behaviour.

"... Fighting racist theories, demonstrating the flexibility of sex roles, promoting respect for exotic traditions, challenging the ethnocentrism of psychologists, sociologists and historians, fighting colonialism, questioning research methods that 'objectify' non-Western people, preserving disappearing cultures and resisting the generalizations of sociobiology. To every one of these genuine *causes célèbres*, Mead made a significant contribution."[26]

"Today, everyone who is not a religious fundamentalist or an unlettered boob of the male sex agrees that Mead was right and the prevailing idea was wrong. Mead's book, which preceded Simone de Beauvoir's *The Second Sex*, Betty Friedan's *The Feminine Mystique* and all the feminist sociology that followed, sowed the seeds of freedom and equal opportunity now enjoyed by millions of women in the West and, increasingly, by scores of millions throughout the world."[27]

Other activist:
Rosemary Gladstar 12 Dec 1948 (no time) California (Sun Mercury conjunction in Sagittarius, Grand Trine in Earth) herbalist, campaigner for plant conservation.[28]

Notes

1. www.perseus.tufts.edu/hopper/text?doc=Perseus%3Atext%3A1999.01.0137%3Ahymn%3D27 accessed 20.7.2020.
2. Nilsson, pp.510–11 .
3. *a-te-mi-to* /Artemitos/ (gen.) and *a-ti-mi-te* /Artimitei/ (dat.), written in Linear B at Pylos. Chadwick, John and Baumbach, Lydia. *The Mycenaean Greek Vocabulary* Glotta, 41.3/4: 1963:157–271. p.176f
4. Goff, Barbara. 2004. *Citizen Bacchae.* University of California Press, Berkley. pp.107–8.
5. Blundell, Sue, Williamson, Margaret. 1998. *The Sacred and the Feminine in Ancient Greece.* Routledge, London. p.33.
6. See Brooke, Elisabeth. 2019. *Women Healers through History. Aeon Books, London.* For examples of women-centred midwifery practice and male attempts to control it.
7. Goff, 2004, p.113 suggests the ritual teaches women how to function in a patriarchy, by i) they learn they are an object of desire and which mael gaze they may attract, ii) they may be sexual but only as sanctioned by marriage iii) as women they are vulnerable to male desire and need protection from men, all of which necessitate their control by men to 'protect their asset'.
8. Brooke, Elisabeth. 2018. *A Woman's Book of Herb*s. Aeon Books, London. p.67.
9. Xenophon of Ephesus, *An Ephesian Tale* 1.2.5–7. http://www.perseus.tufts.edu/hopper/text?doc=Perseus%3Atext%3A2008.01.0649%3Abook%3D1%3Achapter%3D2%3Asection%3D5 accessed 23.10.2020.
10. Nilsson, Martin, P. 1971. *The Minoan-Mycenaean Religion.* Biblo and Tannen, New York. p.503.
11. Jane Goodall's Questions & Answers, *Readers Digest*, p.128, September 2010
12. www.janegoodall.org
13. https://www.janegoodall.org/our-story/our-legacy-of-science/ accessed 30.7.2020.
14. Goodall, Jane (1993). *Cavalieri, Paola (ed.). The Great Ape Project: Equality Beyond Humanity Fourth Estate, London.* p.10.
15. *Jane Goodall's Wild Chimpanzees.* March 3 1996. PBS Nature. https://www.pbs.org/wnet/nature/jane-goodalls-wild-chimpanzees-introduction/1908/ accessed 3.2.2021.
16. http://www.rootsandshoots.org/aboutus/history accessed 3.2.2021.
17. See also Sharron Gannon, p.xx
18. Hatkoff, Amy. 2009. *The Inner World of Farm Animals*, Stewart, Tabori and Chang. Lond. p.13
19. Mead, Margaret. 1935. *Sex and Temperament in Three Primitive Societies.* p.191
20. Mead, Margaret. 1972. *Blackberry Winter: My Earlier Years.* Autobiography. *Kodansha International. New York.* p.54
21. Dresser, Sam. Aeon online. 21.1.2020. *The Meaning of Margaret Mead.* https://aeon.co/essays/how-margaret-mead-became-a-hate-figure-for-conservatives. Accessed 1.2.2021.
22. Mead, Margaret. 1949. *Male and Female.* p.84

23. Konner, Melvin. 11.3.1999. *Bursting A South-Sea Bubble.* Nature: 398, 117–8. https://www.nature.com/articles/18145 accessed 1.2.2021.

24. Mead, Margaret. 1935. *Sex and Temperament in Three Primitive Societies.* p.321.

25. Horgon, John. 25.10.2010. *Margaret Mead's Bashers owe her an Apology.* Cross Check, Scientific American. https://blogs.scientificamerican.com/cross-check/margaret-meads-bashers-owe-her-an-apology/ accessed 1.2.2021.

26. Konner, Melvin. 11.3.1999. *Bursting A South-Sea Bubble.* Nature: 398, 117–8. https://www.nature.com/articles/18145 accessed 1.2.2021.

27. Konner, Melvin. 11.3.1999. *Bursting A South-Sea Bubble.* Nature: 398, 117–8. https://www.nature.com/articles/18145 accessed 1.2.2021.

28. See Brooke, Elisabeth. 2019. *Women Healers Through History.* Aeon Books, London. p.233.

Capricorn: Hecate

High on a mountainside outside a cave you sit in the dappled sunshine of autumn. Sounding your drum, slowly you pick out a beat and the animals gather around as your song summons them, mountain lions sit at your feet, you are queen of all you survey.

Your old bones are stiff and your hair is white, but the ancient wisdom burns brightly within you. You do not have the concerns of the young, but you are the bright one, the ancient one, the wise one.

The weight of history can bear down on you, then you pick up the drums and the cymbals on your ankle tap out an ancient rhythm, taught by the grandmothers of grandmothers. As you dance in the dust, your feet make patterns and as the beat increases sometimes you lose control. The hills and mountains echo back to you. Across the way a sister picks up her drum and then, on another hill another, and another, until sisters pick up the rhythm and together they weave an ancient sacred web with their drums which spreads from mountainside to mountainside, from crone to crone. The web holds up the world. It is light and dark, hard and soft, life and death. It is spun of the past, it holds every story, every prayer, every song, every dance, every triumph, every failure, knitted together by the holders of the web.

Pick up your drum now and join us.

" ... Honoured Asteria who then Perses brought into his great home to be called his beloved wife. And she fell pregnant and brought into the world Hecate, who among all, Zeus son of Kronos, honoured. And he gave to her many splendid gifts to have as her portion; the earth and the unharvested sea, and in the starry heavens she received honour from the immortal gods who valued her especially." (Hesiod *Theogony* 409–415[1])

Hesiod has a completely different story of Hecate at odds with later accounts of her status and areas of influence.[2] Tracing her genealogy Hesiod writes her grandmother was Leto, her parents Asteria and Perses the Titans. Hesiod also reports she would answer prayers, for favours and happiness.

> "Whenever one of earthly mankind offers a beautiful sacrifice and asks for favour according to custom, he invokes Hekate. Then much honour follows effortlessly for the sincere person whose prayers the goddess welcomes. She sends happiness since the power is hers to give." (416–420)

Hekate was a Titan, when they were defeated in the battle of the Titans and the Olympians, Zeus, "Neither deprived nor took away that which she obtained by lot from the former Titan gods." (423–5)

Why should this be? We have already seen that many of the Olympian gods 'married' the native goddesses as a way of subduing them and appropriating their powers and spheres of influence. Yet Zeus gives Hekate massive areas of influence; the sea, and the land. Furthermore, she becomes an arbiter of justice.

> "And she is willing, greatly supporting and helping, she sits as judge in the court with compassionate kings. And in the assembly of men, she distinguishes herself, if she is so minded to." (*Theogony* 428–430)

Hekate is wise counsel and justice and fairness. There is a sobriety here, she is not out on the mountainsides, not at home, nor married with children. Hekate takes on the role of the Crone, who sees all and sits in compassionate judgement.

Because her realm includes the sea, Hekate supports, fishermen, (Capricorn is the she-goat in later astrology).

> "And for those whose work in the gleaming rough and stormy sea, they pray to Hekate and the booming earth-shaker (Poseidon). Effortlessly, the lusty goddess sends more fish." (*Theogony* 440–443)

Finally, Hekate is protectress of the young.

> "And the son of Kronos made her a nurse for all the young, who saw with their eyes the light of all-seeing Dawn. And thus, from the beginning, she rears children." (450–453)

Her protective function echoes her actions later with Persephone. Hekate becomes the companion of the young Queen and advises her when Persephone sits in judgement of the dead.

Hecate appears in the myth of Persephone.

"Neither the mortals nor the gods of men heard her voice (Persephone's), not the fruit laden olive trees, only daughter of Persaeus (Perses) noticed it and listened from a cave. Tender hearted Hecate of the shining headdress." *Homeric Hymn to Demeter,* 22–25[3]

Here she is 'tender hearted,' not wicked and evil as she is later depicted. She cares, she has a soft heart. Perhaps she is the kindly crone. She has a shining headdress-showing her august status. She is in a cave, listening. This embodies Capricorn, who does not usually like the limelight, often in fact, prefers simple an unostentatious life. But she is listening, attentive, she does not rush out, Hecate is cautious or controlled. She listens, she understands and then she waits.

"But then on the tenth day when she came upon the light of dawn, Hekate came to her [Demeter], holding a torch in her hands and bearing a message for her. She related the message and said, 'I will speak with you, Queen Demeter, you who bring the fruits in their season, bestowing splendid gifts. Who of the gods of heaven or mortal men kidnapped Persephone and put your beloved heart in mourning? For a sound was heard but I did not see with my eyes what it was. To you now, I tell all I know.' So said Hecate, but the lovely haired daughter of Rhea did not answer but quickly with flaming torches in their hands, they came to Helios." *Homeric Hymn to Demeter.* 51–61

Capricorn does have this darkness about it, which is some way is reminiscent of Scorpio, but without the drama. Capricorn hates drama, which is why Hekate did not rush out of her cave waving her torches aloft but sat quietly waiting for Demeter to arrive. The Crone has seen it all and so does not react like either a young woman or a mother; she bides her time and waits, conserving her energy and thinking things through. It is Hekate who brings the torches, and suggests they speak to Helios.

Hekate has the answer, and torches to guide them. Knowledge then, or wisdom and leadership skills, are part of Capricorn's gifts. Service too, not the emotional service of Pisces, but practical.

Hekate elects to be with Persephone in Hades, perhaps because as an older woman, she has experience of those dark and desolate places. She both understands and appreciates the need for seclusion from the bright light of day, she was in a cave, and will accompany Persephone as protector, or companion and guide in those months of darkness. Hades is a barren place and perhaps it is fitting a barren Crone should be there as guide and confidant.

" … And from nearby came Hekate of the bright headband, and she embraced with love the hallowed daughter of Demeter and from then on the queen was her devoted companion." *Homeric Hymn to Demeter,* 434–439

It is her association with Hades which later gives Hekate her baleful powers. She became the deity presiding over magic and spells, she was linked to the Shades, she appeared to magicians and sorceresses with a torch in each hand or in the form of animals; a bitch or she-wolf. She was credited with the invention of sorcery, and rules superlative magicians such as Medea. Later she was said to be Circe's mother, Circe was Medea's aunt. As a magician Hekate presided over crossroads, the best locations for magic, statues were erected here in the form of a woman with three bodies or three heads.[4] (Fig. 27)

Fig. 27 Hecate, Attic vase, 500 BCE.

It is good to reflect on who Hecate was previously. Her powers are those of a wise elder, the goddess who protects travellers, goddess of the crossroads, whose shrines are lit outside houses at night to keep away evil. All of which ties in with Capricorn. They are often born old souls who have difficult or lonely childhoods, where they don't fit in with boisterous children. They may have to take on caretaker roles for sick or absent parents, raising their siblings. For this reason, they can seem harsh and judgemental. Most realise early on that life is tough, if they want to survive, they will have to work at it and work hard. Many see financial independence and wealth as a way of protecting themselves from harm and gaining security. Both Scorpio and Capricorn amass wealth, but their motives are different; Scorpio enjoys the power and risk of money making, Capricorn is seeking the security and status affluence brings; Libra often gets to spend wealth others have made.

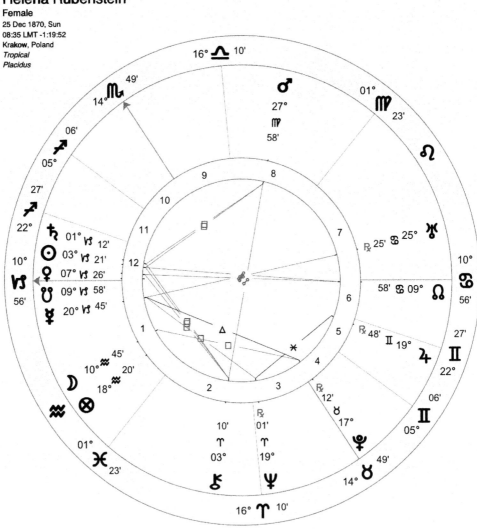

Helena Rubenstein

Female

25 Dec 1870, Sun
08:35 LMT -1:19:52
Krakow, Poland
Tropical
Placidus

Helena Rubinstein: Entrepreneur
25 December 1870[5] (08:35) Krakow, Poland

Helena has a stellium in Capricorn. Ruler Saturn, Sun, Venus and Mercury all conjunct her Ascendant. With Moon in Saturn-ruled Aquarius, also in the First House. Saturn as well as ruling both her Sun and Moon signs, is the almuten (the most powerful planet) of the chart. Her hard working, frugal, Venus in Capricorn sums up her belief about beauty:

> "There are no ugly women, only lazy ones."[6]

Born the eldest of eight daughters, to a middle-class family, Helena had to care for her siblings; a common Capricorn experience, they often have to grow up quickly and take on responsibility. There were no boys, and Helena was good with figures, so she helped out her businessman father, taking her first business meeting at 15, when he was ill. She was sent to study medicine in Switzerland but did not like dealing with sickness and left. Her father said she should marry, but she refused his choice while he rejected hers.

Helena went to visit relatives in Australia and took twelve pots of Modjeska cream, made from a formula of herbs, almond oil, and extracts from the bark of the Carpathian fir tree, made by Dr Lykusky. Women loved it and Helena borrowed $250 to open a beauty salon in Melbourne. By working long days, up to eighteen hours long, she turned this debt into $12,000. Capricorns are brilliant at business, they take risks, work really hard and persist. Helena developed her skills, studying dermatology in Paris with Dr. Berthelo, (serious in her work, needing expert help, also very Saturnian). Helena left family members in charge of her Australian business (Capricorn takes family responsibility seriously and often employs family members). She opened a salon in London, then Paris and then moved to New York in 1916.

> "All the American women had purple noses and gray lips and their faces were chalk white from terrible powder. I recognized that the United States could be my life's work."[7]

Her business was a massive success. Helena married but overworking brought her close to divorce so she sold her American business to Lehman Brothers 1928, for $7.3 million, ($108 million in 2020[8]) while secretly buying back stock. When the Stock Market collapsed in 1928, she was able to buy the company for less than $1 million and eventually turned the shares into a multimillion fortune. Her marriage did not survive. Work always comes first with Capricorn and they are astute, hard-nosed business women.

> "Hard work keeps the wrinkles out of the mind and spirit."[9]

Rubinstein was incredibly frugal, eating a packed lunch to work, watching expenditure carefully in true Capricorn fashion (Saturn hates excess). In 1957 she started the Helena Rubinstein travelling art scholarship in Australia.[10] In 1953, she established the philanthropic Helena Rubinstein Foundation to provide funds to organizations specializing in health, medical research and rehabilitation which operated until 2011. It gave out nearly $130 million over the course of six decades, primarily to education, arts and community-based organizations in New York City supporting children's education and adult employment and training.[11] Capricorns take their civic responsibilities seriously and feel duty bound to give a helping hand up to their sisters. When Helena Rubinstein died in 1965, her cosmetics business was worth somewhere between $17.5 million and $60 million, with international holdings, including laboratories, factories, and salons in fourteen countries.[12]

Other female entrepreneurs:
Madame C. J Walker, 23 December 1867. First Black woman multimillionaire (Sun, Mars, Venus in Capricorn)
Elizabeth Arden, 31 December 1878. (Sun, Venus in Capricorn).

Dolly Parton

Female
19 Jan 1946, Sat
20:25 CST +6:00
Alcoa, Tennessee
Tropical
Placidus

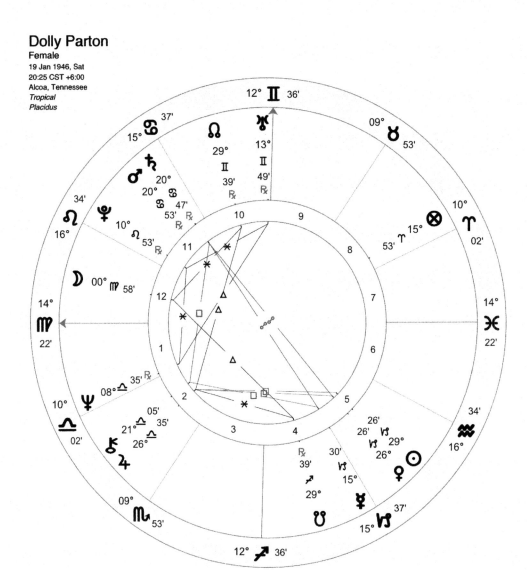

Dolly Parton: Singer and philanthropist
19 January 1946. (20:25) Sevierville TN

"It costs a lot of money to look this cheap."[13]

Born in a one-room cabin, in rural Appalachia, Dolly was the fourth of twelve children. Parton credited her father for her business savvy, and her mother's family for her musical abilities. She began singing in church when she was six, and at seven started playing a homemade guitar. When she was eight, her uncle bought her first real guitar. Parton moved to Nashville the day after she graduated High School. Her initial success was as a songwriter; she signed with Combine Music Publishing shortly after her arrival. Again the serious Capricorn realising it was her job to earn money and get responsible early on.

"You'll never do a whole lot unless you're brave enough to try."[14]

Her Sun Venus conjunction in Capricorn in the fifth house of creativity shows hard work, honing her skills and serious approach to life.

Dolly developed a professional partnership with country music singer Porter Wagoner, who promoted her career on his TV show, they recorded duets for his record label. Her breakthrough song *Jolene* was released in 1973 and she decided to go solo, writing another best-seller, *I Will Always Love You* about their partnership, which went to number one in the country music charts. Elvis was interested in recording the song. Dolly was told by his manager that it was standard procedure for the songwriter to sign over half of the publishing rights to any song recorded by Presley. Parton refused.

"As soon as I could, I started my own publishing company, got my own record label. I think it's important, if you can, to keep all of your goods close to home where you can control them and know what's happening with them."[15]

Dolly's Sun, Venus and Mercury in Capricorn show her business acumen and how she would earn her wealth, Venus ruling the voice and Mercury music and writing. Dolly made millions of dollars in royalties from both songs. Her decision to leave Wagoner, was another hard-headed business decision. Parton moved into pop music by working with producer Gary Klein for her next album, *Here You Come Again*. It was her first million-seller, topping the country album chart and reaching number twenty on the pop chart. Dolly wrote the song *9 to 5* for the film of the same name in which she starred with Jane Fonda and Lily Tomlin. It reached number one in the country chart, but also, in February 1981, reached number one on the pop and the adult contemporary charts, making it a triple number-one hit, one of the few female country singers to have a number-one single on the country and pop charts simultaneously.

151

In 1998, *Nashville Business* ranked her the wealthiest country-music star. As of 2017, her net worth is estimated at 500 million dollars.

> "If your actions create a legacy that inspires others to dream more, learn more, do more and become more, then you are an excellent leader."[16]

She married in 1966 and, unable to have children, she raised several of her younger siblings. Since the mid-1980s Parton has supported many charities, particularly in the area of literacy, primarily through her Dollywood Foundation. Her literacy program, Dolly Parton's Imagination Library, a part of the Dollywood Foundation, posts one book a month to each enrolled child from the time of their birth until they enter kindergarten. Currently, over 1,600 local communities provide the Imagination Library to almost 850,000 children each month across the U.S., Canada, the UK, Australia, and the Republic of Ireland. In 2018 she sent out its one hundred-millionth book.

The Sun Venus is opposed by a Saturn Mars conjunction in Cancer again showing hard work, (Saturn) dynamism (Mars) and compassion for the less fortunate (Cancer). These form a T square with Jupiter in Libra in the second showing wealth (Jupiter in the second) and a glitzy lifestyle (Jupiter in Libra).

> "Being a star just means that you just find your own special place, and that you shine where you are."[17]

The Dollywood Foundation, funded by Dolly, brings jobs and tax revenue to a poor area. Dolly also has worked to raise money for several other causes, including the American Red Cross and HIV AIDS charities. She supported the Vanderbilt University School of Medicine including the Monroe Carell Jr. Children's Hospital at Vanderbilt Paediatric Cancer Programme in honour of a lifelong friend, Professor Naji Abumrad and by way of thanks to the staff of the children's hospital for the successful treatment of her niece for leukaemia.

Her Ascendant and Moon in Virgo show the very feminine persona she presents which masks a shrewd businesswoman.

> "You know, I look like a woman, but I think like a man. And in this world of business, that has helped me a lot. Because by the time they think that I don't know what's goin' on, I then got the money, and am gone."[18]

Notes

1. http://www.perseus.tufts.edu/hopper/text?doc=Perseus%3Atext%3A1999.01.0129%3Acard%3D404 accessed 2.07.2020.
2. The creation myth in Hesiod has long been held to have Eastern influences, such as the Hittite Song of Kumarbi and the Babylonian Enuma Elis. This cultural crossover

would have occurred in the eighth and ninth century Greek trading colonies such as Al Mina in North Syria. (For more discussion, read Robin Lane Fox's *Travelling Heroes* and Walcot's *Hesiod and the Near East.*)

3. https://www.perseus.tufts.edu/hopper/text?doc=Perseus%3Atext%3A1999.01.0137%3Ahymn%3D2 accessed 12.4.2020.

4. Grimal, 1987:181–2.

5. There is some debate about her year of birth, I have used www.jwa.org and Encyclopaedia Britannica as sources and they both say 1870. Most of the biographical details come from: https://jwa.org/encyclopedia/article/rubinstein-helena.

6. *Green, Penelope (February 15, 2004). "The Rivals". The New York Times.*

7. https://www.brainyquote.com/quotes/helena_rubinstein_362582 accessed 7.8.2020.

8. https://www.dollartimes.com/inflation/inflation.php?amount=1000000&year=1928 accessed 5.8.2020.

9. https://www.brainyquote.com/quotes/helena_rubinstein_286540. Accessed 7.8.2020.

10. *Poynter, J. R. "Rubinstein, Helena (1870–1965)". Australian Dictionary of Biography. Australian National University.*

11. http://philanthropynewsdigest.org/news/helena-rubinstein-foundation-to-close-at-year-s-end 7 Nov. 2011.PND. by Candid, accessed 5.8.2020.

12. https://jwa.org/encyclopedia/article/rubinstein-helena accessed 5.8.2020.

13. "Dolly Parton Biography". *thebiographychannel.co.uk.*

14. https://www.goalcast.com/2019/02/21/dolly-parton-quotes/ accessed 7.8.2020.

15. https://www.biography.com/musician/dolly-parton accessed 7.8.2020.

16. https://www.goalcast.com/2019/02/21/dolly-parton-quotes/ accessed 7.8.2020.

17. https://www.goalcast.com/2019/02/21/dolly-parton-quotes/ accessed 7.8.2020.

18. https://www.goalcast.com/2019/02/21/dolly-parton-quotes/ accessed 7.8.2020.

Aquarius: Athena

You walk in the ancient city, stark, white marble columns, clear lines, high buildings, their elegance and symmetry pleases you. The silence and space gratifies you. You mount the steps of a shimmering temple and sit in the shade to dream up future palaces, spinning your inspiration into ideas.

You wander the marble halls, your footsteps echoing, deep in the centre of the city. Other spinners and weavers wait for you to join them. You approach without speaking and sit, silently joining their circle. Your minds connect as one. You breathe, in unison, the trance deepens and you fly, you soar, far from your body as visions flow. Cool, clear ideas present a template for a future of harmony, equity and justice, of honesty and integrity.

Your minds weave the future and connect with other webs, other visionaries, your web become part of the greater web that you all weave over this beautiful blue planet. Together you dream a future into being, a mesh of peace, fairness and community.

Athene, the most controversial of the goddesses, marks the defeat of the matriarchal line and the victory of god-the-father, or does it? Looking back we find an earlier story.

The best known myth of Athena is that Zeus swallowed her mother Metis, because he had been warned that her children by him would be more powerful than he was. Metis, the goddess of wisdom was duly swallowed, and Athena was born from his head along the shore of Lake Triton in Libya.

"Zeus, the king of the gods took Metis goddess of wisdom, wise counsel, skill and craft as his first wife, she was the greatest skilful-minded among both gods and mortal men. But when she was destined to bring into the world the goddess of the shining eyes, Athena, he with treachery deceived her heart with wily words he put her down in his own stomach, following the cunning of Gaia and starry Ouranos. For in this way they had advised him, so that Zeus and no other might have royal honour over the everlasting gods. For from Metis, it had been fated to bring in very thoughtful children; the first, the shining eyed maiden Tritogenia [Athena][1] having equal strength to the father and sage in counsel and deliberation. But Zeus then put her into his own stomach so that the goddess might be able to point out to him both good and evil." Hesiod, *Theogony*, 886–90.[2]

Nothing could be more explicit. Zeus, jealous of Metis, goddess of skill and crafts, wisdom and cunning, swallowed her when she was pregnant with Athena, because he feared she would be cleverer than him and he wished to have complete control over the other gods.

The Pelasgians say Athene was born by Lake Tritonis in Libya, where the women and girls dress in goatskins. She was raised by the three nymphs of Libya. Playfighting with her friend, Pallas (daughter of the river Triton) she accidentally killed her. Heartbroken she put Pallas' name before hers, (Pallas Athene). Graves cites a late patriarchal story, in which the girls were sword fighting, and Athene was distracted when Zeus put his aegis (a shield or animal skin carried by Athena and Zeus with the head of the Gorgon on it) on her (Fig. 28). In reality, the aegis[3] was a magical goat skin

Fig. 28 Gorgon mask 525 BCE.

bag containing a snake. It was protected by a Gorgon mask and was Athene's long before Zeus claimed to be her father. Goat skins were the habitual costumes of Libyan girls and Pallas means maiden. (Graves: 2011:44)

"The clothing and aegis of honour of Athene was taken by the Hellenes from the Libyans. For, except that the Libyan's clothing is made from leather and the tassels of the goatskins of the women are not serpents but leather thongs, in all other ways it is arranged like theirs. Moreover, the very name signifies that the clothing of the statues of Pallas came out of Libya. For they put the tasselled wraps over their dresses, this is a hairless goatskin stained red with madder. The Hellenes they gave the new name *aegides* to these goatskins." Herodotus *Histories* 4:189[4]

Unmarried girls of the Auseans who lived around lake Tritonis (or priestesses of Neith) fought in armed combat for the position of High Priestess. At the festival of Athena, the unmarried girls separated into two groups and throw sticks and stones at each other,

"An ancestral obligation they have to the goddess who is their patron, who we know as Athena. Those who die from their wounds were said not to be virgins. Before this, the most beautiful maiden is dressed in Egyptian armour and driven around the lake in a chariot. They claim Athena is the daughter of Poseidon and the lake Tritonis … [for these people] there is no marriage, they have sex with many partners, often in the open air, and when a child is born, the men decide among themselves which one most closely resembles the child and he is named the father." (Herodotus, 4:180)

The loud cries of beseeching called out in prayer to Athene (*Iliad* vi. 297–301) were of Libyan origin.[5]

It is believed there was a Libyan exodus into Crete as early as 4000 BCE when many goddess-worshipping Libyan refugees from the Western Delta arrived in the island, bringing their goddesses with them. First, she lived in the city of Athenae by the river Triton in Boetia. Plato associated Athene with the matriarchal Libyan goddess Neith who had a temple at Sais. Graves, (2011:176–7), claims there was a pre-Hellenic medical cult[6] presided over by Moon priestesses at the shrines of heroes who re-incarnated as serpents or crows or ravens. Athene was the head of the cult. Athene was called 'Coronis' because of the crow oracle and Hygeia, because of her healing arts. Athene's gift to Asclepius suggests her healing remedies were secret, guarded by the priestesses. The Gorgon's head was intended to terrify the curious and keep them away. Athene gave Asclepius two vials of Gorgon blood. One drawn from the veins of the Gorgons left side, could raise the dead, that from the right side could kill instantly, or they divided the blood between them, he used it to save life and she to destroy it and instigate wars. (Graves, 2011:175). Apollo took over the healing sanctuaries, the serpents were the original oracles.

Fig. 29 Tree Goddess with snakes, Minoan, Knossos, 1600–1500 BCE.

In Minoan Krete Athena was associated with the Snake Goddess and also the Tree Cult. (Fig. 29) The Minoan goddesses changed into animals,

" ... Flashing eyed Athena, she left in the form of a sea eagle" *Odyssey* iii:371.

Elsewhere in the Odyssey Athene is represented as a heron or eagle (αωοπαια) (*Od.* i:320) and a swallow (*Od.* xxii:239). (Fig. 30)

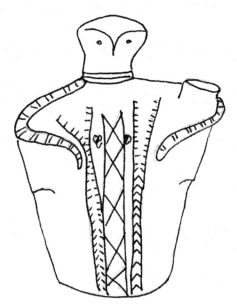

Fig. 30 Bird snake goddess Koumasa Krete, 2300 BCE.

Athene invented the flute, the trumpet, the earthenware pot, the plough, the rake, the ox-yoke, the horse-bridle, the chariot and the ship. She first taught the science of numbers and all women's arts such as cooking and weaving and spinning. Some of the finest Cretan pots were known to have been made by women. Athene helped Prometheus bring fire to mankind after Zeus had forbidden it. Athene opened a back door entrance to Olympus and Prometheus lit a torch at the fiery chariot of the sun and broke from it a fragment of charcoal which he hid in a hollow giant fennel stalk.[7]

In Classical Greece Athene becomes the ultimate warrior, who defeats Ares with her marital skills. Zeus says to Hera,

"Take Athene the spoiler pit her against him (Ares) for she is especially disposed to cause suffering in the body for him." *Iliad*, 5:765–6[8]

In her Greek form, Athena becomes the agent of Zeus in his war against the matriarchy. Athena is a man manqué and also a better fighter than Ares, who loses himself in rage. Athene backs the Greeks and they win the Trojan war. She wins the battle with Poseidon to rule Athens. The final nail in the coffin of matriarchy is the law that Athene exemplifies; the end of the mother-right, policed by the *Furies*, replaced with father-right, trial by jury and the valuing of the father over the mother.

In Aeschylus' play *The Eumenides*[9] vividly recounts the loss of power of the matriarchal, chthonic gods and the establishment of father-right. It is arguable that the blood-guilt system did lead to endless bloodshed, but then patriarchal eternal warfare sheds more blood, senselessly. The shame of abusing the mother is here removed and the rights of men are now paramount. Crimes of murder are no longer punished by the female chthonic goddesses, they are adjudicated by an all-male jury of Greek citizens, who naturally would be expected to favour the father over the mother (see Mars the Furies).

What then, can we take from all this for Aquarius?

A love of truth, a need for justice, diplomatic and conciliatory skills, logic not passion, the importance of the collective over individual rights, revolution, skilful with words, calm, measured, thoughtful, fighters for justice. Cool, analytical, iconoclasts, a fighter, fair, honest, and reasonable. Often unmarried and without children, freedom is vital to them.

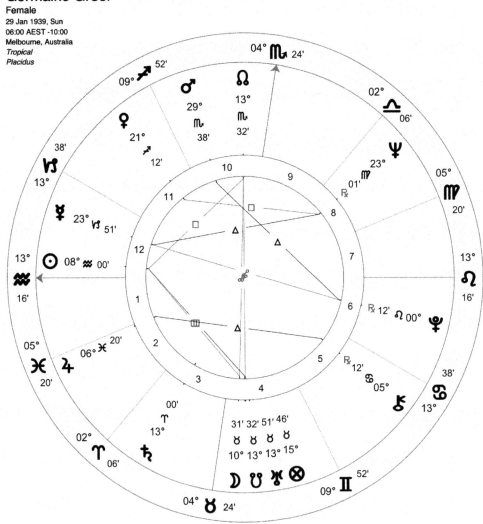

Germaine Greer

Female

29 Jan 1939, Sun
06:00 AEST -10:00
Melbourne, Australia

Tropical
Placidus

Germaine Greer: Revolutionary Feminist
29 January 1939. (06:00) Melbourne Aus.

"Do what you want and want what you do."[10]

Greer is a writer, journalist, Shakespearian scholar, and one of the most important feminist thinkers of the second wave of feminism. A true Aquarian, her ideas created controversy both within and without the Women's Liberation Movement. *The Female Eunuch* (1970) argued that women were forced into submissive roles to fulfil male fantasies about what women were (just like patriarchal Athene).

"This is impossible, you can't live this way. So I've got to invent another way to live."[11]

Germaine argued that women's lives were made unworkable by patriarchy.

"When a woman may walk on the open streets of our cities alone, without insult or obstacle, at any pace she chooses, there will be no further need for this book."[12]

As a true revolutionary Aquarius, Germaine was radical even for the feminists, she was scathing in her putdowns.

"Reaction is not revolution. It is not a sign of revolution where the oppressed adopt the manners of the oppressors and practice oppression on their own behalf."[13]

And,

"Privileged women will pluck at your sleeve and seek to enlist you in the 'fight' for reforms, but reforms are retrogressive. The old process must be broken, not made new. Bitter women will call you to rebellion, but you have too much to do. What *will* you do?"[14]

She was vilified in the press,

"I was told then [after the publication of *The Female* Eunuch] that I had removed the basis of Western Civilisation. And I thought, well if that is the basis of Western Civilisation get rid of it! Because it means it is resting on the shoulders of 51% of oppressed people. It's crap, get rid of it."[15]

Her analysis of marriage and the family was blunt,

> "The nuclear family is a bad environment for women and for the raising of children, and that the manufacture of women's sexuality by Western society is demeaning and confining. Girls are feminised from childhood by being taught rules that subjugate them. Later, when women embrace the stereotypical version of adult femininity, they develop a sense of shame about their own bodies and lose their natural and political autonomy. The result is powerlessness, isolation, a diminished sexuality, and a lack of joy."[16]

Aquarians being air signs are intellectually gifted, like Aries, Aquarius lives in the future and waits impatiently for everyone else to catch up.

"Most of what I say is blindingly obvious."[17]

At the centre of her arguments are the need for freedom, personal freedom for both men and women and political freedom.

> "In 1970 the movement was called 'Women's Liberation' or, contemptuously, 'Women's Lib'. When the name 'Libbers' was dropped for 'Feminists' we were all relieved. What none of us noticed was that the ideal of liberation was fading out with the word. We were settling for equality. Liberation struggles are not about assimilation but about asserting difference, endowing that difference with dignity and prestige, and insisting on it as a condition of self-definition and self-determination. The aim of women's liberation is to do as much for female people as has been done for colonized nations. Women's liberation did not see the female's potential in terms of the male's actual; the visionary feminists of the late sixties and early seventies knew that women could never find freedom by agreeing to live the lives of unfree men. Seekers after equality clamoured to be admitted to smoke-filled male haunts. Liberationists sought the world over for clues as to what women's lives could be like if they were free to define their own values, order their own priorities and decide their own fate. *The Female Eunuch* was one feminist text that did not argue for equality."[18]

Germaine is the author of *Sex and Destiny: The Politics of Human Fertility* (1984); and *The Change: Women, Ageing and the Menopause* (1991), and most recently *Shakespeare's Wife* (2007). She has also purchased and is restoring Tropical Rainforest in Northern Australia to save virgin land from the developers.

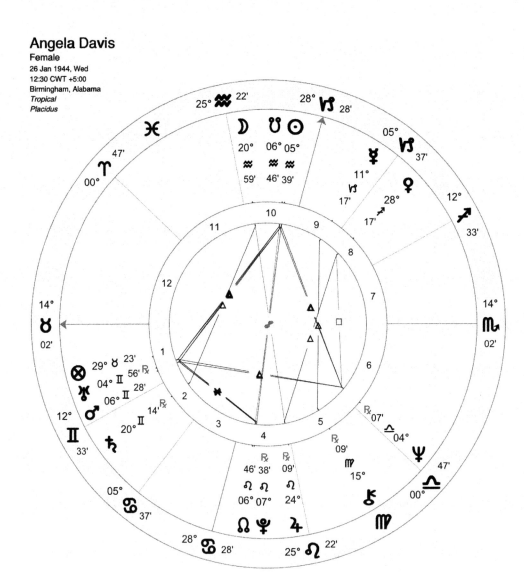

Angela Davis
Female
26 Jan 1944, Wed
12:30 CWT +5:00
Birmingham, Alabama
Tropical
Placidus

Angela Davis: Revolutionary, abolitionist and feminist
26 January 1944. (12:30) Birmingham AL

Angela is an American political activist, philosopher, academic, and author. She is a professor emerita at the University of California Santa Cruz. A Marxist and long-time member of the Communist Party USA and founding member of the Committees of Correspondence for Democracy and Socialism. She is author of over ten books on class, feminism and the prison system.

> "Our very survival has frequently been a direct function of our skill in forging effective channels of resistance. In resisting, we have sometimes been compelled to openly violate those laws which directly or indirectly buttress our oppression."[19]

A true radical, Angela Davis with her Moon and Sun in Aquarius lives the future and fights against racism, misogyny and social justice. Her Mars, Uranus conjunction in Gemini shows her fight (Mars) against tyranny and violence (Uranus) through her words (Gemini).

> " … Racism is integrally linked to capitalism. And I think it's a mistake to assume that we can combat racism by leaving capitalism in place."[20]

Born to an African-American family in Birmingham Alabama. Davis was friends with some of those who died in the 16th Street Baptist church bombing in 1963 in which Ku Klux Klan terrorists murdered four girls, but no one was prosecuted until 1977.

> "We knew that the role of the police was to protect white supremacy,"[21]

Davis studied French at Brandeis University and philosophy at the University of Frankfurt under Herbert Marcuse. She took her doctorate at the Humbolt University of Berlin in what was then communist East Germany. On returning to the United States, she joined the Black caucus of the Communist Party and was an activist in the Woman's Movement, the Black Panther Party, and the campaign against the Vietnam War.

In 1969 she was hired as an acting assistant professor of philosophy at the UCLA. She was fired soon afterwards, due to her Communist Party membership. Angela took UCLA to court and won. The university fired her again, this time for her use of inflammatory language.

In August 1970, members of the Black Panthers tried to escape from a court. The judge who was taken hostage was killed, Jonathan Jackson, who tried to free the two defendants, also died. Angela was charged with aggravated kidnapping and first degree murder because she had (legally) bought the gun. Angela fled underground and was the subject of an intense FBI manhunt as one of 'America's Most Wanted.'

After eighteen months as a fugitive, Angela was captured, arrested, tried, spent eighteen months in jail and eventually acquitted in one of the most famous trials in recent USA history. Her case became a cause célèbre, Aretha Franklin helped publicise her case by offering to stand bail; the Rolling Stones and John Lennon wrote songs about her.

> "When I was in jail, solidarity coming from Palestine was a major source of courage for me. In Ferguson, Palestinians were the first to express international solidarity. And there has been this very important connection between the two struggles for many decades."[22]

Of her continued activism she said,

> "I could have been sentenced to spend the rest of my life behind bars. [as many Black Panthers were]. And it was only because of the organising that unfolded all over the world that my life was saved. So, in a sense, my continued work is based on the awareness that I would not be here had enough people not done the same kind of work for me. And I'll continue to do this until the day I die."[23]

A committed feminist, Angela is determined the role of women in history be celebrated,

> "This masculinisation of history goes back many decades and centuries. Discussions about lynching, for example, often fail to acknowledge not only that many of the lynching victims were black women, but also that those who struggled against lynching were black women, such as Ida B Wells."[24]

As a feminist Angela has worked in collective movements and is pleased that the 2020 rebellions have collective leadership, "I see these young people who are so intelligent, who have learned from the past and who have developed new ideas," she says. "I find myself learning a great deal from people who are 50 years younger than me. And to me, that's exciting. That keeps me wanting to remain in the struggle."[25] Considering the future, she says, "The most important thing from where I stand is to begin to give expression to ideas about what we can do next,"[26] and on the 2020 Black Lives Matter protests,

> "I've often said one never knows when conditions may give rise to a conjuncture such as the current one that rapidly shifts popular consciousness and suddenly allows us to move in the direction of radical change."[27]

Notes

1. Tritogenia *Trito-born*, a name for Athena, Iliad, 4:515, 8: 39. Odyssey 3:378, Hesiod, *Theogony*: 895, 924. It probably comes from the lake Tritonis in Libya where she is said to have been born. Interestingly, the Pythagoreans gave the name Athena to the equilateral triangle.

2. http://www.perseus.tufts.edu/hopper/text?doc=Perseus%3Atext%3A1999.01.0129%3Acard%3D886 Accessed 12.8.2020.

3. Graves writes it would have been death for a man to try to remove the aegis-goat-skin chastity tunic worn by Libyan girls without the owner's consent., hence the Gorgon mask set above it and the serpent within. It is also possible that it was a bag cover for a sacred disk, like the one which contained Palamede's alphabetical secret which he was said to have invented, these shields are described by both Homer and Hesiod (Graves, 2011, p.47).

4. Holland, 2013 p.331.

5. Graves, 2011, p.45 when Upper and Lower Egypt were forcibly united under the First Dynasty about 3000 BCE. The First Minoan Age began soon afterwards, and Cretan culture spread to Thrace and Early Helladic Greece.

6. There was a women's medical school at Sais, see Brooke, Elisabeth. 2019 *Women Healers through History.* Aeon Books, London, p.3.

7. (Graves, 2011, p.144) (Virgil, *Eclogues,* vi.42.) it is possible Prometheus was her lover (Graves, 2011, p.149.)

8. http://www.perseus.tufts.edu/hopper/text?doc=Perseus%3Atext%3A1999.01.0134%3Abook%3D5%3Acard%3D764 accessed 13.8.2020.

9. Aeschylus (524/5-465 BCE) writer of tragedy, the *Eumenides* is the final part of his trilogy *Oresteia.*

10. https://www.youtube.com/watch?v=CN2xhrEJCxs accessed 10.2.2021.

11. https://www.youtube.com/watch?v=CN2xhrEJCxs accessed 10.2.2021.

12. *Wlodarczyk, Justyna (2010). Ungrateful Daughters: Third Wave Feminist Writings. Cambridge Scholars Publishing, Newcastle upon Tyne.p.24 quoting first draft of The Female Eunuch.*

13. Festival of Dangerous ideas: Germaine Greer Interview. 2.10.2012. https://www.youtube.com/watch?v=cCzilf_o6fg&t=1m0s accessed 10.2.2021.

14. Greer, Germaine. 1971. *The Female Eunuch.* Farrar Straus and Giroux, New York p.13.

15. Festival of Dangerous ideas: Germaine Greer Interview. 2.10.2012. https://www.youtube.com/watch?v=cCzilf_o6fg&t=1m0s accessed 10.2.2021.

16. Greer, Germaine, 1971. *The Female Eunuch.* p.371

17. Festival of Dangerous ideas: Germaine Greer Interview. 2.10.2012. https://www.youtube.com/watch?v=cCzilf_o6fg&t=1m0s accessed 10.2.2021.

18. Greer, Germaine, 1999. *The Whole Woman.* Doubleday, London. p.2

19. Davis, Angela. *If they come in the Morning.* 1971 (no page no.) https://en.wikiquote.org/wiki/Angela_Davis accessed 9.2.2021.

20. 12 June 2020. *Angela Davis on Abolition, Calls to Defund the Police, Toppled Racist Statues & Voting in the 2020 Election.* Interviewed by Amy Goodman. Democracy Now. https://www.democracynow.org/2020/6/12/angela_davis_on_abolition_calls_to accessed 9.2.2021.

21. https://www.theguardian.com/us-news/2020/jun/15/angela-davis-on-george-floyd-as-long-as-the-violence-of-racism-remains-no-one-is-safe

22. 12 June 2020. *Angela Davis on Abolition, Calls to Defund the Police, Toppled Racist Statues & Voting in the 2020 Election.* Interviewed by Amy Goodman. Democracy Now. https://www.democracynow.org/2020/6/12/angela_davis_on_abolition_calls_to accessed 9.2.2021.

23. Bakare, Lanre. 15 June 2020.Interview Angela Davis. *We Knew that the Role of the Police was to Protect White Supremacy.* The Guardian Newspaper. London. https://www.theguardian.com/us-news/2020/jun/15/angela-davis-on-george-floyd-as-long-as-the-violence-of-racism-remains-no-one-is-safe

24. Bakare, Lanre. 15 June 2020.Interview Angela Davis. *We Knew that the Role of the Police was to Protect White Supremacy.* The Guardian Newspaper. London. https://www.theguardian.com/us-news/2020/jun/15/angela-davis-on-george-floyd-as-long-as-the-violence-of-racism-remains-no-one-is-safe

25. Bakare, Lanre. 15 June 2020.Interview Angela Davis. *We Knew that the Role of the Police was to Protect White Supremacy.* The Guardian Newspaper. London. https://www.theguardian.com/us-news/2020/jun/15/angela-davis-on-george-floyd-as-long-as-the-violence-of-racism-remains-no-one-is-safe

26. Bakare, Lanre. 15 June 2020.Interview Angela Davis. *We Knew that the Role of the Police was to Protect White Supremacy.* The Guardian Newspaper. London. https://www.theguardian.com/us-news/2020/jun/15/angela-davis-on-george-floyd-as-long-as-the-violence-of-racism-remains-no-one-is-safe

27. 12 June 2020. *Angela Davis on Abolition, Calls to Defund the Police, Toppled Racist Statues & Voting in the 2020 Election.* Interviewed by Amy Goodman. Democracy Now. https://www.democracynow.org/2020/6/12/angela_davis_on_abolition_calls_to accessed 9.2.2021.

Pisces: the Pythia

Through the mists you walk, long robes flowing behind you. The ground is soft underfoot and the sparkling river runs beside you as you make your way to the place of power.

A light appears in the gloom and you make your way towards it, drawing you in, welcoming you.

You take your seat and light the incense, billows of perfumed smoke fill the space. Candles flicker giving off a soft light. With water from the sacred stream you make your libation, invoking the goddess, you settle as she speaks.

She tells of a better time to come. She shows cities of light where peace lives and love reigns. She speaks of sorrow and suffering and washes them away. She speaks of betrayal and hurt and washes them away. She speaks of forgiveness and compassion and she fills your heart with a longing for a time before, a yearning for a time to come. She stretches you wide until you are boundless and free, filled with love, you dissolve in the mists and are one.

At the foot of mount Parnassus, was a chasm in the earth where a stream flowed. In the cave sanctuary was a priestess, the Pythia, a shamanic priestess of Gaia, the Earth Goddess. The Pythia presided over divination at the shrine at Delphi long before the upstart Apollo came along. The shrine at Delphi was sacred to Aegean earth goddess, later called Ge/Gaia by the Greeks. Here, the Pythia invokes the goddess at Delphi.

> "I begin with a prayer to the oldest of the gods, the first prophet Gaia and from her, Themis and then of the mother of the second sits at this oracle, so the story goes, and in third place in the allotted portion, by consent and not by force, another Titan child of the earth Phoebe, sat here." *Eumenides*, 1–10[1]

169

Themis and Gaia were pre-Hellenic goddesses, Titans who predated the patriarchal gods. Gaia was called protomantis (πρωτομαντις) the first prophet.[2] Themis was goddess of justice, law, rights, judgement. In the patriarchal pantheon, Zeus 'marries' her, and she gives birth to children who have her powers under his supervision. (see Themis, Jupiter). From this we can glean that Themis was Justice, Peace, Fate, and Order, rather like the astrological planet Jupiter.[3] Notice the mother-line from goddess to goddess for the Sibyl of Delphi.

> "A cult was carried on in Mycenaean times on exactly the same spot as in the Greek age, the very site of the temple and the altar of Apollo … A female deity appeared at Delphi sometime after the Neolithic period, both in the place afterwards dedicated to Athena and on the site where later the temple of Apollo was erected."[4]

It is believed the original Pythia came from Libya and was the daughter of the goddess Lamia. The shrine at Delphi was founded by Kretans, who brought their sacred music, ritual, dances and calendar. The new male priests at Delphi, the *Labryadae* were named after the Kretan *labrys* the sacred double headed axe. The first temple was a rustic hut made from laurel branches. The second was built from beeswax and feathers by the *Melissae* (bees).[5]

> "It is said, the most ancient temple of Delphi was made from laurel, the branches of laurel were brought from the valley of Tempe.[6] This temple would have taken the form of a hut. The second they say, the Delphinians made a temple of the Melissae,[7] from beeswax and feathers and they say this was sent to the Hyperboreans[8] by Apollo … And the story they have of the fern that grows on the mountains, from these fresh blooming herbs, they wove a temple." Pausanias, 10:5:9–10[9]

The Pythia chewed Laurel leaves from a sacred tree growing inside the temple complex to induce the *enthusiasmos* (trance) from which she uttered the prophecies.[10] Some accounts describe her as shaking a laurel branch while delivering her divinations. (Fig. 31) In Kretan iconography there are many examples of 'tree shakers' engraved on small gold signet rings[11] which supports this contention. Laurel is a hallucinogenic plant, reputedly it brought spirits out and allowed discourse with them. The Melissae were oracular bees who brought messages and prophecies (see Gemini Melissae). Fern seeds are believed to confer the power of invisibility if ingested.[12] The oracle, then had association with magical plants.

Others claimed the Sibyl's prophecies came from the she-dragon in the Castalian Spring (the daughter of Hera perhaps). She sat on a tripod in an underground chamber, the *adyton*, built where the two fault lines intersected, set over a cleft in the earth. She inhaled the vapours, falling into a trance. The Castilian spring flowed underneath creating a chasm where *pneuma* (πνευμα-air, spirits, inspiration) wafted up from the fissure. Modern science suggests these vapours could have contained the anaesthetic

Fig. 31 Themis/Pythia 5thC BCE.

and sweet-smelling ethylene or other hydrocarbons such as ethane which produce powerful trances.[13]

Herophile, one known historical Sibyl would stand on the *omphalos* rock at the shrine, which marked the place where two eagles, who flew in opposite directions around the earth met (it signified the centre of the earth) and declaim her prophecies some time before the Trojan War (twelfth or eleventh century BCE).

Plutarch, (d.119 CE) a late source for the Pythia, was a priest at Delphi. He said the spirits breathed into the Pythia, inspired her, giving her a beautiful fragrance [ethylene?], she was inspired by the god[ess] who gave her visions and, "Creates a light in her soul in regard to the future; for inspiration is precisely this." *De Pythiae Oraculis*:6[14]

He continues,

> "We reached a point opposite the rock which lies over against the council-chamber, upon which it is said that the first Sibyl sat after her arrival from [Mount] Helicon where she had been reared by the Muses (though others say that she came from the Malians and was the daughter of Lamia[15] whose father was Poseidon) ... she sang of herself that even after death she would not stop prophesying, but that she shall go round and round in the moon, becoming what is called the face that appears in the moon; while her spirit, mingled with the air, shall be for ever borne onward in voices of presage and portent; and since from her body, transformed within the earth, grass and herbage shall spring, on this shall pasture the creatures reared for the sacred sacrifice, and they shall acquire all manner of colours and forms and qualities upon their inward parts, from which shall come for men prognostications of the future." (Plutarch, *De Pythiae Oraculis* 9)[16]

Other ancient sources suggest it was vapour from the rotting corpse of the serpent which inspired her (see Themis). Or perhaps the messages from the voiceless, the mantic wind (πνευμα μαντις). Later historians claimed that her utterances had to be 'translated' by male priests, but there is no contemporary evidence of this, indeed she was said to sing her divinations in poetical metres (dactylic hexameters).[17]

Before prophesying, The Pythia fasted and bathed herself in the Castalian Spring. She burned laurel leaves and barley on her altar where an everlasting fire burnt and the spring bubbled up from the ground. She drank the spring water and sat on to the tripod holding a laurel branch in one hand and a bowl of spring water in the other.

The Pythia prophesied for nine months of the year, stopping in the winter months, she worked on the seventh day of each month. Querents had to fast, seclude themselves (probably to meditate on the question), immerse themselves in the Castilian spring, put on special robes, join a sacred procession, offer sacrificial cakes and an animal sacrifice. They then entered the dark shrine and asked their question, which was recorded by the male priest.

There exist records of these prophesies, Herodotus (1:47:3) reports the voice of the Pythia in response to an enquiry from King Croesus (c 6thC BCE).

> "I know the number of the grains of sand and the measure of the ocean, I can understand the speechless and hear those with no voice."[18]

The oracle at Delphi was taken by force by Apollo, who was jealous of its power and prestige. In the *Homeric Hymn to Apollo,* the upstart god describes how he achieved this.

"And Phoebus Apollo boasted, 'now then, you listen here, you will no longer be a mischief to men by living on this earth that nourishes mankind, and the harvest of the bountiful earth which they eat. [Instead] they will bring [offerings] here, offering me a hecatomb. Neither cruel death nor *Typhoeis* [the she-dragon] will help you nor the hateful she-goat Chimera. You will rot in the black earth [burnt] by him, the shining son, Hyperion [the Sun]. This Apollo said boasting and the darkness covered her eyes. And she putrefied under the sacred force of the sun and so now it is called *Pytho* (πυθο-rot) and the lord [Apollo] they call Pythia. And then she rotted there, this monster, by the might of sharp Helios." *Homeric Hymn to Apollo* 364–374[19]

This aetiological myth shows how the name Pythia comes from the Greek pytho (πυθω-to rot) referring to the she-dragon Apollo killed. The bones of the she-dragon were buried under the Omphalos stone.

When she was ejected Themis began prophesying via dreams, helped by her mother Gaia. Apollo ran to daddy Zeus. Euripides recounts the myth,

"But when he came and sent Themis, the child of Earth, away from the holy oracle of Pytho, Earth gave birth to dream visions of the night (Nux)[20] and they told to the cities of men the present, and what will happen in the future, through dark beds of sleep on the ground. Thus Gaia took the office of prophecy away from Phoebus [Apollo], in envy, because of her daughter [Themis]. The lord [Apollo] made his swift way to Olympus and wound his baby hands around the throne of Zeus, to take the wrath of Gaia from the Pythian home [Delphi]. Zeus smiled that the child so quickly came to ask for worship that pays in gold. He [Zeus] shook his locks of hair, to put an end to the night voices, and took away from mortals the truth that appears in darkness and gave the privilege back again to Loxias [Apollo]. In this way, [brought] confidence to men in the songs of prophecy at the throne visited by many [Delphi]." (Euripides, *Iphigenia in Taurus*, 1259–1289)

To placate the Goddess Themis, Zeus initiated the Pythian Games. These were originally choral competitions, of poetry and dance and music, played on the *cithra* (lyre/harp/lute) and *aulos* (wind instrument). Winners were presented with laurel leaf crowns and women were allowed to participate in some areas. They were held every four years. Eventually sports and chariot racing were added to the games. Part of the celebration was a re-enactment of the killing of the she-dragon. Eventually, women were forbidden to participate.

Apollo, after seizing the shrine at Delphi killed the water goddess Telphousa, the spirit of the sacred spring who had persuaded him not to build his temple on her sacred land.

"And then bright Apollo knew in his spirit how the beautiful flowing spring had deceived him utterly and he came upon *Telphousa* angrily, and when quickly he reached her, he stood close to her and he gave this speech to her, 'Telphousa, you were not destined to have for yourself this lovely place, pouring forth this beautiful water, deceiving my mind. For here my fame will not be yours alone. And lord Apollo working from afar, pushed her from the mountain top onto the rocks and flowers, hiding her streams. And he made an altar in the woody grove, right by the beautiful spring. All men now worship the lord *Telphousian*, for he broke in spirit and dishonoured the streams of the serpent *Telphousa*." *Homeric Hymn to Apollo*: 375–388.

In this way, the most famous and influential oracle in Greece was seized by the upstart god Apollo, who took control with violence, both 'breaking and dishonouring her.' As any invader knows, the easiest way to subdue a people is to dishonour its women and suppress or conceal their spiritual practices with the imported one.[21]

"The oracle of Thelphousa no longer invokes the Earth or nymphs of the waters." (Dashu 2009:4)[22]

The Pythia then, as representative of the goddesses of prophesy, Gaia and Themis, gives us the Piscean clairvoyance and mediumship as well as the arts of song, music, poetry and dance. Modern day Pisces may find much in common with the Pythia, they are often subject to powerful chthonic influences from which their utterances emanate. Often the sign of artists, singers particularly, but also actresses, dancers and of course psychics who hear what others cannot and connect with Spirit or the Goddess, communicating with the unseen, and bring to light messages from other realms. Sometimes the porosity of their psyche is such that Pisces uses mind altering substances to both enhance and dampen down the multitude of messages she gets.

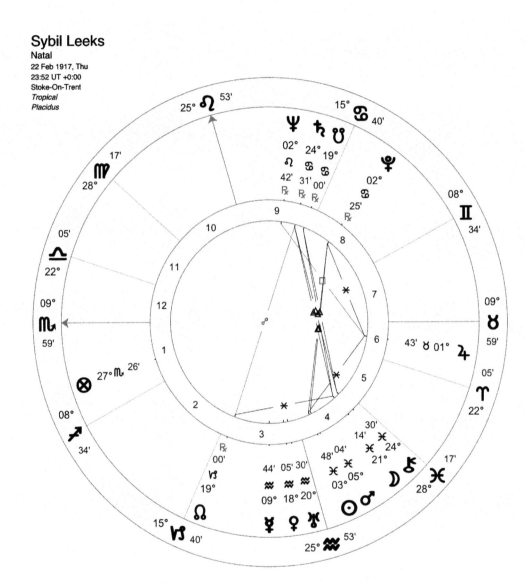

Sybil Leeks
Natal
22 Feb 1917, Thu
23:52 UT +0:00
Stoke-On-Trent
Tropical
Placidus

Sybil Leek: Psychic
22 February 1917. (23:52)
Normacot/Stoke on Trent Staffs

"All human beings have magic in them. The secret is to know how to use this magic." *Sybil Leek, 1972.*[23]

Sibyl has a Sun Mars conjunction in Pisces and her Moon in Pisces, with a witchy Scorpio Ascendant. The Sun, Mars and Moon in the fourth house shows she was working from Tradition, which came from her family line. The Mars trine Saturn in Cancer in the ninth describes her love of and craft in Astrology. A Scorpio Ascendant indicates a natural aptitude and interest in the occult, as well as a fearlessness in spreading her message. Pisces shows her great sensitivity and powerful psychic skills, as well as her ability to translate those messages for others.

Sybil claimed to be a descendant of Molly Leigh (1685–1746) who was accused of witchcraft by the local priest and whose ghost was believed to haunt the town where Sybil grew up. In *The Complete Art of Witchcraft* (p. 21) Sibyl says her family belongs to a 800 year old dynasty of Ancient Celtic Witchcraft and occultism. Like her alleged ancestor Molly Leigh, who had a pet blackbird, Sybil walked around with a pet jackdaw (crow) on her shoulder that she named Mr. Hotfoot Jackson.[24]

Sybil Leek wrote more than sixty books, one of the most prolific authors of the tradition. She had an overtly eccentric personality, often wearing her trademark cape, flowing gowns, and large crystal necklaces.

"There is alchemy in love-the mysterious feeling which no one is ever quite sure about but which contains all kinds of magical ingredients. There is magic which drives illness from bodies in pain, there is magic in a great name, of music, of Spring. Magic is a joyous exceptional experience which leads to a sense of well-being, and there is nothing we witches love more."[25]

Sybil said her entire family is descended from English and European covens and could trace her mother's lineage to Irish witches from 1134, and her father's occultists in Czarist Russia. Her family's interest in astrology and the occult brought H.G. Wells, T. E. Lawrence, and Aleister Crowley to her family home. Crowley, a frequent visitor, instructed her in magical practice.[26]

Sybil spent some time living amongst the New Forest Gypsies whose covens, she claimed, had existed in the forest for over 700 years. She was initiated by them; they taught her herbal medicine, and other plant magic, some of which is to be found in her books, *Sybil Leek's Book of Herbs* (1973), *Herbs, Medicine and Mysticism* (1975).

Sybil describes the privations of war, and her involvement in the war effort vividly in her book, *My Life in Astrology,* (1972), claiming she was recruited by the British Government. Author Michael Salazar wrote her role was to provide phony horoscopes for the Germans. Sybil cast a horoscope which apparently convinced the Nazi Rudolf Hess to fly to England, where he was captured. Michael says,

> "World War II was a battle between good and evil and Sybil was in the middle of it."[27]

After the war, the women were awarded medals.

> "I ceremonially buried mine in the New Forest at the first sabbat I was able to attend after the war. Perhaps it was theatrical to do this, but it was like burying myself, and then, through the help and the renewal of psychic forces, being reborn in my beloved New Forest."[28]

A clear example of Earth magic and cleansing of the bloodshed of war.

In 1951 the Witchcraft Act was repealed and Sybil became a celebrity. As media attention grew, her home became a focus for tourists. A local man, Dionis MacNair commented, 'People either thought she was a bit of a joke or a fraud.'[29] Eventually, her landlord refused to renew her lease and Sybil moved to America.

In America, Sybil became known as an astrologer, which she said was her 'first love'.[30] She was in great demand, appeared on many TV shows, including with para-psychologist Hans Holzer who invited her to join him investigating hauntings and psychic phenomena.

Sybil was interviewed by Krezkin and on Satanism she said,

> "It was due to bad publicity in the Middle Ages."
> "When anything goes underground a mystique is built up around it … the things we don't understand are the things we are afraid of."[31]
> "Reincarnation is a fact … The Spirit is indestructible."[32]

Sybil had strong opinions; she disapproved of nudity in rituals, a requirement in some reconstructed traditions, and strongly against the use of drugs. She was at odds with most other witches in that she did believe in hexing. Her book, *Sybil Leek's Book of Curses* (1975) was controversial in the Craft.

> "It seems to me that the orthodox religions always know more about the Devil than I do and can describe him in more detail, and if I hadn't a nice type of mind, I'd begin to wonder what company they keep when the moon rides high in the sky and good witches are doing simple little incantations and asking for spiritual guidance."[33]

Sybil promoted environmental causes, claiming this as integral part of the practice of witchcraft. A brilliant self-publicist, Sybil spent her life writing and doing interviews on the tradition. Her legacy is the fact that witchcraft is thriving in America and the UK.

A coven of white witches in the New Forest are following in Sybil's footsteps. High Priestess Julie Forest said,

"She was a pioneer of her time and she is an inspiration to modern day witches."[34]

Sybil understood that the Craft comes with responsibilities,

"We are about to move into the Aquarian age of clearer thinking. Astrology and witchcraft both have a contribution to make to the new age, and it behooves the practitioners of both to realize their responsibilities and obligations to the science and the religion."[35]

Other psychics:
Barbara Brennan (see Themis).

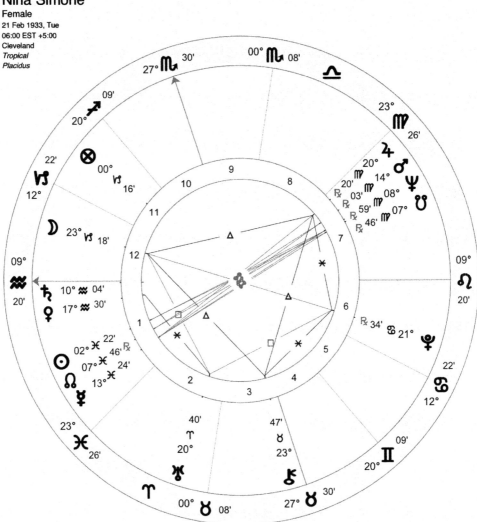

Nina Simone

Female
21 Feb 1933, Tue
06:00 EST +5:00
Cleveland
Tropical
Placidus

Nina Simone: The high priestess of soul
21 February 1933. (06:00) Tryon NC

"I am a real rebel with a cause."[36]

Named Eunice Kathleen Waymon, Nina's mother was a minister, working as a maid, and her father was a handyman. Nina excelled musically and, aged six, became the official pianist of the Methodist Chapel of Tryon.

At her first public recital aged eleven, when her parents were moved out of the front row seats, because they were Black, Nina stood up and announced she would not play unless they were re-seated. She felt,

"As if I had been flayed, and every slight, real or imagined, cut me raw. But the skin grew back a little tougher, a little less innocent, and a little more black."[37]

Collectively funded by people from Tyron for lessons and musical studies, in 1950, she won a scholarship to study the piano at the summer school at Juilliard in New York.

Nina had Sun, and Mercury in Pisces opposite Neptune, Jupiter and Mars in Virgo, which shows both her poetic inspiration (Pisces) and her technique (Virgo). Her ambition, to be the first black concert pianist is shown by a forward thinking revolutionary Saturn on her Aquarius Ascendant as well as a super ambitious Moon in Capricorn. The Moon is opposed by Pluto in Cancer and Square Uranus in Aries, which shows how the blocks to her dreams (both musical and revolutionary) caused explosive moods and ultimately a mental illness. She experienced terrible disappointments both personally, professionally and politically. Her brilliance, (Saturn in Aquarius) gave her a so called 'haughtiness' but to my mind it was simply the knowledge of her own genius. Racism and misogyny denied her full expression of her gifts, (Saturn is unaspected by any planet).

In 1954, Nina took a job at a bar and grill in Atlantic City, where she adopted the stage name of Nina Simone, knowing her mother would not approve of her working there. Her success at the club led to other gigs in the area and, in 1957, she got a recording session with Bethlehem Records. Her first jazz album, *Little Girl Blue*, was a success.

Nina was radicalised by a woman friend, and came to regard her music as a powerful tool in the struggle. Of her performances she said her intention was,

"To shake people up so bad that when they leave a nightclub where I performed, I just want them to be in pieces."[38]

In 1964 Nina wrote and recorded her most potent critique of American racism, *Mississippi Goddam* in response to the firebombing of a Black church in Mississippi which killed four little girls. First performed in front of a mainly White audience in Carnegie Hall, the song lyrics mocked Whites' view of Black people, 'Too damn lazy!' Government promises 'Desegregation/Mass participation', and the caution of black leaders to 'Go slow.'

Mississippi Goddam was rejected by southern radio stations, and boxes of the records were returned broken into pieces. Nina performed the song outside Montgomery, Alabama, in March 1965, as 3,000 marchers were walking the fifty-four-miles from Selma. Two weeks earlier, marchers on the same route were driven back by state troopers with clubs, whips, and tear gas. The concert, on the fourth night of the march, was organised by Harry Belafonte at Martin Luther King's request. The makeshift stage was built on stacks of empty coffins lent by local funeral homes. The audience grew to 25,000 and they cheered on the line, "Selma made me lose my rest."[39]

As a Black woman, Nina also spoke to the new Black feminist and Womanist movements. She presented a portrait of Black women addressing race, colour, caste, sexuality and gender in her song, *Four Women*.[40]

Her friend, Langston Hughes, wrote the campaigning lyrics for *Backlash Blues* in 1967, which Nina set to music; she said of her political activism at that time,

> "I felt more alive then, than I feel now because I was needed, and I could sing something to help my people."[41]

In Detroit, on 13 August 1967, two weeks after a five-day riot had left forty-three people dead, hundreds injured, and the city in ruins, Nina, sung *Just in Time*, and said, to the crowd, "Detroit, you did it. ... I love you, Detroit—you did it!" The crowd went wild.[42]

In 1969 she recorded *Young, Gifted and Black*. Writing in the Los Angeles Times, Meshell Ndegeocello said,

> "Nina Simone was a messenger to our heart and conscience ... No telling how many lives she touched with the simple affirmation of the beauty of being."[43]

In the early 1970s, Simone was feeling manipulated by the record companies, fed up with show business and racism, and experiencing serious financial problems. Her drinking became problematic and she began suffering from bipolar disorder. Nina left the US and spent time in Barbados, Liberia (encouraged by her friend, civil rights activist Miriam Makeba), Switzerland, Paris, Great Britain, and the Netherlands, before eventually settling in the south of France where she continued to record.

> "As a political weapon, it [music] has helped me for 30 years defend the rights of American blacks and third-world people all over the world, to defend them with protest songs. To move the audience to make them conscious of what has been done to my people around the world."[44]

Other musicians:

Miriam Makeba: 4 March 1932. (no time) Johannesburg SA. (Sun, Mercury, Mars in Pisces).

Billie Holiday: 7 April 1915. (02:30) Philadelphia. (Sun Aries, Venus, Jupiter, Mars and Mercury in Pisces).

Notes

1. Aeschylus, *Eumenides,* http://www.perseus.tufts.edu/hopper/text?doc=Perseus%3A text%3A1999.01.0005 accessed 2.8.2020.
2. Strolonga, Polyxeni. (2011) *The Foundation of the Oracle at Delphi in the Homeric Hymn to Apollo.* Greek, Roman and Byzantine Studies 51 p.529.
3. See Graves, 2001, p.27.
4. Nilsson, Martin, P. 1968. *The Minoan-Mycenaean Religion and its Survival in Greek Religion.* C.W.K.Gleerup, Lund. p.487.
5. Pausanias, (110–180 CE) Geographer, *Description of Greece* http://www.perseus. tufts.edu/hopper/text?doc=Perseus%3Atext%3A1999.01.0159%3Abook%3D10%3A chapter%3D5%3Asection%3D9 accessed 21.8.2020.
6. Tempe was a valley full of lush vegetation, including the laurel trees.
7. The Melissae or bee maidens were priestesses/goddesses found in Krete, see (xx)
8. Peoples who lived in the far north.
9. Pausanias (c150 CE) a geographer wrote his *Guide to Greece* in 10 books on the layout and features, antiquities, legends and history of the places he visited. http://www. perseus.tufts.edu/hopper/text?doc=Perseus%3Atext%3A1999.01.0159%3Abook%3D 10%3Achapter%3D5%3Asection%3D9 accessed 23.8.2020.
10. Scott, Michael (2014). *Delphi. Princeton University Press, Princeton.* p.20
11. See Dashu, Max, www.suppressedhistories.net for examples.
12. Himmelein, Paul, *Ferns and Fairy Tales,* issue 30, 2020, Enchanted living. Frazer, J.G. *The Golden Bough* 1983, Macmillan press, London. p.922 https://enchantedlivingmagazine.com/ferns-and-fairy-tales/ accessed 23.8.2020.
13. Spiller, Henry; de Boer, Jella; Hale, John R.; Chanton, Jeffery (2008). *"Gaseous emissions at the site of the Delphic Oracle: Assessing the ancient evidence".* Clinical Toxicology. 46 (5): 487–488. doi:10.1080/15563650701477803. PMID 18568810 accessed 23.8.2020.
14. Plutarch, *De Pythia Oraculis:6.* http://www.perseus.tufts.edu/hopper/text?doc=Pers eus%3Atext%3A2008.01.0247%3Asection%3D7 accessed 17.2.2021.
15. Lamia was Neith (see Athena) the Love and War goddess whose worship the Achaeans suppressed and she became a female monster who sucked the blood of young men as they slept and could remove her eyes at will [this might refer to her clairvoyance]. Graves, 2011 p.205.
16. Plutarch, (46–126CE) a Greek essayist. http://www.perseus.tufts.edu/hopper/text? doc=Perseus%3Atext%3A2008.01.0247%3Asection%3D9 accessed 23.8.2020.
17. Morford 2015, p.258.
18. http://www.perseus.tufts.edu/hopper/text?doc=Perseus%3Atext%3A1999.01.0125 %3Abook%3D1%3Achapter%3D47%3Asection%3D3 accessed 23.8.2020.
19. http://www.perseus.tufts.edu/hopper/text?doc=Perseus%3Atext%3A1999.01.0137 %3Ahymn%3D3%3Acard%3D349 accessed 3.3.2020.

20. Graves, 2011, p.30, writes black winged Night was a goddess who even Zeus stood on awe.

21. For example, Zeus at Dodona, Amon at the oasis of Siwwa Graves 2011:181.

22. Dashu, Max, (2009) *The Pythias and other prophetic women* from The Secret History of Witches. https://www.academia.edu/9745250/The_Pythias_and_other_prophetic_women accessed 3.5.2020.

23. https://web.archive.org/web/20060814012322/http://solsticepoint.com/astrologersmemorial/leek.html Ravin, Carlo, 2000, accessed 20.8.2020.

24. https://www.traciyork.com/revisiting-late-sybil-leek-birthday/ accessed 17.2.2021.

25. Quoted from *The Diary of a Witch*. 1968. Prentice Hall, New York (no page number) in https://www.traciyork.com/revisiting-late-sybil-leek-birthday/ accessed 17.2.2021.

26. https://100witches.tumblr.com/post/178621669988/31-sybil-leek accessed 17.2.2021.

27. BBC Inside Out South, October 28th, 2002. http://www.bbc.co.uk/insideout/south/series1/sybil-leek.shtml accessed 18.2.2021.

28. Leek, Sybil, (1972) *My Life in Astrology,* Prentice Hall Book Club. p.35.

29. BBC Inside Out South, October 28th, 2002. http://www.bbc.co.uk/insideout/south/series1/sybil-leek.shtml accessed 18.2.2021.

30. Iles, Juduka. 2005. *Encyclopedia of Witchcraft*, Element Books, Shaftesbury. p.746

31. YouTube interview with Kreskin, https://www.youtube.com/watch?v=ahBA3uqLwdg accessed 17.2.2021.

32. YouTube interview with Kreskin, https://www.youtube.com/watch?v=ahBA3uqLwdg accessed 17.2.2021.

33. https://www.azquotes.com/quote/1403941 accessed 17.2.2021.

34. BBC Inside Out South, October 28th, 2002. http://www.bbc.co.uk/insideout/south/series1/sybil-leek.shtml accessed 18.2.2021.

35. *The Diary of a Witch*. 1969. Prentice Hall, New York p.186

36. https://www.ninasimone.com/ accessed 19.2.2021.

37. Pierpont, Claudia, Roth. 4.8.2014. *A Raised Voice: How Nina Simone turned the movement into music.* The New Yorker Magazine. https://www.newyorker.com/magazine/2014/08/11/raised-voice accessed 19.2.2021.

38. Lynskey, Dorian. 22.06. 2015. The Guardian newspaper. *Nina Simone: Are you ready to burn buildings?* https://www.theguardian.com/music/2015/jun/22/nina-simone-documentary-what-happened-miss-simone accessed 20.2.2021.

39. Pierpont, Claudia, Roth. 4.8.2014. *A Raised Voice: How Nina Simone turned the movement into music.* The New Yorker Magazine. https://www.newyorker.com/magazine/2014/08/11/raised-voice accessed 19.2.2021.

40. Neal, Mark, Anthony. 4.6.2003. *She cast a spell and made a choice.* www.SeeingBlack.com http://www.seeingblack.com/2003/x060403/nina_simone.shtml accessed 20.2.2021.

41. Cohodas, Nadine (2010). *Princess Noire: The Tumultuous Reign of Nina Simone. Pantheon Books New York.* p.345

42. Pierpont, Claudia, Roth. 4.8.2014. *A Raised Voice: How Nina Simone turned the movement into music.* The New Yorker Magazine. https://www.newyorker.com/magazine/2014/08/11/raised-voice accessed 19.2.2021.

43. Neal, Mark, Anthony. 4.6.2003. *She cast a spell and made a choice.* www.SeeingBlack.com http://www.seeingblack.com/2003/x060403/nina_simone.shtml accessed 20.2.2021.

44. https://www.brainyquote.com/quotes/nina_simone_843312 accessed 19.2.2021.

The Planets: the Sun

Tradition has it that all solar deities are male. In the Greek pantheon, Helios, the Sun god is brother to Selene the Moon goddess.

It may be that the Sun goddess was female in Krete.[1] Queens in Egypt, Syria and Anatolia in the second half of the second millennium were high priestesses of the Sun goddess, this has been overlooked due to the influence of later Greek mythology where the sun was assumed to be male. It is possible that the high priestess of the Sun was the Queen in Krete and that the double axe was her symbol. (Marinatos, 2010:47). (Fig. 32). The design of the griffin around the throne room in Knossos suggests it was

Fig. 32 Goddess of the labrys, Knossos, 1500 BCE.

Fig. 33 Goddess and griffins, seal, Mycenae 1600 BCE.

used for a female deity as griffins are generally used to depict goddesses. Marinatos (2010:60) suggests that both the palm tree and the griffin are symbols of the Sun in Syria, Egypt, and Mesopotamia. A seal from Mycenae shows a female goddess standing on top of a stylised palm tree, flanked by two griffins. (Marinatos 2010:63) (Fig. 33)

A solar goddess is also a fertility goddess as sunshine makes crops grow and ripen. (Marinatos 2010:65) suggests this is why Minoan wall paintings show lush plants, flowers and trees, as the sun's gift to mankind. There are many symbols of the sun with women dancing (Fig. 34) and the large courts of Minoan palaces are aligned to

Fig. 34 Sun dancers, Thessaly, 1600 BCE.

Fig. 35 Woman on boat or loggia, fresco, Mycenean, 1400 BCE.

gain maximum sunlight in wintertime. Like the *tholos* tombs they aligned on an east-west axis.

The Sun was connected to funerary rites with death and rebirth, mirroring sunset and sunrise, the cycle of life. The burial *tholoi* (beehive shaped tombs) were rounded like the womb shapes of Neolithic goddess statues. Their entrances were often situated in line with the rising sun at certain times of the year, particularly on the winter solstice. Bodies were laid out in an east west [sunrise, sunset] orientation. The Temple Tomb at Knossos has its entrance in the east. Furthermore, paved areas have been found around these tombs, suggesting they may have been areas for ritual and dance; objects depicting women performing a circular dance have been found in grave sites. Interestingly, what appear to be mirrors are found in tombs placed on the belly, these so called 'frying pans' may have been filled with water for scrying or another sacred purpose [perhaps reflecting the Sun]. Fire was also used in funerary rites, not to burn the body, but remains of braziers were found beside the corpse; their significance is unknown [perhaps to burn incense or sacred herbs]. Images of priestesses (or goddesses) travelling on boats may show funerary rites where the deceased is taken across water [like the sun during its daily passage] (Fig. 35). Women were shown performing funerary rituals with arms raised in a mourning gesture. Goodison, 1989:84–94

Arinna was the Hittite Sun goddess (Fig. 36). She was goddess protector of the Hittite kingdom and was called 'the Queen of all lands.' Her cult centre was the sacred city of Arinna. A fragment tells us her myth,

> "An apple tree stands at a well and is covered all over with a blood-red colour.
> The Sun goddess of Arinna saw (it) and she decorated (it) with her shining wand."
> KUB 28.6 Vs. I 10'–13' = II 10'–13'[2]

The king of the Hittite Old Kingdom referred to Arinna as 'Mother' The goddess was shown as a solar disc, with a great halo. During the New Kingdom Arinna is mentioned in the Queen's prayers,

"Sun goddess of Arinna, my lady, queen of all lands! In the Land of Ḫatti, you ordained your name to be the "Sun goddess of Arinna", but also in the land which you have made the land of the cedar, you ordained your name to be Ḫepat."[3]

The Hittite Kingdom (c1680 BCE) covered Anatolia (Turkey) and some of Mesopotamia; its high point was in the mid fourteenth century. After the Late Bronze Age collapse, (c1180 BCE) the kingdom merged with Assyrian and Egyptian empires. Ceramics from that period show bull-leaping, which may refer to common cultic rituals with Krete. The deer was sacred to the Sun goddess and Queen Puduḫepa promised to give her many deer in her prayers. Cultic vessels in the shape of a deer were probably used for worship of the Sun goddess. It is also believed that the golden deer statuettes from the Early Bronze Age, which were found in the middle of the Kizilirmak River were associated with the cult of the Sun goddess.

Fig. 36 Sun Goddess, Arinna, Hittite, 15th–13thC BCE.

Perhaps, because in Patriarchal cultures women were considered to only have an identity related to the men in their lives, (fathers and husbands particularly), the idea of solar autonomy, self-actualisation and self-determination were anathema.

Hesiod describes the Sun, Helios as,

> "The brilliant sun never looks at them [sleep and death] neither as he rises up to the heavens nor as he descends. The former, Sleep (*Hypnos*) roams peacefully all over the earth and the wide arching sea and is kind to mankind, but the other, Death, (*Thanatos*) has a heart of iron and his inner spirit is a pitiless as bronze [the sword] once he has taken hold of men, he does not release them, so he is hateful even to the deathless gods." *Theogony: 760–65*

In the Greek pantheon the feminine became fixed as Moon, dark, chaos, confusion, serpents, madness and instinct and nature, while the masculine was Sun, light, order, mind, clarity, Spirit and rule. The solar deities of patriarchy embody the myth of the Hero.

> "Solar deities, … give expression to the religious values of autonomy and power, of sovereignty, and intelligence … the hero is assimilated into the sun; like the sun, he fights darkness, descends into the realm of death and emerges victorious … darkness … symbolises all the god is *not*."[4]

To have a female Sun goddess was, then, irrational; women were not seen to have the capacity for solar attributes. Gone was the inclusive dance between night and day, darkness and light, heaven, and earth, and instead it becomes a battle between Solar hero and the Lunar mother, between male and female, sharing and dominance.

Where does this leave Goddess Astrology? It could suggest that the Moon in a woman's chart was more important than the Sun but I do not think this is the case. The Sun is that inner core of our identity, which is often not apparent, nor embodied, (or sometimes not really discovered) until after the first Saturn return (see Transits) when people leave the life intended for them and carve out their own path. This path, the journey of the Hero, is represented by the Sun in the horoscope. The Solar journey becomes the dance of the Hero.

The Hero gives clues how to survive and thrive in patriarchy. Susanna Barlow writes on the qualities of the Hero[5] which can be used as guidelines for best living out your Sun sign.

Determination or identifying where action is needed and implacably moving towards the goal, trusting your deepest impulses and inspiration (from the Latin *inspiro* -breathing in the breath of the gods) to lead you to your best life.

Humility, accepting that all journeys are spiral, there will be progress and reversals, which will teach you valuable lessons and allow you to gain strength and wisdom.

Supporting others: The Hero understands nothing is achieved alone and gives back a hundred-fold in inspiration, encouragement, and time. She realises through reversals any success or progress is a joint endeavour, no one journeys alone. Understanding this, the Hero supports other people in their quests, by giving freely of their time and by encouraging and inspiring them.

Spiritual wisdom: the Hero understands all journeys are spiritual ones. Real transformation comes from work on the inner self as the outer world is a mirror of the inner landscape.

Vulnerability: they understand that honesty about their shortcomings and willingness to listen and learn give them great strength.

Honesty: they are often role models and so exercise this power with humility and kindness, being a role model, honest about both their achievements and their failures, their strengths and their weaknesses as this gives hope to others.

They take responsibility for their lives and are modest.

This then is how women might embody the Solar Hero archetype without its life-denying ideology or sense of separateness.

The Hero has a shadow side. Self-confidence can be replaced with egotism, where minor achievements are exaggerated, there is a lack of humility and self-awareness, denying the help others gave them, pretending it was all their own efforts.

Fear of failure can be displayed as pushing/bullying others to do what they cannot. To compensate, there may be escape into addictions, distractions, and fantasy, where the work is done in the imagination without any personal effort or risk (armchair warriors).

Fear brings the need to feel superior. A huge arrogance is seen, where the person is both hyper competitive and ruthless, with the shadow fear of weakness and vulnerability, where competitors are crushed ruthlessly.

The negative Hero will act alone, ostensibly because no-one can match their high standards, but in reality, because they do not wish to be exposed. Consequently, they may display aggression and use intimidation and bullying to reach their goal 'by any means necessary'. Any achievement is fragile as it is not built on strong foundations. The massive fragile ego.

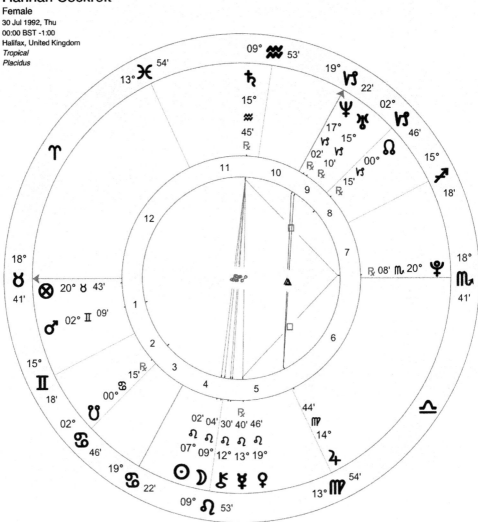

Hannah Cockroft

Female
30 Jul 1992, Thu
00:00 BST -1:00
Halifax, United Kingdom
Tropical
Placidus

Hannah Cockroft (Hurricane Hannah): Wheelchair athlete
30 July 1992. (No time) Halifax, England

Hannah, born in Halifax, West Yorkshire suffered two cardiac arrests at birth which damaged her occipital lobe. She was left with permanent brain damage, resulting in weak hips, deformed feet and legs, and mobility problems affecting the fine motor skills in her hands, but with normal upper body strength. Hannah's disability means she uses a wheelchair for long distances but she can walk for short distances. Some people have attacked her disabled status.

> "It has really got to me in the past, people have said some really nasty things and tried to get me to quit."[6]

At primary school Hannah was not encouraged to try sport. Luckily, her Secondary school introduced her to seated discus and wheelchair basketball. She started wheelchair racing at the age of thirteen; her father, a welder, built her first racing chair.

She won a silver medal in the seated discus at the UK School Games and was invited to a British Paralympic Talent Day at Loughborough University in October 2007. She was given her first opportunity to try an elite racing wheelchair by Dr Ian Thompson, husband of former wheelchair racer Tanni Grey-Thompson. Hannah fell in love with the sport. Tanni was her coach for five years.

> "I want to win gold medals. I don't think you should ever come to a championship and wanting anything less than the best."[7]

In 2008 a dance academy she attended donated the proceeds from its annual show programme sales to help her buy her own racing chair but, when it arrived, its made-to-measure set up was incorrect, so her father modified the wheelchair to fit. After returning to the UK School Games that year, and taking gold in her first competitive 100m race, she was subsequently invited to join the Great Britain Paralympic Team after the Beijing Paralympics in 2009. Hannah participated in her first ever road race; the London Mini Marathon, and won the Champion title in the girls 14–19 age group category.

> "I'm not going to lie, I love winning."[8]

Hannah won two gold medals, breaking four Paralympic records, in the T34 100m and 200m in the 2012 Paralympic games, where she earned the title 'Hurricane Hannah.'

> "This summer has been breath taking, this is what all the training has been for."[9]

In the 2013 New Year's Honours, Hannah was awarded a MBE for her services to sport. She won three further gold medals at the 2016 Paralympics in Rio de Janeiro. In addition to her performances on the track, Hannah has also competed at national level in seated discus and wheelchair basketball.

Hannah has Sun, Moon, Mercury, Venus in Leo showing her courage, sense of fun, drive to be the best, endurance (Leo is fixed earth) glamour and humour. Hannah always has her nails painted to match her kit, when competing for the British team she wears red, white and blue nails.[10]

She has won five Paralympic gold medals, twelve World Championship gold titles, three European championships. She is also a world record holder 100m, 200m, 400m, 800m and 1500 metre events in wheelchair racing. By 2017 Hannah had been unbeaten at the Paralympic, European and World level for six years. She was the first disabled athlete to be named Sports Journalists Association Sportswoman of the Year in 2017.

Her creative, indomitable spirit (Sun Leo) has plans for a life after athletics. Hannah studied journalism and media at Coventry University in 2013. In October 2014 she launched 17 Sports Management Limited, a sports management company. She has ambitions to work in television media after her athletics career. In 2018 she began presenting Countryfile for the BBC and in 2019 appeared in The Great British Bake Off for Channel 4.

"Find something you love and make it your life. That is the only way to be successful."[11]

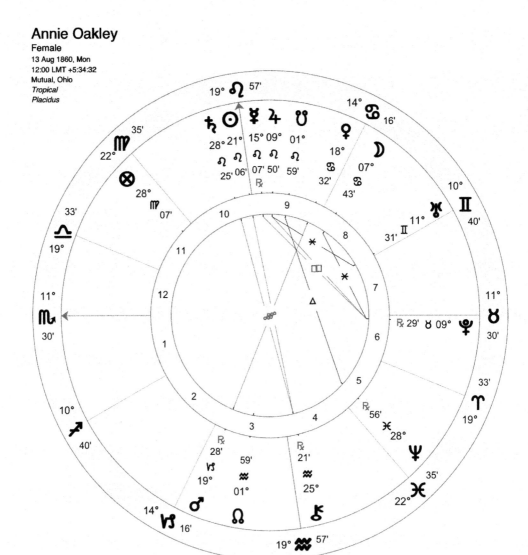

Annie Oakley

Female

13 Aug 1860, Mon
12:00 LMT +5:34:32
Mutual, Ohio
Tropical
Placidus

Annie Oakley: Sharpshooter
13 August 1860. (12:00) (DD[12]) North Star Ohio

"My mother … was perfectly horrified when I began shooting and tried to keep me in school, but I would run away and go quail shooting in the woods or trim my dresses with wreaths of wildflowers."[13]

Annie was born into poverty in rural Ohio. She developed her hunting skills at a young age to feed her family. She was sent as bonded servant aged eight to a family she later described as 'wolves' who physically and emotionally abused her. Her hunting and trapping skills not only fed her family but she earned enough by selling game to pay off the family's mortgage by the time she was fifteen. She entered a shooting competition in 1881[14] against Frank Butler who bet $100 he could beat any local marksman. Butler later ungraciously said,

"I was a beaten man the moment she appeared, for I was taken off guard."[15]

They married and eventually she replaced Butler's shooting partner who fell ill on May Day in 1882. Annie became the star of the show.

Annie had Jupiter, Mercury, Sun, Midheaven and Saturn in Leo. Sun at the MC, especially in its own sign, Leo, shows fame and success. Jupiter gives luck and helpful friends, Saturn the ability to work hard and frugality, Mercury the ability to spread your message far and wide. She was a hero to many and certainly a hero in her own life, coming from such a difficult background and shining in an arena traditionally reserved for men. Fearless and charming, proud and generous, hardworking and dedicated.

"Aim for the high mark and you will hit it. No, not the first time, not the second time, and maybe not the third, but keep on aiming and keep on shooting, for only practice makes you perfect. Finally, you'll hit the bull's eye of success."[16]

Butler soon began managing the act, leaving the spotlight to Annie. Around this time Annie adopted the professional name 'Oakley,' apparently from the town of Oakley, Ohio. Other sources say it was the name of a man who paid her train fare when she ran away from the 'wolves'. She arrived at the train station[17] but didn't have enough money for a ticket. A man listened to her story, bought her food, and then bought her ticket. Afterwards she remembered him in her daily prayers.

"I prayed to God each night to keep the good man who helped me away from the wolves."[18]

In St. Paul, Minnesota, in 1884, Annie attracted the attention of legendary Native American warrior Sitting Bull, who adopted her and named her *Watanya Cicilla* or 'Little Sure Shot.' The nickname stayed with Annie as she rose in the show business ranks. She joined Buffalo Bill Cody's Wild West in 1885 and performed in the show for most of the next seventeen years. Annie captivated audiences with her shooting skills; splitting cards on their edges, snuffing out candles, and shooting the corks off bottles. She maintained a modest wardrobe, unlike other women performers. Annie was a natural performer; she knew how to please the crowd, blowing kisses and pouting theatrically whenever she intentionally missed a shot.

> "A crowned queen was never treated with more reverence than I was by those whole-souled southern boys."[19]

At the American Exhibition in London in 1887, Annie met Queen Victoria, who called her a, "Very clever little girl." When she was presented to Prince Edward and Princess Alexandra after a command performance, she ignored Edward's outstretched hand and first shook the hand of Princess Alexandra, making a statement about the democratic equality of American women.

Annie wowed the British papers. Despite her success, rivalry with a fellow sharpshooter, Lillian Smith, had grown so tense that Annie left at the end of the London run (Leo so needs to be the star of the show). Annie returned to the theatre and toured with a rival wild west show until Smith left the Buffalo Bill show. She then embarked on a successful three-year tour of Europe starting with the 1889 Paris Exhibition. After it ended, Annie was recognised as America's first female superstar.[20]

Careful with money all her life and a great philanthropist, Annie explained,

> " ... People have asked me 'But why do you give as you do? Why do you not spend more on yourself?' If I spend one dollar foolishly, I see tear-stained faces of little children, beaten as I was."[21]

Annie supported women's rights. She understood that women should learn to use a gun for the power and independence it gave them.

> "I ain't afraid to love a man. I ain't afraid to shoot him either."[22]

And,

> "Even in the best and most peacefully civilized countries many occasions arise when a woman versed in the knowledge and use of firearms may find that information and skill of great importance."[23]

Annie used her influence to support education and independence for women. She created the image of the American cowgirl which proved women are as capable as men when offered the same opportunities. Annie was a strong advocate of shooting sports.

She made it a mission to teach girls and women to be comfortable with firearms and to enjoy the outdoor life. It is estimated that she taught more than 15,000 women how to shoot. Annie saw the physical and mental benefits of shooting and hunting. She strongly believed that it was crucial for women to learn how to use a gun, as not only a form of physical and mental exercise, but also to defend themselves. She said,

> "I would like to see every woman know how to handle guns as naturally as they know how to handle babies."[24]

In 1898 Annie wrote to the President, McKinley offering, "To place a company of fifty lady sharpshooters" at his disposal during the Spanish American War. She went on, "Every one of them will be an American and as they will furnish their own arms and ammunition will be little if any expense to the government." Her offer was not accepted. Twenty years later, in 1917, she made a similar offer to President Wilson, during World War 1, "I can guarantee a regiment of women for home protection, every one of whom can and will shoot if necessary." He turned down her offer, so instead Annie raised money for the Red Cross by giving shooting exhibitions.[25]

Annie and Butler were in a train accident in late 1901 and afterwards she left Cody's show for good. In 1902 she appeared in a stage play, *The Western Girl*. Her fierce leonine pride was outraged in 1903, when newspaperman William Randolph Hearst published a false article claiming she was in jail for stealing to support a cocaine habit. Oakley, whose 'highest ambition' was 'to be considered a lady,' was furious and pursued each and every newspaper that libelled her. She won or settled in fifty-four cases, often hardly covering her costs, but her reputation was restored.[26]

Notes

1. Blobrana, 14 April 2010: Female deities appear to outnumber the male deities. Linear B tablets name some of the goddesses worshipped in Crete: Eleuthia/Eileithyia, goddess of childbirth; Diktynna/Artemis, the Mistress of the Animals; Pipituna of the Doves, who may be a form of Aphrodite; Atana Potinija, who might be an early Athena; an unnamed Mistress of the Labyrinth; Rhea, who might be a form of the Great Mother Goddess; and Qe-ra-sija (pronounced "Therasia"), a minor goddess associated with the Thera eruption. Hera was also worshipped, and there seems to have been a female version of Poseidon named Po-se-dana. Keep in mind that these are all Mycenaean Greek names. Because Linear A, the unique Minoan language, remains undeciphered, we don't yet know what the Minoans called their gods or goddesses. The popular Snake Goddess could be an aspect of the Mistress of the Animals, who also seems to be represented as the Mistress of Horses and the Mistress of Birds. Again, we don't know whether they're the same goddess or several minor goddesses. https://astronomy.activeboard.com/t35272386/minoan-deities/?sort=oldestFirst&page=1 accessed 5.12.2020.

2. Dietrich Sürenhagen: *Zwei Gebete Ḫattušilis und der Puduḫepa. Textliche und literaturhistorische Untersuchungen*; A of **8** (1981), pp. 83–168. https://en.wikipedia.org/wiki/Sun_goddess_of_Arinna#cite_note-5 accessed 19.3.2021.

3. Laroche, Emmanuel. *(1971). Catalogue des textes hittites. Études et commentaires, 75 (in French). Paris. 384.* The first edition came out in 1956. A supplement was published in 1972: *Laroche, Emmanuel (1972). "Catalogue des Textes Hittites, premier supplément". Revue hittite et asianique.* **XXX:** *94–133.*

4. Eliade, 1959, *The Sacred and the Profane* 157–8.

5. Adapted from: https://susannabarlow.com/on-archetypes/understanding-the-hero-archetype/ accessed 8.9.2020.

6. Marsh, Jenni. 29.8.2012. *London 2012 Paralympics: Ten Essential Facts about Hannah Cockroft.* The London Evening Standard. https://www.standard.co.uk/sport/sport-olympics/london-2012-paralympics-ten-essential-facts-about-hannah-cockroft-8091750.html accessed 7.4.2021.

7. https://tokyo2020.org/en/paralympics/news/hannah-cockroft-in-full-speed-for-tokyo-2020-paralympic-games-x9089 accessed 2.8.2020.

8. https://tokyo2020.org/en/paralympics/news/hannah-cockroft-in-full-speed-for-tokyo-2020-paralympic-games-x9089 accessed 2.8.2020.

9. http://paralympics.org.uk/gb/athletes/hannah-cockroft accessed 7.4.2021.

10. Marsh, Jenni. 29.8.2012. *London 2012 Paralympics: Ten Essential Facts about Hannah Cockroft.* The London Evening Standard. https://www.standard.co.uk/sport/sport-olympics/london-2012-paralympics-ten-essential-facts-about-hannah-cockroft-8091750.html accessed 7.4.2021.

11. https://scoop-hockey.com/2017/06/20/17-inspiring-and-motivational-quotes-from-women-in-sport/ accessed 7.4.2021.

12. DD = dodgy data, not established this was her birth time.

13. https://www.azquotes.com/quote/705928 accessed 17.3.2021.

14. Because of poor record keeping at the time, dates are hard to verify, other sources say it happened in 1875, it is known she took six years off her age later on in her career because of a younger female rival. https://www.pbs.org/wgbh/americanexperience/features/oakley-butler/ accessed 17.3.2021.

15. https://www.pbs.org/wgbh/americanexperience/features/oakley-butler/ accessed 17.3.2021.

16. https://www.azquotes.com/quote/589800 accessed 17.3.2021.

17. Annie Oakley Foundation Inc. http://www.annieoakleycenterfoundation.com/faq.html accessed 17.3.2021.

18. Annie Oakley Foundation Inc. http://www.annieoakleycenterfoundation.com/faq.html accessed 17.3.2021.

19. https://www.azquotes.com/author/29928-Annie_Oakley accessed 17.3.2021.

20. https://www.pbs.org/wgbh/americanexperience/features/oakley-butler/ accessed 17.3.2021.

21. https://www.pbs.org/wgbh/americanexperience/features/oakley-butler/ accessed 17.3.2021.

22. https://www.azquotes.com/author/29928-Annie_Oakley accessed 17.3.2021.

23. https://www.azquotes.com/quote/938632 accessed 17.3.2021.

24. https://www.azquotes.com/author/29928-Annie_Oakley accessed 15.3.2021.

25. Annie Oakley Foundation Inc. http://www.annieoakleycenterfoundation.com/faq.html accessed 17.3.2021.

26. https://www.pbs.org/wgbh/americanexperience/features/oakley-butler/ accessed 17.3.2021.

The Moon: Selene

"Sweet sounding Muses, sing in praise, tell of the long winged Moon … From her immortal head the brilliance of the heavens dances around on the earth. With great beauty she rises, radiant in splendour. As she lights up the dark sky, her rays shine clear. When she bathes her beautiful body in Oceanus' waters, Selene clothes herself in heavenly, far glittering robes. She yokes her arch-necked horses, she sets them moving, hurrying forwards, radiant, these exquisite maned horses. In the evening at mid-month, when her great orbit is complete, her beams glisten down from heaven the brightest. Thus she makes a marker and a sign to mortal men. When the son of Kronos mingled and lay in friendship with her, she conceived Pandia[1] (all brightness-πανδια) the maiden was born, she most lovely among the deathless gods. Greetings, goddess of the white arms, goddess Selene, gracious, with golden locks."[2] *Homeric Hymn to Selene 32*

The ever changing, but predictable phases of the Moon give people a yardstick to measure the passage of time and the waxing and waning of light brings phases to her people. The Palaeolithic moon gave times to hunt (bright Moon) and rest (dark Moon),[3] while in the Neolithic Era, the phases mirrored the crops they grew, times of growth and decay, fullness and fertility, barrenness, and death. In the Bronze Age, phases of the Moon gave rise to myths of descent and fullness.[4]

Cashford (1991:147) suggests the fullness of the Moon came to represent the Great Mother of All who marries or gives birth to a son or daughter at the New Moon, and they are lost or taken at the dark moon and the Great Mother searches for them, they are reunited at the new crescent moon. This cycle, repeated each month represents, birth, growth, fullness, death, and decay. The unchanging life, which the Greeks called *zoe* (ζωη) is divided into segments or phases or *bios* (βιος). Cashford suggests (148) that the Great Mother represents *zoe* while the changing phases of the moon the son/lover or daughter are *bios*. Thus, the moon cycle represents life which, collectively, is unchanging and eternal while, individually, it is impermanent and mutable. It follows then, that the moon at her fullest, would be celebrated, as would the return shown by the crescent moon, while the dark of the moon would be a time of retreat and fear to be propitiated and respected.

The omnipresence of the moon suggests the Great Mother Goddess is everywhere and in everything. Her great shining orb at the full moon shines light on all things and guides us in the darkness. Because she later retreats it reminds us of the impermanence of life, and the need to take advantage of the light nights to expand and explore and respect the dark ones to withdraw and go inwards.

Selene is the daughter of the Titans Theia and Hyperion. Selene was part of the triple goddess of the Moon, she was the full moon, Artemis the crescent moon and Hekate the dark moon. Her name may come for the word for bright light (selas, σελας). Selene shows the full Moon Goddess who rode across the night sky on her sacred horses and bathed herself in the oceans, both rising and setting.

The moon of course, is central to life, even in our artificially illuminated world, she still pulls the tides and is a source of wonder as she waxes full. Of all the planets, she is seen as our Mother, constant yet changing. The Moon who is our loyal companion as we step through each month. There are thirteen lunar months in each solar year, the gestation cycle is counted in months, crops are sown and harvested in tune with the phases of the moon, our emotions wax and wane as she does. Women's monthly cycle, full-empty-new, mirrors Selene's passage through the heavens. Conscious of her or not, our emotions wax and wane and peak with the full moon madness well testified by frontline workers.

So the Moon is the essential nature of a person, which waxes and wanes, changes and remains constant; their instincts, their safety (the Mother) their clan, she is fertility, fecundity, life giving and also life denying, light and darkness.

The moon gathers her tribe together and holds them close with bonds of sympathy and kindness. The Moon is where we find solace, like in a mother's embrace, how we rest and recharge, where we go to heal and regroup.

The Moon has her Mysteries: her light bathes the earth but distorts and shape-shifts so that objects in moonlight appear strange, distorted and magical.

Selene was also known as Mene (Μηνη) which means Moon and refers to the Lunar month (Μην). In early times a month was divided into two parts; the month rising (μην ἱσταμενος), the month waning (μνην φθινων) then later on her cycle was divided into three, μην ἱσταμενος (waxing), μεσων (full/middle), φθινων (declining/waning).[5]

In early Greek myth the sun yields to the moon, which inspires greater superstitious fear. The Moon does not grow dimmer as the year wanes and was credited with the power to grant or deny water to the fields. (Graves, 2011:13)

The moon's phases, new, full and old reflect the matriarchal maiden, nymph and crone. Also, spring maiden, summer nymph, winter crone, and so the moon was identified with seasonal changes in nature. (Graves, 2011:14)

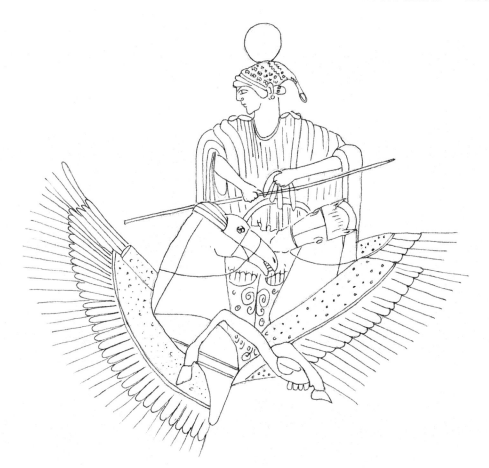

Fig. 37 Selene, kylix pot, 5thC BCE.

Time was first reckoned by lunations and every important ceremony took place at a certain phase of the Moon (even today, Christian Easter, Chinese New Year and Islamic Ramadan are related to the full moon). The solstices and equinoxes were calculated roughly to the nearest new or full moon. The moon cycles gave seven days for each of the four quarters of the Moon (7/28) and related to the seven visible planets, one for each day.[6] Graves suggests this system may have evolved in matriarchal Sumeria. (Graves, 2011:16).

At Laussel, a figure of a woman (see intro Fig. 1) 43cm tall, cut from limestone holds a crescent shape (perhaps a horn) which has thirteen notches on it. The figure points to her swollen belly. There are thirteen days of the waning moon and thirteen is the number of months in a lunar year.

The Moon is also related to time measurement in a woman's life, menstruation and, menarche and menopause as well as the more relatable monthly cycle of menstruation. I have talked about the Moon and how it is postulated that hunting and the full moon equated with the fertile time, while retreat, bleed time corresponded with the dark moon. (See above). Fig. 37

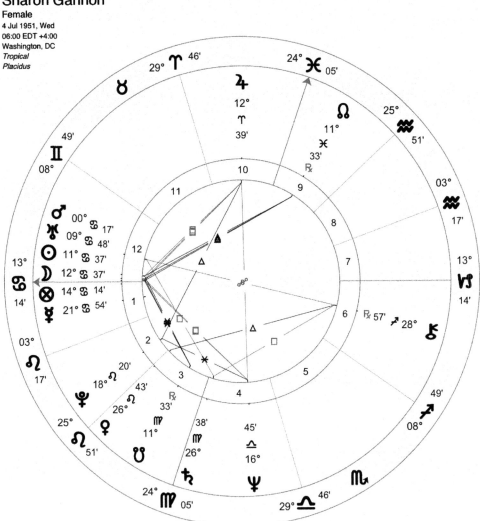

Sharon Gannon

Female

4 Jul 1951, Wed
06:00 EDT +4:00
Washington, DC
Tropical
Placidus

Sharon Gannon: Caring for humans and animals
4 July 1951. (06:00) Washington DC

"Jivamukti yoga is a path to enlightenment through compassion for all beings. Jivamukti is a Sanskrit word that means to live liberated in joyful, musical harmony with the Earth. The Earth does not belong to us—we belong to the Earth."[7]

Sharon Gannon is a yoga teacher, animal rights defender, musician, author, dancer and choreographer. She is the co-founder of the Jivamukti Yoga Method with David Life. She studied Dance at the University of Washington. She began her yoga, meditation and bhakti journey in 1969. Her gurus are Shri Brahmananda Saraswati, Swami Nirmalananda, and Sri K. Pattabhi Jois. She met her partner David Life in 1982 and started teaching yoga in 1984. She and Life studied Sivananda Yoga in India in 1986 and co-founded the Jivamukti Yoga Centre in New York on their return.[8] In 1990 they studied Ashtanga Yoga in Mysore under with Pattabhi Jois.

Sharon has a Stellium in Cancer (the sign ruled by the Moon) including her Moon, Sun, Ascendant, Uranus, Mars and Mercury. Compassion and kindness for all beings is her life's work.

"When we have a choice it is always best to choose kindness. Veganism is simply the kinder choice."[9]

Gannon is a lifelong and outspoken advocate for the rights of animals and ethical veganism. She developed anorexia as a young woman and used cooking and selling vegan food as part of her healing process. Sharon considers modern factory farming as slavery and believes a yogi must be against all types of enslavement, including the slavery of animals.

"To be a joyful vegan in the world today is to become involved in the most radical, positive, political revolution ever … By choosing kindness over cruelty, we contribute to the sustainability of our planet Earth and can even change the destiny of our species and all the species on Earth."[10]

In 1999 she helped to set up the Animal Mukti Free Spay & Neuter Clinic at the Humane Society of New York City.[11] It reduced the number of unwanted pets that had to be put down in the city by thirty percent.[12]

Sharon is both an empath and a shapeshifter. Her radicality is shown by Uranus (the planet of revolution) conjunct her Sun, Moon and Ascendant which are all part of a T square with fiery Jupiter in Aries in her house of career (making a new Yoga school) and idealistic Neptune in Libra who uses her spirituality intellectually to transform (Uranus) herself and her world.

205

"The most courageous act any of us can do at this time is to dare to care about others-other animals, the Earth, and all beings."[13]

The enormous sensitivity to the suffering of others, animals especially, compels her to fight (Jupiter in Aries) for their liberation (Uranus). Saturn in Virgo gives her the organisational skills to put her vision into practical reality (like spaying stray animals).

"To become a vegan is by far the best way we have at this time in history to contribute to peace on Earth. Being a vegan in the world today is to be involved in a nonviolent, direct-action protest against cruelty and an affirmation of kindness."[14]

Kindness is an attribute of the Moon, the mother as well as non-violence.

"Ahimsa is yogic non-violence and compassion to all beings, while the most popular form of yoga *asana* means how we relate to and connect with the earth, it should be steady (*sthira*) and joyful (*sukham*) according to Patanjali *Yoga Sutras*."[15]

Her care for animal welfare is part of her yoga practice.

"Some people, many who profess to be yogis, argue that vegetarianism not a healthful diet for everyone. We agree that vegetarianism is not for everybody; it is only for those who desire happiness and peace. It is definitely a must for those who are interested in enlightenment."[16]

The Moon illuminates our emotional life and shines a light on areas we can increase peace and kindness. She shows us we are all connected, all valuable, all one family.

"A yogi is someone who strives to live harmoniously with the Earth and all beings."[17]

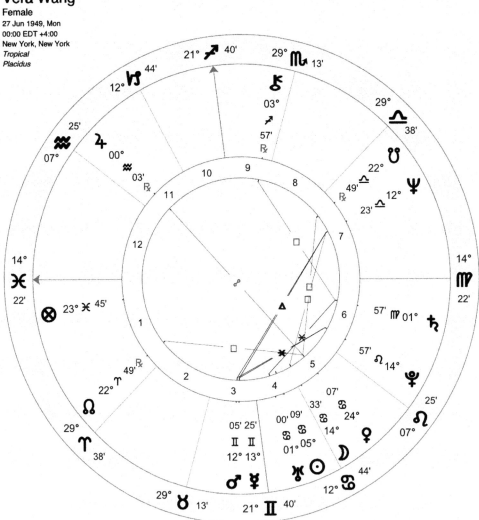

Vera Wang
Female
27 Jun 1949, Mon
00:00 EDT +4:00
New York, New York
Tropical
Placidus

Vera Wang
27 June 1949. (11:30) New York

"I want people to see the dress but focus on the woman."[18]

Designer of the ultimate feminine wedding dress, Vera Wang originally wanted to be an Olympic ice skater, but after failing to get into the team, she went into fashion.

"Whether you are a skater or a dancer, without sounding narcissistic, it is all about looking in the mirror."[19]

The Moon, of course is the ultimate reflection (it reflects the light of the Sun) so it fits that Vera with her super powerful Moon in Cancer would be in the business of illusion, fantasy, and ultra-femininity. Although recently her collections have included more spare wedding dresses, her signature look is the 'princess dress' or meringue which is a massive, white, fluffy extravaganza of a wedding dress. The whole business of weddings is a multi-million-pound industry centred around the 'fantasy' of the 'best day in a woman's life'. Certainly, the bride is on display in a way many women never have been before. The recent reality television shows of brides choosing their wedding dresses opens up the world of fairy-tale weddings and stress, and both heartache and joy that comes from the experience. How better to express a stellium in Cancer than to invest, expand and mirror the impossible fantasy of the blushing bride as princess as she moves into her married state?

Between 1970–87 she was an editor at Vogue, then she left to work with Ralph Lauren 1987–9 after which she became a bridal wear designer.

"When I decided to get married at forty, I couldn't find a dress with the modernity or sophistication I wanted. That's when I saw the opportunity for a wedding gown business."[20]

Her signature style is soft, feminine, flowing, and comfortable, all fitting in with her feminine, emotional, creative, and dreamy Sun, Moon, Venus in Cancer, while her down to earth, ambitious Jupiter in Capricorn made her the thirty-fourth richest self-made women in 2018, with an estimated net worth of $630 million. Vera shows the Moon's illusion and softness in her beautiful, white, fantasy wedding dresses.

Vera Wang is the by-word for wedding gowns, the ultimate extravagance and fantasy, they run into tens of thousands of pounds, but Cancer is also a canny business-woman, Vera has created a line of reasonable priced dresses so that everyone can 'remember the dress for ever'.[21] Cancer loves her tribe, and what is a better evocation of the tribe or family than gathering together to celebrate nuptials? There is food, music and dressing up, all Cancerian concerns, they love nothing better than to bring loved ones together over a meal in a beautiful setting.

Of course, the Moon in all about magic and Vera uses this imagery in her advertising, 'seize the magical moment'[22] the copy runs, and indeed, the fantasy becomes reality for some brides, weddings are pure make-believe, a time to escape the mundane and dream a little.

Notes

1. Pandia was the festival of the full Moon in Athens.
2. https://www.perseus.tufts.edu/hopper/text?doc=Perseus%3Atext%3A1999.01.0137 %3Ahymn%3D32 accessed 22.9.2020.
3. A fascinating PhD thesis argues that the moon, menstruation and hunting were all connected. Hunting, always done by men, as women were watching the children, would be done around the full moon (for light at night). Women who synchronistically menstruated and would bleed and not have intercourse before the hunt, to prepare males for hunting. The blood of the dead game, like menstrual blood was taboo, the women cooked the meat and their blood time ended and sexual relations resumed and women shared the meat, as the moon waned to dark. Knight, Chris (1987) *Menstruation and the Origins of Culture*. University College, London. (Thesis unpublished). http://radicalanthropologygroup.org/sites/default/files/pdf/pub_chris_thesis.pdf accessed 3.6.2020.
4. For my thoughts on the Astrological/Magical Moon see: *A Woman's Book of Shadows*. 2019. pp.69–85. On the Moon in Health and Sickness: *Traditional Western Herbal Medicine*. 2019. pp.141–7.
5. Liddell & Scott, 1944. p.444.
6. For an extended discussion of how the Moon's cycles work in Medical Astrology see: Brooke, *Traditional Western Herbal Medicine*. (2019) pp.139–40.
7. Gannon, Sharon and Life, David. 2014. *Simple Recipes for Joy*. Penguin, New York. Introduction.
8. Hammond, Holly. *Meet the Innovators: Sharon Gannon & David Life*. Yoga Journal August 28th 2007. https://www.yogajournal.com/lifestyle/meet-the-innovators-sharon-gannon-david-life/
9. Silverstone, Alicia. 17th September 2014. *An Interview with World-Renowned Yogini Sharon Gannon*. http://thekindlife.com/blog/2014/09/an-interview-with-world-renowned-yogini-sharon-gannon/ accessed 21.9.2020.
10. Gannon, Sharon and Life, David. 2014. *Simple Recipes for Joy*. Penguin, New York. Introduction.
11. Hoffman, Jan. 7th September 1999. *Celebrities' Yoga Centre Aids Furry Friends*. New York Times. https://www.nytimes.com/1999/09/07/nyregion/celebrities-yoga-center-aids-furry-friends.html?scp=19&sq=jivamukti&st=nyt accessed 21.9.2020.
12. Schneider, Carrie (2003). *American Yoga: The Paths and Practices of America's Greatest Yoga Masters*. Barnes and Noble, New York. pp.144–151.
13. Gannon, Sharon and Life, David. 2014. *Simple Recipes for Joy*. Penguin, New York. Introduction.
14. Gannon, Sharon and Life, David. 2014. *Simple Recipes for Joy*. Penguin, New York. Introduction.

15. Gannon, Sharon and Life, David. 2014. *Simple Recipes for Joy*. Penguin, New York. Introduction.
16. Gannon, Sharon and Life, David. 2002. *Jivamukti Yoga: Practices for Liberating Body and Soul*. Ballantine Books, New York. p.65.
17. *Simple Recipes for Joy*. Introduction.
18. https://www.brainyquote.com/authors/vera-wang-quotes accessed 21.12.2020.
19. https://www.brainyquote.com/authors/vera-wang-quotes accessed 21.12.2020.
20. https://www.brainyquote.com/authors/vera-wang-quotes accessed 21.12.2020
21. https://www.davidsbridal.co.uk/Content_Bridal_VeraWangUK accessed 21.4.2022.
22. https://www.davidsbridal.co.uk/Content_Bridal_VeraWangUK

Mercury: the Melissae

In the *Homeric Hymn to Hermes,* Apollo speaks of the three *Melissae.*

"For there are certain august goddesses born as three sisters, maidens, blessed with wings and on their head is scattered white barley meal. They live in their house under the cliffs of Mount Parnassus. They are teachers of the power of divination … For they fly about, here and there, feeding on honeycombs and each bringing matters to pass. And when they become inspired, from eating green honey,[1] readily they are willing to proclaim the truth [speak as oracles], but if they are denied the pleasant food of the gods, they tell lies as they buzz in and around each other. So, then I insist that when you ask them, do so precisely, and your heart shall be delighted … " (*Homeric Hymn to Hermes* 552–566)

Apollo, who had already seized the Delphic oracle, (see Pisces) 'gifts' the Melissae to Hermes to enable him to travel into the underworld and return, an attribute of the goddesses since time out of mind. By 'gifts' of course I mean steal, as he stole the shrine at Delphi.

Bee images are found with images of the goddess (Fig. 38). It was believed that bees hatched out of the dead carcass of a bull as far back at the Neolithic times; there is a representation of a stylised bull's head with the shape of a bee picked out on its head.[2] Together with the butterfly, the bee is one of the oldest symbols of transformation. The complexity of beehives show the interconnection and co-operation of nature. The myth of the gods being fed on honey (Zeus and others) is an aetiological myth explaining the super nutritive powers of honey.

213

Fig. 38 Bee goddess, Gold plaque, Kameiros, Rhodes, 800–700 BCE.

The image of the buzzing bees, headfirst in the nectar and pollen of flowers, suggests hard, but pleasant work which humankind had to undertake to survive. The queen bee was a representation of the Great Mother and the goddess, whose humble workers humans were, just like the bees. There are three types of bees, the queen, workers and drones. Worker bees are all female and the only bees with stingers. The drones fertilise the queen and then die; they are all male. To avoid predators, worker bees create a distraction zone near the hive. They avoid any flowers growing in that area, but feed on flowers further away. Their foraging patterns are systematic and predictable. In the hive they dance special dances which show the location of flowers while the other bees watch and learn. The dancing bee has the scent of the flowers she has found to aid identification and she allows the watching bees to taste the nectar she has gathered. Theirs is a complex self-regulating community. If there is a shortage of young worker bees, older workers age backwards and become more energetic to pick up the slack, until more young workers are hatched.

In Crete, the goddess and her priestesses dressed as bees, or became the bees and are shown dancing and worshiping embodying the mystery of the bees. Gimbutas[3]

Fig. 39 Melissae, Gold ring, Isopata, Knossos 1500–1450 BCE.

suggests that both the sacrificed bull and the bee (its product) belonged to the regenerative power of the Moon (Fig. 39). May show her descending into the underworld with snake and flowers (lilies, crocus/saffron) with the priestesses' arms raised in a gesture of benediction or invocation or mourning. Another Melissae appears to be dancing. Thus, the bee, bull and Moon suggest death and rebirth, or life that comes from death.

Honey was used to embalm the dead and the large jars, pithoi (πιθοι) found in Knossos were used to store honey. The tombs at Mycenae were shaped like beehives, as was the *omphalos* at Delphi (see Pisces) where the Pythia was known as the Delphic bee. Because it is preservative, nutritive and purifying, honey was used to embalm the dead, both providing nourishment in the afterlife and preventing decay of the body.

Pictograms of Linear A (as yet undeciphered) show beehives, while other gold seals depict the bee goddess with horns of consecration (or the Moon) and gods or wolves with bee-like wings.[4]

Honey was at the centre of the Cretan New Year celebrations which began on the Summer Solstice, the hottest time, and lasted until 20th July when the star Sirius rose conjunct the Sun. The Minoan palaces were built orientated towards Sirius. The rising of Sirius marked the end of a forty-day ritual during which honey was gathered from beehives in caves and the woods. The honey was fermented into mead which was drunk during an ecstatic ritual, which possibly celebrated the return of the daughter of the goddess and the New Year, or from the labyrinth underground. A bull was sacrificed to coincide with the rising of the star. The bees represented the re-birth of the soul of the bull and the constant round of eternal life.[5] The humming of the bee was perhaps the voice of the chthonic goddess or the hum of life itself.

The Ancient Greek word for honey is melissa (plural melissae-μελισσα) and possibly of Minoan origin.[6] The Minoans were renowned for their beekeeping. The Linear B tablets record huge quantities of honey stored at the Knossos temple complex, while the Minoan fresco of the fleet at Akrotiri depicts a hillside covered with beehives.[7] In classical times there was a god called Melissus who protected the infant Zeus from his father. This probably represents the patriarchal take over from the Melissae.[8]

Cashford[9] writes that the word 'fate'; ker (Κηρ) is an Ancient Greek word for the goddess of death or fate, as well as the heart. Kerothi (κεροθι) means with all the heart, while meli-keron (μελι-κερον) is honeycomb and keros (κερος) is beeswax. Thus, the common root ker links, the goddess of the underworld, fate, the bees and the heart. While kerodomeo (κηροδομεω) means to build with wax, which is how the first shrine at Delphi was built.

Bachofen [10]describes the bond between the Goddess and the bee,

> "The beehive a perfect prototype of the first human society, based on the gynocracy… The bee was rightly looked upon as a symbol of the feminine potency of nature. It was associated above all with Demeter, Artemis, and Persephone. Here it symbolised the earth, its motherliness, its never-resting, artfully formative, busyness, and reflected the Demetrian earth soul in its supreme purity."

In the Syracusan *Thesmophoria,* the participants were called *mylloi.* Cakes made of sesame and honey formed into the shape of the vagina. Honey and milk belong to motherhood.

Honey intoxication is a result of eating honey containing grayanotoxins.[11] Honey produced from flowers of laurel and azaleas may cause honey intoxication. There were laurel forests in Greece and Crete. Symptoms include dizziness, weakness, excessive perspiration, nausea, and vomiting. Less commonly, low blood pressure, shock, heart rhythm irregularities, and convulsions. Perhaps also hallucinations or receiving messages from Spirit.[12]

Porphyry (3rdC CE) writes that Melissae were priestesses of Demeter and initiates of her chthonic rites.[13] Souls were symbolised by bees (and butterflies) and it was the Melissae who drew down souls to be born, and so the Melissae are connected with both birth and death.

There are two expressions of the Melissae; Mercury is the ruler of both Gemini and Virgo.

Gemini: the divine messenger who will give messages, depending on how they are treated, honeyed or not, a tiny bit tricky, very busy buzzing or dancing about.

Virgo: as the food of the gods and the beginning and end of life, nourishment, the mother, the earth, death and burial.

Isadora Duncan

Female
26 May 1877, Sat
02:20 LMT +8:09:40
San Francisco
Tropical
Placidus

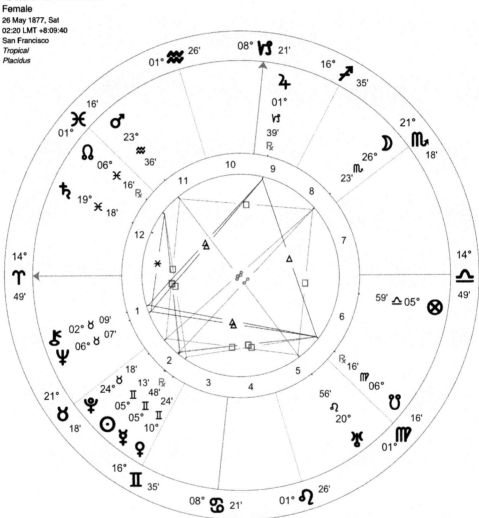

Isadora Duncan: Gemini-Dancer
26 May 1877. (02:20) San Francisco

"My inspiration has been drawn from trees, from waves, from clouds, from the sympathies that exist between passion and the storm, between gentleness and the soft breeze, and the like, and I always endeavour to put into my movements a little of that divine continuity which gives to the whole of nature its beauty and its life."[14]

Isadora, had Sun, Mercury and Venus all conjunct in Gemini. She encapsulated that connection to the divine dancer, who used the winds and the waves and the creatures of the earth as inspiration for her dance. Her Aries Ascendant is boundary breaking and pioneering, she foresaw the relaxed, naturalistic styles of Martha Graham and the spiritual dance of Gabrielle Roth. Her life had tragedy and death, which can be seen with her fixed Grand Cross (see Aspects).

She was a pioneering dancer, who defied convention by dancing barefoot and free-form, in a way that shocked audiences used to the formal rigidity of ballet. She briefly studied dance in New York but was underwhelmed by traditional ballet. She moved to London in 1898 and, inspired by the collections in the British Museum she danced in the drawing rooms of the wealthy, wearing flowing robes evoking ancient Greek dance. She used her earnings to create larger works for the stage. In Paris, she was equally inspired by the *Exposition Universale* of 1900 and her fame grew. *La fête de Bacchus* on 20 June 1912, re-created the Bacchanalia of Louis XIV at Versailles. Isadora entertained the over 300 guests wearing a Greek styled evening gown designed by Poiret. She performed dancing on the tables it was estimated over 900 bottles of champagne were drunk before dawn.[15]

Isadora imagined she had traced dance to its roots as a sacred art.

"I spent long days and nights in the studio seeking that dance which might be the divine expression of the human spirit through the medium of the body's movement."[16]

She aimed to connect emotions with movement and elevate dance to a spiritual practice rather than simple entertainment. She used natural movements, folk dances, ancient Greek art, and the rhythms of nature as her inspiration.

"To seek in nature the fairest forms and to find the movement which expresses the soul of these forms—this is the art of the dancer."[17]

Isadora believed dance could encapsulate all areas of life, from joy to sadness, by dancing in a simple white Greek tunic and bare feet she was able to express her emotions and connect with the spiritual essence of dance.

She taught that all movement originated from the solar plexus which she believed was the source of a dancer's power.[18] It is this philosophy and her innovative dance techniques which made Isadora 'the mother of dance'. Isadora toured all over Europe and opened a school in Berlin in 1904 to teach her method and philosophy of dance. She adopted six young women who became her acolytes and spread her message. After ten years she moved to Paris and opened another school which was closed when war broke out. Like many visionaries, she found the moneymaking aspect of dance, problematic and distasteful.

"But the dance of the future will have to become again a high religious art as it was with the Greeks. For art which is not religious is not art, is mere merchandise."[19]

Her connection to nature, her need to communicate through physical expression and her emphasis on the spiritual nature of movement made her unique. She believed all movement in nature, including human, beats to the same rhythm, which is reminiscent of the dance of the bees.

"Man has not invented the harmony of music. It is one of the underlying principles of life. Neither could the harmony of movement be invented: it is essential to draw one's conception of it from Nature herself, and to see the rhythm of human movement from the rhythm of water in motion, from the blowing of the winds on the world, in all the earth's movements, in the motions of animals, fish, birds, reptiles, and even in primitive man, whose body still moved in harmony with nature … All the movements of the earth follow the lines of wave motion. Both sound and light travel in waves. The motion of water, winds, trees, and plants progresses in waves. The flight of a bird and the movements of all animals follow lines like undulating waves. If then one seeks a point of physical beginning for the movement of the human body, there is a clue in the undulating motion of the wave."[20]

She wrote, *The Art of the Dance*, a group of essays, and an autobiography, *My Life*.[21]

Carlotta Perez
Female
20 Sep 1939, Wed
00:00 VET +4:30
Caracas, Venezuela
Tropical
Placidus

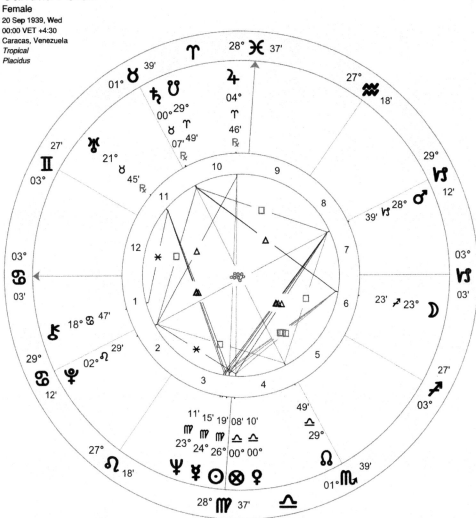

Carlotta Perez: Virgo, economic transformation[22]
20 September 1939. (No time, used 12:00) Caracas Venezuela

"In a world of capital gains, real estate bubbles and foreign adventures with money, all notion of the real value of anything is lost. Uncontrollable asset inflation sets in while debt mounts at a reckless rhythm; much of it to enter the casino."[23]

Economist and scholar on technology and socio-economic development, Perez is visiting professor at the Institute of Innovation and Public Purpose at University College London, and to the London School of Economics. She is a co-founder of The Other Canon, a centre and network for unorthodox economies.

As a Sun, Mercury and Neptune in Virgo (and possibly Venus depending on her birth time) meticulous research, analysis and data made her conclude that a deeper integration and more equitable sharing of resources is the only way forwards. Like the thrifty economy of the beehive, Virgo sees the connection between behaviour and outcomes, and rejects greed and selfishness, for the wellbeing of all.

Perez argues,

"There is also ample scope for redirecting business imagination and technological innovation towards the deeper transformation of world society, through developing truly knowledge intensive ways of producing and living."[24]

Writing in 2002, after the financial collapse, she warned that systemic, fundamental change was needed to prevent economic collapse. It was too easy to blame external factors for economic crisis, but this detracts from the underlying, structural problems which precipitated the crisis.

"Explanations based on exogenous shocks (often, in fact, partly symptoms of the same deeper causes) lead to an impotent insistence on applying old economic recipes to new structural problems. Such recipes can only lead to fragile and short-lived successes, vulnerable to relatively minor events." (2002:168)

Eighteen years later, as I write (2021) we are again in such a crisis, brought on by external factors (Covid-19) but precipitated by industrial pollution, poverty and wealth inequalities of the casino variety describe above.

Perez writes that the 'casino economy' needs to be restrained by regulation (she cites corrupt accounting practises, but examples of greed and selfishness are legion). Perez has a Grand Trine in Earth, (see Aspects) analytic, academic Sun, Mercury in Virgo, an ambitious and forensic Mars in Capricorn (working with the establishment) with a radical and revolutionary Uranus in Taurus which shows her concern and life's work on conserving the world's resources and sharing them out fairly.

223

"… Short-term financial criteria, apart from the risk of stimulating dishonesty, can
no longer serve to guide investment." (2002:169)

Perez argues that lower profits can be seen as a benefit to society, as it will encourage
long term planning, not get rich quick practices. Secondly, technology is a growth
area needs to be expanded into developing economies. Following on from this is the
need to create more equity between the rich and the poor, and stimulate the global
economy, to expand wealth generation across the world.

"Not reversing global polarization, in itself, poses serious threats to the safety and
stability of the prosperous countries. These include massive migrations, various
forms of violence and the outbreak of serious economic crises." (2002:170)

Perez wrote this in 2002, and her prediction has been realised, with the influx of
millions of refugees into both Europe and the USA. She argues that sharing the world's
wealth has many benefits and that business and technology can change direction for
the greater good as well as their own personal benefit.[25]

"There is a growing sense of urgency that leads to many proposals coming forth,
of greater or lesser scope, with greater or lesser ambition, going from alternative
economic theories to practical measures and policies. There is also ample scope for
redirecting business imagination and technological innovation towards the deeper
transformation of world society, through developing truly knowledge intensive
ways of producing and living." (2002:171)

In her latest work, Perez calls again for worldwide co-operation to raise the living
standards of the poor and to curb 'casino' economics.[26] Interestingly, an editorial by
the Financial Times (not a byword for radical economics) argues the same points,
focussing on climate change. It argues that fundamental change is needed, or we will
all go down together. And that the time has arrived for a radical shift.[27]

Like the economy and community of the Melissae, Carlotta argues that cooperation
and fair sharing of resources is the only way we can survive. That economics needs to
serve the many not the few.

Notes

1. Green or unripe honey
2. Baring & Cashford, p.74
3. Gimbutas, *Goddesses and Gods of Old Europe*. p.181.
4. Baring & Cashford, p.118.
5. Baring & Cashford, p.119.
6. Perry, Laura. *The Melissae: A bit of Minoan Honey*. December 5th 2017 in http://witchesandpagans.com/pagan-paths-blogs/the-minoan-path/the-melissae-a-bit-of-minoan-honey.html

7. https://commons.wikimedia.org/wiki/File:AKROTIRI_SHIP-PROCESSION-FULL_PANO.jpg accessed 1.8.2020.

8. Perry, Laura, December 5th 2017. *Modern Minoan Paganism: Walking with Ariadne's Tribe* in http://witchesandpagans.com/pagan-paths-blogs/the-minoan-path/the-melissae-a-bit-of-minoan-honey.html accessed 2.8.2020.

9. Baring & Cashford, p.120.

10. Bachofen, p.114

11. Jansen, Suze A.; Kleerekooper, Iris; Hofman, Zonne L. M.; Kappen, Isabelle F. P. M.; Stary-Weinzinger, Anna; van der Heyden, Marcel A. G. (2012). "Grayanotoxin Poisoning: 'Mad Honey Disease' and Beyond". *Cardiovascular Toxicology*. 12 (3): 208–215. https://www.ncbi.nlm.nih.gov/pmc/articles/PMC3404272/ accessed 4.9.2020.

12. Xenophon the Greek warrior-writer wrote in 401 BC in *Anabasis* " … the swarms of bees in the neighbourhood were numerous, and the soldiers who ate of the honey all went off their heads, and suffered from vomiting and diarrhoea, and not one of them could stand up, but those who had eaten a little were like people exceedingly drunk, while those who had eaten a great deal seemed like crazy, or even, in some cases, dying men. So, they lay there in great numbers as though the army had suffered a defeat, and great despondency prevailed. On the next day, however, no one had died, and at approximately the same hour as they had eaten the honey they began to come to their senses; and on the third or fourth day they got up, as if from a drugging" *Anabasis* 4:8:20 http://www.perseus.tufts.edu/hopper/text?doc=Perseus%3Atext%3A1999.01.0202%3Abook%3D4%3Achapter%3D8%3Asection%3D20 accessed 12.9.2020. see also: Abdulkadir Gunduz, MD; Suleyman Turedi, MD; Hikmet Oksuz, PhD *The Honey, the Poison, the Weapon*. Wilderness and Environmental Medicine, 22, 182–184 (2011) https://www.wemjournal.org/article/S1080-6032(11)00043-3/pdf accessed 8.12.2020.

13. No primary source, Gimbutas, *Goddesses and Gods of Old Europe*, p.182.

14. Flitch, John Earnest Crawford *Modern Dancing and Dancers* (1912) p.105.

15. Desti, Mary. *The Untold Story: The Life of Isadora Duncan 1921–1927* (1929) p.102

16. Kurth, Peter. *Isadora: A Sensational Life*. (2001) Little Brown, New York, p.57

17. Flitch, John Earnest Crawford *Modern Dancing and Dancers* (1912) p.105

18. Kurth Peter. *Isadora: A Sensational Life*. (2001), Little Brown, New York, p.57

19. Duncan, Isadora, Cheyney, Sheldon (ed). *The Art of the Dance*. (1928) New York: Theatre Arts, p.62.

20. Duncan, Isadora. Cheney, Sheldon (ed) 1928 *The Art of the Dance* New York: Theatre Arts, p.78

21. Duncan, Isadora. *My Life*. New York: Boni and Liveright, 1927, Duncan, Isadora; Cheney, Sheldon (ed.) *The Art of the Dance*. New York: Theater Arts, 1928.

22. https://thecorrespondent.com/466/the-neoliberal-era-is-ending-what-comes-next/61655148676-a00ee89a?fbclid=IwAR2B0GixsqD4pYB-ObYYIjBbDIXvvxL-rVF4q3W4CtKdyAEmBCLrMYA3X1sE accessed 12.11.2020.

23. Perez, Carlotta. *Technological Revolutions and Financial Capital, The Dynamics of Bubbles and Golden Ages*. London: Elgar 2002 p.75

24. Perez, 2002: 171.

25. Lisa Feldman in her book, *Seven and a Half Lessons About the Brain*. Houghton Mifflin Harcourt, 2020. Agues that it is cheaper to remove all children out of poverty than to treat the health problems and social problems which come from having a deprived childhood.

26. http://www.carlotaperez.org/pubs?s=dev&l=en&a=handbookongreengrowth accessed 8.12.2020

27. Cavendish, Camilla. June 26 2020. *We must build back Greener after Covid-19*. The Financial Times. https://www.ft.com/content/d4aa350e-d082-4aa7-bef2-a717b4a053f1 accessed 8.12.2020.

Venus: Aphrodite

There are two types of Venus, Earthy, ruling Taurus and Airy ruling Libra.
Earthy Venus *Pandemos* (pan-demos, of all the people πανδεμος).
Aphrodite *Pandemeos* was the Venus who brought lust and unconquerable passions which wrecked lives and kingdoms.

> "Muse, tell me the deeds of golden Aphrodite the Cyprian, who stirs up sweet passion in the gods and subdues the tribes of mortal men and birds that fly in air and all the many creatures [5] that the dry land rears, and all that the sea: all these love the deeds of rich-crowned Cytherea (Fig. 40)." *Homeric Hymn to Aphrodite* 5: 1–6

Fig. 40 Kore with 2 companions, drawing on a cup, Minoan, 2000 BCE.

This Aphrodite made the daughters of King Tyndareus libidinous because the king did not sacrifice to her on one occasion. His daughters were Helen, Klytemnestra and Timandra who became notorious for their adulteries, and in Helen's case the Trojan War which destroyed a wealthy kingdom, Queen Klytemnestra who murdered her husband, Agamemnon to stay with her lover Aegisthus. (Graves:2011:631)

Helen (she of the thousand ships) complains,

> "Maiden Aphrodite don't destroy me! Daughter of Dione. You have mistreated me enough, with an abundance of insults. Handing over my name, though not my body, to barbarians. So, allow me to die in the land of my ancestors. Why are you so greedy for wickedness, working your deceits and love spells with inventions of love potions for this most blood stained of houses? If you were only moderate, for otherwise you are the sweetest of the gods for all mankind." (Euripides *Helen* 1097–1106)

Aphrodite Pandemos is the hurricane of love which knocks us off our feet and can leave disaster in its wake. Arguably she is the Aphrodite of youth (although not necessarily) who makes us lose our minds to passion. Aphrodite can bring exquisite suffering to those who fall under her spell. Sappho invokes the goddess:

> "Immortal Aphrodite, shimmering mind
> Weaver of wiles
> Please, I beg you do not crush my spirit
> With agony and anguish." (1)[1]

Aphrodite Pandemos is sexually curious, as are many women.[2] Patriarchy despises female sexuality and denigrates its life giving force. For them, it is something to be bought, sold, stolen (rape) and regulated (marriage). The sexually independent woman is a terrifying prospect.

> "Women's libidos are far stronger and more adventurous than we thought ... Until recently, women have tended to blame themselves for a lack of desire. [Oh really!] Psychologists and other experts are suggesting, however, that it's not that women lose interest in sex per se—it's that they simply stop being interested in sex with their other half ... this contradicts what we're told so often about a women's sexuality—that it's women who have lower libidos than men or are the ones who go off sex in relationships ... But new research is now helping us rediscover the truth about the female libido that had been forgotten due to hundreds of years of social convention and strict morality codes that ostracised women who are unfaithful or merely sexual."[3]

Women get bored with the same partner. Since the advent of paternity testing it has been found that large numbers of women have extramarital affairs. One random survey of 5,000 DNA results showed that forty-eight per cent of the men were shown not to be the father of their supposed children. Women are curious and sexually adventurous.[4]

Pre-patriarchy there was no marriage, which is the natural state of Aphrodite, free to love where she fancies.

Aphrodite *Pandemos* is earthy love, comfort, the physical body, sensuality and sexuality. She rules Taurus/Kore.

Aphrodite Urania is the patriarchal idealised airy Aphrodite who was not born of woman but from the genitals of a male and fertilised in the seafoam. (Fig. 41)

Plato writes in the *Symposium* that Aphrodite Urania is the older of the two (not so according to Homer—see above). She has close links with the Semitic goddess Ishtar, Astarte, worshipped in Mesopotamia and Phoenicia, she was the Heavenly (Urania) Astarte who was honoured with incense altars and sacrifices of doves. Herodotus

Fig. 41 Aphrodite Urania, kylix pot, Rhodes, 460 BCE.

(1:105) wrote the oldest cults of Aphrodite in Greece were established by Phoenician settlers. Her close association with Cyprus may relate to the colonising of the island by Phoenicians in the ninth century BCE.

As Aphrodite, who emerges from the ocean at the separation of earth and sky (Ouranos and Gaia), she is a pre Olympian deity. Love as a vital cosmic force is recorded by Empedocles (5thC BCE),

> "Love is in the middle, equal in length and breadth. Gaze on her with your mind, and do not sit with dazzled eyes. For she is recognised as being inborn with mortal limbs; through her they think kind thoughts and perform the deeds of friendship, calling her Joy by name and Aphrodite." *On Nature* fr. 349 20–4[5]

Aphrodite Urania becomes the goddess of 'spiritual love' versus the 'physical love' of Aphrodite *Pandemos*. This split between the physical female love (nature, the body, animals, reproduction) and the spiritual is the bedrock of patriarchy. The female body is despised, debased, and devalued, while the female manqué who is not 'sullied' by physical birth and is the creation of and loyal to the male, is superior.

In the *Symposium* the playwright Aristophanes gives his opinion,

> "… If a male united with a female, they would propagate the race and it would survive, but if a male united with a male, they might find satisfaction and freedom to turn to their pursuits and devote themselves to the other concerns of life." (191c2–191d3)[6]

Socrates recounts how he was instructed about the nature of love and desire (Eros, Ἔρως) by Diotima a woman from Mantinea.[7] (*Symposium* 210d1–212c3). These were her teachings; the lover desires who they do not possess, the beautiful and the good, so they are pursuing happiness. Love aims to reproduce or create that which is beautiful, both physically and spiritually and this brings them in touch with the divine. Procreation grants immortality through one's children, love then is the pursuit of immortality as well.

Diotima continues; the young fall in love with physical beauty embodied in one person and this love creates an outflowing of creativity or beautiful ideas. Later it is realised physical beauty is to be found in everyone (if looked for) and so one can love all people equally. The mature person realises that the beauty of the soul is more precious than physical beauty (which fades) and therefore loves the soul more than the physical sheath. Later in life, the beauty of ideas is valued above all others[8] (Plato calls this morals and laws) and deemed to be the ultimate form of love. (210a4–210c5)[9]

Plato, using what was later called *Diotima's Ladder*, wrote there was a hierarchy (like a ladder) from love for a particular body (romantic love), to love for all bodies (universal love), to love for souls (spiritual and moral beauty are loved), then love for laws and institutions (the society created by beautiful souls), the love of knowledge (or wisdom) and finally, the love of love itself (enlightenment when love is all).

To my mind it is not a hierarchy but a spiral where all aspects of love are experienced and one is not placed above another, a bit like the Zen saying,

> "Before enlightenment, fetch water, cut wood,
> After enlightenment, fetch water, carry wood."

We do live in bodies in a physical world and now, more than ever (writing in 2021 in the midst of a worldwide pandemic probably caused by abuse of nature) we need to honour, value and respect our physical home, or bodies and the earth. While at the same time stopping the abuse, degradation and exploitation of women, children, and animals (pornography and femicide, child rape, factory farming). As Empedocles understood, Love is life and Life is love, all life all love.

These philosophical musings are the terrain of Venus Urania as is the *Symposium* or Salon where the refined celebrations and cerebral discussions of Aphrodite Urania are held (of course Greek women were not allowed in the *Symposium*). Aphrodite Urania is cooler, more cerebral (being airy) than Aphrodite Pandemos; she looks for harmony and peace, pleasure and good company.

> "Come, Cyprian goddess [Aphrodite]
> Pour a libation
> Gracefully into luxurious goblets,
> Nectar
> Mixed for our rites." Sappho (2)[10]

Sheila Kitzinger

Female
29 Mar 1929, Fri
00:00 UT +0:00
Taunton, United Kingdom
Tropical
Placidus

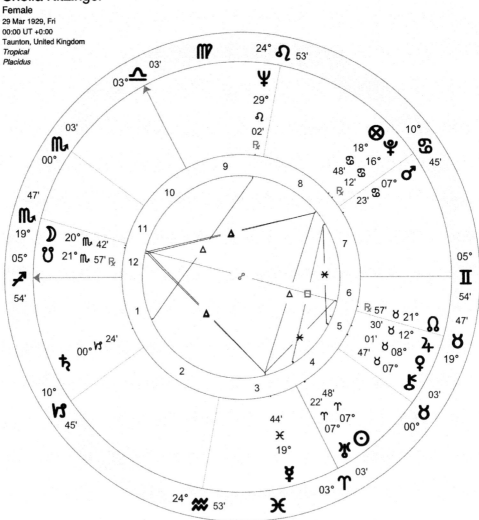

Sheila Kitzinger: Aphrodite Pandemos, high priestess of natural childbirth *29 March 1929. (No time) Taunton Somerset*

"Women know how to give birth."[11]

Sheila was a social anthropologist specialising in pregnancy, childbirth and the care of babies and young children. A mother of five herself, who went against convention to have all her babies at home, she was a fierce advocate of women's right to choose their labour and birth. At the time labour was managed by obstetricians[12] and birth was medicalised, women were even rendered unconscious during labour, while enemas, shaving, episiotomies and forceps deliveries were routine.

Sheila has Venus and Jupiter conjunct in Taurus. Aphrodite Pandemos supports women in their physical bodies to be strong, autonomous, and to delight in their strength. She understands the importance of how we treat women in labour, and how the experience of childbirth colours the society we live in.

"Birth isn't something we suffer but something we actively do and exult in!"[13]

Sheila argued that labour can be a sensual and even erotic experience for women (she was speaking from personal experience) and should not be medicalised and controlled by doctors.

"In achieving the depersonalisation of childbirth and at the same time solving the problem of pain, our society may have lost more than it has gained. We are left with the physical husk; the transcending significance has been drained away."[14]

Sheila researched childbirth practices in the Caribbean, US, Canada (among the Inuit), China, South America and in Africa. She trained teachers and couples in the new Natural Childbirth Trust, and taught and lectured in North and South America, Israel, Europe and Australia. Her book, *The Experience of Childbirth* (1962) transformed childbirth practices in hospitals worldwide and she encouraged home birth which in many countries is now an established option. Because of her pioneering work (Aries Sun, Uranus) women in the UK, rather than unhelpfully lying on their backs (pushing against gravity), now routinely have a birth plan, are able to walk around in labour, use water baths, have friends or partners present and use birth suites which are softly lit and non-medical.

A strong feminist Sheila understood that solidarity among women was crucial.

"In most societies birth has been an experience in which women draw together to help each other and reinforce bonds in the community."[15]

Sheila's Aries Sun conjunct Uranus shows her then radical views, which are mainstream now (Aries seeing the future). While her Venus in Taurus has the sweetness to put across her ground-breaking ideas without ruffling too many feathers, Sheila insisted that birth educators should rock the boat to change birthing practice, in her article in 'Birth' in 1993.[16]

> "Kitzinger was an intensely likeable woman—warm, intelligent, funny and youthful to the end. She was also unashamed and forceful about being a feminist social revolutionary, her belief centred on the opportunity for women to reclaim their bodies."[17]

Like Aphrodite Pandemos, Sheila understood the strength of women and how, if left alone, their bodies knew exactly what to do.

"... Her absolute belief that the experience of giving birth and the first hours together between mother and child were crucially important to the way that precious relationship would develop. She wanted women to be given the chance to love and trust their bodies; give birth in the way that felt right to them and breastfeed in comfort, without having to worry about offending anyone. 'After all, dear,' she said, her face wreathed in her familiar, slightly naughty smile, 'it is what breasts were designed for.'"[18]

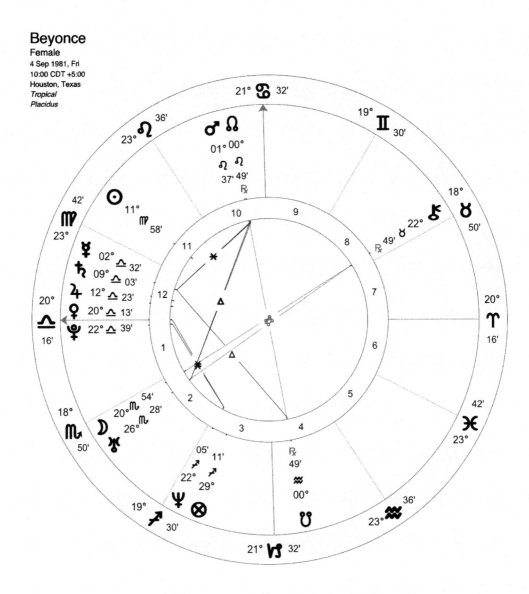

Beyonce
Female
4 Sep 1981, Fri
10:00 CDT +5:00
Houston, Texas
Tropical
Placidus

Beyoncé: Aphrodite Urania, goddess
4 September 1981. (10:00) Houston TX

"I don't have to prove anything to anyone, I only have to follow my heart and concentrate on what I want to say to the world. I run my world."[19]

Although she is a Sun Virgo, Beyonce has five planets in Libra plus her Ascendant. On stage she dresses in fantastic, bejewelled costumes which form part of a spectacular musical experience. It is interesting that she has created an alter ego who is described as being, "Sexy, seductive and provocative" when performing on stage, Beyoncé has said that she originally created 'Sasha Fierce' to keep that stage persona separate from who she really is. She described Sasha as being, "Too aggressive, too strong, too sassy [and] too sexy," stating, "I'm not like her in real life at all. I'm not flirtatious and super-confident and fearless like her. What I feel onstage I don't feel anywhere else. It's an out-of-body experience. I created my stage persona to protect myself so that when I go home, I don't have to think about what it is I do. Sasha isn't me. The people around me know who I really am." Beyoncé said she doesn't need celebrity or crave fame.

"I do normal things, walk in the park," she told *Parade*. "I don't want to be off on my own diva planet. I want to be on Earth. I want to be normal. I think I am past needing celebrity. I don't want to feel the void I see in a lot of celebrities … the unhappiness underneath the smile."[20]

Being true to her Virgo Sun, but like Aphrodite Urania knowing what the people want and giving it to them.

"The most alluring thing a woman can have is confidence."[21]

Beyonce is of course a massively successful singer and performer and one of the most powerful women in the music business. Love, beauty and music, as well as a powerful message.

"I truly believe women should be financially independent from their men. And let's face it, money gives men the power to run the show. It gives men the power to define value. They define what is sexy. And men define what is feminine. It's ridiculous."

Notes

1. https://www.sacred-texts.com/cla/usappho/sph02.htm accessed 9-5-2020.
2. https://leighnoren.com/human-sexuality-blog/who-has-more-sexual-desire-men-or-women-according-to-science/

3. Wednesday Martin For The Daily Mail Published: 22:05, 26 September 2018 | Updated: 16:35, 27 September 2018.

4. Roue, Lucy. 3 Jan 2017. *Nearly Half of Men who take Paternity tests are not the real father.* Manchester Evening News. https://www.manchestereveningnews.co.uk/business/business-news/paternity-test-father-bioclinics-group-12399580 accessed 1.12.2020.

5. Kirk, G.S., Raven, J.E., Schofield, M. 1983. *The Presocratic Philosophers.* Cambridge University Press. London. frag 349 20–4.

6. In Morford, 2015, p.209.

7. Her name, Maninea, may refer to a city in the Peloponnese or it may refer to her being a famed (τιμη) seer or mantis (μαντις). It has been claimed she was an invention, but Plato, in his writings mentions people who were alive at the time, like Aristophanes, and Alcibiades, so there is no reason why she was not a real person living in Athens. It was not until the 15thC that her existence was doubted, by Ficino, probably due to the misogyny of his time.

8. Plato was writing about what Socrates (allegedly) said. Socrates was reputedly fantastically ugly, so perhaps his dismissal of the physical beauty was more a personal reaction.

9. In Morford, 2015, p.2213.

10. https://www.sacred-texts.com/cla/usappho/sph07.htm accessed 2.6.2020

11. https://www.lamaze.org/Connecting-the-Dots/remembering-sheila-kitzinger-an-amazing-advocate-for-women-babies-and-families

12. To read the sorry tale of how midwives were pushed out by male doctors in the 17thC see, Brooke, Elisabeth (2019) *Women Healers through History.* Aeon Books, London, p.111–145.

13. https://www.azquotes.com/author/22313-Sheila_Kitzinger accessed 5.4.2021.

14. Kitzinger, Sheila, 1978 *Women as Mothers.* (no page number given) quoted in https://www.azquotes.com/author/22313-Sheila_Kitzinger accessed 5.4.2021.

15. https://www.azquotes.com/author/22313-Sheila_Kitzinger accessed 5.4.2021.

16. Birth Journal. Vol20:issue4, p.216-6. https://onlinelibrary.wiley.com/doi/abs/10.1111/j.1523-536X.1993.tb00230.x accessed 5.4.2021.

17. Hayman, Suzie. 12.4.2015. *Guardian Obituary.* https://www.theguardian.com/life-andstyle/2015/apr/12/sheila-kitzinger. Accessed 5.4.2021.

18. Murray, Jenni. 13.4.2015. Obituary, Daily Mail. https://www.dailymail.co.uk/news/article-3036293/As-childbirth-expert-Sheila-Kitzinger-dies-86-JENNI-MURRAY-pays-tribute.html accessed 5.4.2021.

19. https://www.goalcast.com/2017/06/27/top-18-most-empowering-beyonce-quotes-2/ accessed 2.6.2020.

20. Johnson, Caitlin A. (December 13, 2006). *"Beyoncé On Love, Depression, and Reality".* CBS News. https://web.archive.org/web/20081208151348/http://www.cbsnews.com/stories/2006/12/13/entertainment/main2258069.shtml accessed 1.11.2020.

21. https://www.goalcast.com/2017/06/27/top-18-most-empowering-beyonce-quotes-2/ accessed 2.6.2020.

Mars: the Furies

Ispent a long time wondering what a Goddess version of Mars (Ares) would be like, women generally do not go to war, although they can and do fight, but it is usually to defend themselves or their children and loved ones. Then they can be fierce, implacable, and deadly. Or furious.

The Furies or the *Erinyes* (Ερινυες)

"Before this man, slumber an extraordinary armed band of women, asleep upon the oracular seat. Perhaps not women, but I call them Gorgons, although they have not quite the Gorgon shape as far as one can see … they appear wingless and black robed and disgusting, they are snoring, breathing with repulsive breaths and from their eyes drip disgusting discharge." (Aeschylus, *Eumenides*:46–54)

According to Hesiod *Theogony* (183–187) The Erinyes were created when Zeus castrated Uranus his father,

"Gaia (earth) accepted all the bloody drops as they fell. As the seasons passed Gaia gave birth upon the boundless earth, to both the Erinyes and the mighty giants with gleaming armour, long spears in their hands, and the nymphs called Melissae."

So, the Furies belong to the pre-patriarchal deities.

Others say they are the children of Night (Νυξ) the primeval goddess.

"Oh mother! Mother Night who bore me to punish the blind and the seeing, hear me now!" (321–327 *Eumenides*)

239

Either way, they are pre-patriarchal deities. The Erinyes live in Hades with Hecate and Persephone. Sometimes they are seen as a group, others as three separate goddesses: Alecto (endless, punisher of moral crimes, like anger), Megaera (jealous rage, punisher of infidelity, oath breakers and theft) and Tisiphone (vengeful destruction of murderers, retributive justice). They are depicted as powerful, they carry torches to see, whips to punish and serpents wrapped around the wrists, like the Kretan priestesses, (Fig. 42) and in their hair (like Medusa) because they are chthonic goddesses (of the Underworld).

Fig. 42 Erinyes, krater pot, Graeca Magna, 4thC BCE.

They punish criminals and taboo-breakers, especially matricides, and blood guilt.

> "We drive matricides from their homes." (*Eumenides*:210)

They are remorseless, pitiless, and implacable as they stalk their prey.

> "We hunt him down like dogs on the scent of the blood of a wounded fawn, lungs
> panting from many wearying struggles. And now he is here, somewhere cowering.
> The scent of fresh mortal blood greets me." (*Eumenides*:246–51)

Some say they are the ghosts of murder victims seeing vengeance or the embodiment of hexes or curses invoked on the perpetrators.[1]

The Erinyes represent the old moral order of the goddess, which demands blood sacrifice for murder exacted by the family of the victim, an eye for an eye justice, vendetta along blood lines.

> " ... Waft your bloodstained breath over him! By this vapour cause his shrivelling,
> follow him with the fire of your womb, vanquish him!" (*Eumenides*:135–7)

The Erinyes punished parricides as these undermined the integrity of the family, for this reason murderers were banished until someone was able to purify them, usually they were sent mad.[2]

> "A mother's blood once it is shed on the ground is hard to recover, a liquid poured
> on the earth is gone." (*Eumenides*:261)

The Erinyes refused to recognise the authority of the Olympians, even Zeus. They were protectors of the social order and punished crimes which disturbed this order, the forces of anarchy. When Apollo attempts to excuse Orestes, they upbraid him. (Fig. 43)

> "Oh, child of Zeus, you are a thief, a youth who has trampled the gods of old,
> receiving this suppliant, a godless man and evil to his parent. You have stolen
> away a matricide, despite being a god, and you say this is justly done? Would any-
> one call just, what has been done here?" (*Eumenides*:149–54)

They punished *hubris* (overwhelming pride) when men forgot they were mortal. They prohibited diviners from telling the future too accurately lest mankind lost their uncertainty and stopped relying on the gods.[3]

The *Eumenides* describes how they pursue Orestes the matricide to Delphi, driving him to the edge of madness. He depicts them as bestial, crawling on all fours, dressed in black, whining and howling like dogs. It is said at the first performance of this play, the depiction of the Furies was so terrifying that women in the audience fainted and suffered miscarriages.[4]

Fig. 43 Erinye and Apollo, Krater pot, 360 BCE.

"But you must repay me, I sup greedily on the blood from your living limbs. May I feed on you, foul beverage! I will wither you alive and drag you down. Retribution, you pay the price for your murdered mother's agony." (*Eumenides*:264–8)

The Erinyes were summoned thus,

> "Nursing the raw anger of a mother's bitter curses, she prays to the gods, grieving much for the slaughter of her brother and pounding on the bountiful earth she struck it, again and again, sinking utterly to the ground, her bosom drenched in tears, she called upon Hades and dread Persephone to bring death to her child and the Erinyes, of the pitiless heart, walking in darkness in Erebus, heard her." *Iliad* 9:566–572

The ghost of Klytemnestra recounts how she worshipped them,

> "… You have imbibed many libations of mine, wineless offerings and meals in the solemn night on flames in the fire pit. I offered these at a time when no one speaks to any god." (*Eumenides* 106–10)

To placate the Erinyes a wreath called the *leirion* was worn, made from the blue iris, the oil of the root (Oris root has a violet-like smell) is sacred to Demeter and Persephone.[5] Orestes is found lying by a pool crowned with lilies where he tried to purify himself after murdering his mother; the Erinyes refuse to be placated.[6] Both the Iris and the Hyacinth are found in Kretan iconography, they are found in wall paintings and engraved on many gold signet rings.[7]

The Erinyes were not mentioned by name for fear of attracting their attention, in the play they are called the Eumenides (the kindly ones) to placate them. Their name is possibly of Mycenaean origin, in the Linear B tablets are found e-ri-nu and e-ri-nu-we.[8]

Orestes was given a bow made of horn by Apollo to keep the Erinyes at bay, but it was not powerful enough[9] to stop them. In desperation he bit off his finger to placate them and they changed their black clothes to white, he shaved his head and made an offering to both the white and the black goddesses and to the Graces.[10] Purification involved sacrificing a pig and allowing the angry ghost to drink the blood and then washing in running water, shaving the head to change one's appearance and to go into exile for a year to throw the hungry ghosts off the scent. Until this was done, the murderer was shunned, bringing bad luck to all he met, they were forbidden to enter people's homes or share their food. Matricide carried such a curse this was not enough. Heracles even bit off one of his fingers to placate Hera (see Leo Hera). The tradition of wearing black after death was to hide from any angry ghost by changing their appearance and perhaps just merging into the darkness.[11]

After Athene (see Aquarius) throws the casting vote and patricide is deemed more important than matricide the Erinyes rebel, threatening to let fall a drop of their blood, and lay waste the countryside, destroy the crops and kill all the children in the city. (Graves: 2011:434), claims this is the traditional witches curse using their menstrual blood to blight a house, field or children by walking nine times around, west to east, naked while menstruating, particularly during an eclipse of the moon.

In Aeschylus' play the Erinyes are subdued by flattery and become the Eumenides (the kindly ones). (Graves: 2011:435) suggests instead they were given an ultimatum from Zeus born Athene that unless they accepted fathers were more important than mothers and agreed to share their cult with the male underworld gods Hades and Hermes, they would be denied worship altogether.

Other traditions have the Erinyes continue to pursue Orestes. He returns to Delphi and the Pythia sends him across the Black Sea to Taurus to bring back an ancient wooden image of Artemis. What he did not know was that any stranger arriving in that country was decapitated and his head is stuck in a pike. Shipwrecked sailors were sacrificed to Taurian Artemis by Iphigenia her priestess. Iphigenia was the daughter of Agamemnon (who Klytemnestra killed by way of revenge). Agamemnon agreed to sacrifice Iphigenia because the Greek ships were becalmed on their way to fight the Trojans, and they blamed Iphigenia's magic. As they were about to cut her throat, Iphigenia was whisked away by Artemis under cover of a cloud, to serve as her priestess. In Taurus, Iphigenia killed Orestes by cutting his throat, not knowing (or knowing) he was her brother. So, Iphigenia avenged her mother Klytemnestra's death, just as Klytemnestra had avenged hers (supposed).[12]

Mars, the Erinyes have two expressions, Aries which is more combative and Scorpio more defensive.

Valerie Solanas

Natal
9 Apr 1936, Thu
05:37 EST +5:00
Atlantic City
Tropical
Placidus

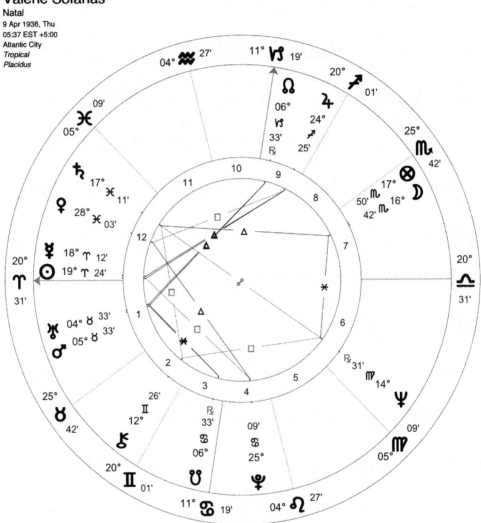

Valerie Solanas: Aries
9 April 1936. (05:37) Ventnor City NJ

Valerie Solanas was a Radical Feminist who wrote the *SCUM Manifesto*, an essay on patriarchal culture published in 1967.[13] It argued that men have ruined the world, and that it is up to women to fix it; "The male as an 'incomplete female'" who is genetically deficient due to his Y chromosome.[14] According to Solanas, this genetic deficiency causes the male to be emotionally limited, egocentric, and incapable of mental passion or genuine interaction. She describes the male as lacking empathy and unable to relate to anything apart from his own physical sensations.[15]

Valerie's astrology shows both expressions of Mars. Sun and Mercury in Aries conjunct the Ascendant and Moon in Scorpio. Aries is the more brutal, aggressive, warrior. Solitary, impulsive, and argumentative, Mercury in Ares gives her a quick wit, which can be violent and cutting, but clever, articulate, and radical. The Moon in Scorpio shows the watery Mars, which is deeper, fixed on resentments and punishment, interested in sexual exploration, power and money, holding on to hurts and slights. Scorpio often experiences loss/brutality early on as well as powerlessness, hence their need to gain autonomy through struggle. While Mars conjunct Uranus shows violence, experienced and enacted by her.

Valerie suggested the formation of SCUM, an organization dedicated to overthrowing society and eliminating the male sex. The *SCUM Manifesto* contends the male spends his life attempting to become female, to overcome his inferiority. Solanas rejects Freud's theory of penis envy, arguing that men have 'pussy envy.' Solanas blames men for turning the world into a 'shit-pile.'[16]

> "The female function is to explore, discover, invent, solve problems crack jokes, make music—all with love. In other words, create a magic world." (*SCUM Manifesto*:6)

In childhood Valerie Solanas was raped by her father and then her grandfather. At fifteen, she became pregnant, and gave the child up for adoption. Described by her high school principal as, "An exceptionally bright girl with lots of courage and determination,"[17] she earned a degree in psychology from the University of Maryland. It has been argued the *SCUM Manifesto* was a brilliant parody of Freud, who Solanas would have studied.[18]

Chavisa Woods suggests,

> "The SCUM Manifesto is a masterwork of literary protest art, which is often completely misread. Much of it is a point-by-point re-write of multiple of Freud's writings. It is a parody."[19]

The bulk of the *SCUM Manifesto* consists of a list of critiques of the male sex, and argued that women must replace the 'money-work system' with a system of complete automation which will cause the collapse of government and women's financial freedom from men.[20]

The *SCUM Manifesto* proposes that a revolutionary vanguard of women be formed, referred to as SCUM, arguing that they should employ sabotage and direct action tactics rather than civil disobedience to destroy the system; violent action is necessary:

> "If SCUM ever marches, it will be over the President's stupid, sickening face; if
> SCUM ever strikes, it will be in the dark with a six-inch blade." (p.7)

Solanas is famous for shooting Andy Warhol and another man in 1968. She claimed she shot Warhol because he was going to steal her play, *Up Your Ass*, which concerns a female prostitute who kills a man. She worked on a few films with Warhol in New York and gave him the script, hoping he would produce it, but Warhol decided it was too pornographic to produce. She complained that Warhol publicly demeaned her, he recorded their phone conversations, and used some of the dialogue in his films uncredited saying, "She was a great talker."[21]

Solanas was charged and sentenced to three years in jail. She did not regret the shooting, "I consider it immoral that I missed, I should have done target practice."[22] Shortly after her release from prison, she became homeless, and never published another work.[23]

Valerie was later diagnosed as a schizophrenic, which may have been the case, but she would have suffered from complex PTSD following prolonged childhood rape.

In a bitter twist of fate Solanas was subjected to non-consensual hysterectomy while hospitalised, in effect a female castration, as if removing a womb would render a woman neuter and therefore 'safe.' Perhaps like the Ancient Greeks, her doctors felt the womb was full of fire which could shrivel men.

> " ... Waft your bloodstained breath over him! By this vapour cause his shrivelling,
> follow him with the fire of your womb, vanquish him!" (*Eumenides*:135–7)

Solanas divided the women's movement. Aries are often pioneers rejected by their peers, they need to go their own way. She is responsible for the Radical Feminist movement[24] which maintains there should be no negotiation with patriarchy, that women should live separate lives, while more mainstream feminism aims to change men within the system. Aries' opinions can be extreme or just wounding and they are scathing of people who do not have the courage to follow their blazing trail. Solanas derided the Woman's Liberation Movement describing it as, 'a civil disobedience luncheon club' and 'for its blind adherence to cultural codes of feminine politeness and decorum which the *SCUM Manifesto* identifies as the source of women's debased social status.'[25]

Aries live in the future. Solanas presented a radical analysis of patriarchy (if not all men) which still stands today, while the need for its demise is ever more urgent. Solanas epitomises the Erinyes, demanding payment for patriarchy's crimes. She was mutilated, discarded and exiled into obscurity. Her isolation might be seen as her undoing; she died alone from pneumonia in a homeless shelter.

Lorena Bobbitt

Female

31 Oct 1970, Sat
00:00 EST +5:00
Quito, Ecuador
Tropical
Placidus

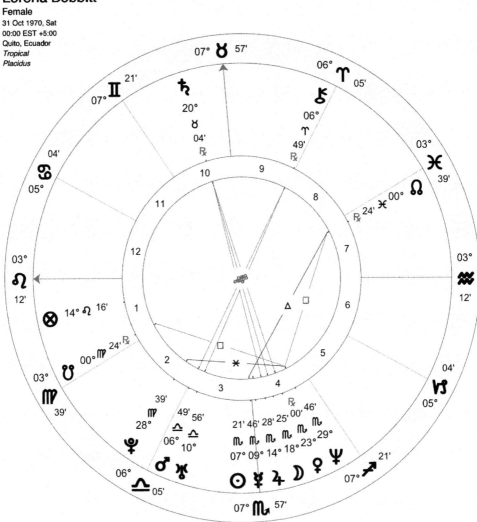

Lorena Bobbitt: Domestic violence
31 October 1970.[26] (No time) Bucay, Quito, Ecuador

Lorena grew up in a middle class family, spent her childhood in Venezuela, and came to the USA to study. She met and married John Bobbitt when she was twenty. Lorena claimed their marriage was abusive from the start; she suffered rape, beatings, and emotional abuse. Although the police were called multiple times, her husband avoided prosecution as 'domestic violence' was not against the law at that time.

On 3 June 1993 Lorena was raped by Bobbitt when he came home drunk. While he was sleeping, she cut off his penis and ran away. Apparently, she threw it from the car window, went to a friend's house and called the police. She told them where she had thrown it and it was successfully re-attached. Both were charged with assault and both were acquitted. Lorena spent a month in a mental hospital under observation but was released as she posed no risk to the public. In later life Lorena began campaigning against domestic abuse; in 2007 she founded the Lorena Gallo institute to help victims of abuse.

Although we do not have the time for her chart I feel this chart is a powerful expression of Scorpionic energy. Lorena has six planets in Scorpio, Sun, Mercury, Jupiter, Venus, Moon and Neptune all forming a powerful stellium which is opposed by Saturn in Taurus. Her marriage must have been a descent into hell for her, yet, despite the beatings and rape, she was finally able to garner the strength to fight back. She retaliated to save her life; she said she feared he was going to murder her.

"It was survival. Life and death. I was fearing for my life."[27]

Most evocative of the act though, is a Mars Uranus conjunction in Libra. Mars, the knife castrates Uranus, the partner/lover Libra.

Afterwards, her Jupiter wanted to speak her truth,

"The media was focusing only on the penis, the sensationalistic, the scandalous. But I wanted to shine the light on this issue of spousal abuse. When I went to Knoxville [to speak at a symposium for Lincoln Memorial University's law review], the president of the school introduced me as a celebrity. I said, 'Thank you, but let me correct you. I am not a celebrity I am an advocate.'"[28]

Lorena turned down a million dollars to appear nude in Playboy magazine. Her husband had a brief career as a porn star, he was arrested several times for assault on his subsequent wives.

Scorpio, then, goes to deeper and darker places than other signs, often unwillingly, but the treasures they discover in Hade's realm make them the strongest of the signs, or the most resilient, and having lived in the dark corridors of the underworld, Scorpio has a conduit to the unconscious and can bring its mysteries into the sunlight.

Notice that both Valerie and Lorena have Mars conjunct Uranus (the planets of violence and castration) and they are in signs ruled by Venus. Taurus in Valerie's case and Libra in Lorena's. The assault and brutality of the male is cut off violently.

Notes

1. Morford, 2015, pp.382–3.
2. Compare this to the indigenous practice of ostracising or 'not-seeing' wrong doers, which often killed them, see Graves, 2011, p.431.
3. Grimal, 1987, p.151.
4. March, 2002, p.165. although as other sources say women were not able to attend the theatre, so it is not clear which story is correct.
5. Sophocles, *Oedipus at Colonus*: 681–686. 'A fed on dew from heaven, the narcissus blooms by day its lovely flowers, it is the ancient crown of the Great Goddesses.'
6. Graves, 2011, p.288.
7. See www.supressedhistories.net Max Dashu.
8. Chadwick, John. 1979. *The Mycenaean World.* Cambridge University Press. Cambridge. p.98. '*Erinus* the later name, usually in the plural for the Furies or avenging spirits believed to pursue murderers. The same name has now been deciphered on the edge of the famous list of Greek gods at Knossos (V52)'.
9. Grave, 2011, p.426.
10. Pausanias, *Description of Greece.* 8:34.1–2. http://www.perseus.tufts.edu/hopper/text?doc=Perseus%3Atext%3A1999.01.0160%3Abook%3D8%3Achapter%3D34%3Asection%3D1 accessed 27.8.2020.
11. Graves, 2011, p.431.
12. This is one version, there are several others, see Grave, 2011:435–441.
13. For a list of her work see: https://web.archive.org/web/20050817015943/http://geocities.com/WestHollywood/Village/6982/solanas.html
14. Harding, James Martin (2010). *Cutting Performances: Collage Events, Feminist Artists, and the American Avant-Garde.* Ann Arbor: University of Michigan Press. p.152.
15. Solanas, 1968, pp.32–33.
16. Solanas, 1968, pp.34–35.
17. https://www.biography.com/news/andy-warhol-valerie-solanas-shot accessed 30.11.2020.
18. Woods, Chavisa (21 May 2019). *"Hating Valerie Solanas (And Loving Violent Men)"* Full Stop. http://www.full-stop.net/2019/05/21/features/chavisa-woods/solanas/ accessed 28.8.2020.
19. Woods, Chavisa (21 May 2019). *"Hating Valerie Solanas (And Loving Violent Men)"* Full Stop. http://www.full-stop.net/2019/05/21/features/chavisa-woods/solanas/
20. Heller, Dana (2001). "Shooting Solanas: radical feminist history and the technology of failure" *Feminist Studies.* 27 (1): 167–189.
21. Solomon, Tessa. 18 June 2020. *Who was Valerie Solanas, the Feminist Revolutionary who shot Andy Warhol?* Art News. https://www.artnews.com/art-news/news/who-was-valerie-solanas-andy-warhol-1202689740/ accessed 30.11.2020.

22. Solomon, Tessa. 18 June 2020. *Who was Valerie Solanas, the Feminist Revolutionary who shot Andy Warhol?* Art News. https://www.artnews.com/art-news/news/who-was-valerie-solanas-andy-warhol-1202689740/ accessed 30.11.2020.

23. Woods, Chavisa (21 May 2019). *"Hating Valerie Solanas (And Loving Violent Men)"* Full Stop. http://www.full-stop.net/2019/05/21/features/chavisa-woods/solanas/ accessed 26.8.2020.

24. Third, Amanda (2006). *"'Shooting from the hip': Valerie Solanas, SCUM and the apocalyptic politics of radical feminism"* Hecate 32 (2): 104–132. Lord, Catherine (2010). *"Wonder waif meets super neuter"*. October (132): 135–136.

25. Heller, Dana (2001). "Shooting Solanas: radical feminist history and the technology of failure" *Feminist Studies.* 27 (1): 167–189.

26. Sources differ about her birthdate, Biography.com has both 1969 and 1970, Wikipedia has 1969, astrologer https://venusinthefifth2.files.wordpress.com/2015/10/lorena-bobbit-attack-chart.jpg has 1970, etc. etc. I have chosen the 1970 chart as it seems to fit the time of the attack when Pluto was transiting her natal Moon Venus conjunction in Scorpio, the North node was conjunct her natal Saturn and Saturn was widely conjunct her Venus. Whereas the 1969 chart has Jupiter conjunct her Uranus and Mercury conjunct her Moon/Lilith, Uranus/Neptune opposite her Moon which also fits but perhaps not so well.

27. https://www.vanityfair.com/style/2018/06/lorena-bobbitt-john-wayne-bobbitt-25-years accessed 26.1.2021.

28. https://www.vanityfair.com/style/2018/06/lorena-bobbitt-john-wayne-bobbitt-25-years accessed 26.1.2021.

Jupiter: Themis

Themis was Goddess of justice, law and order, one of the Titans, daughter of Uranus and Gaia,

> "She [Gaia] lay with Uranus and bore deep-swirling Oceanus, Coeus and Crius and Hyperion and Iapetus, Theia and Rhea, Themis and Mnemosyne and gold-crowned Phoebe and lovely Tethys." (Hesiod *Theogony* 132–6)

Like the other Greek goddesses, she was co-opted or 'married' to Zeus and gave birth to the three Horae (seasons) and the Fates (who personified aspects of order in the universe).

> "By Themis, daughter of Ouranos, he had daughters, the Seasons, Peace, Order, and Justice; also the Fates, Clotho, Lachesis, and Atropus." (Apollodorus 1.1.3)

With Zeus she presided over divine assemblies in Olympus, Zeus,

> "... told Themis to summon all the gods into assembly. She went everywhere and told them to make their way to Zeus' house." (*Iliad* 20:4–5)
>   "Themis who breaks up the assemblies of men and calls them into session." (*Odyssey* 2:68–9)

Clearly this was a function of Themis before the rise of the father-god. It is said Themis planned the Trojan war to deal with over population on earth. Themis had prophetic powers and, like Gaia, was the goddess of the Delphic oracle.

255

"The Priestess of Pythian Apollo:

First, in this prayer of mine, I give the place of highest honour among the gods to the first prophet, Earth; and after her to Themis, for she was the second to take this oracular seat of her mother, as legend tells. And in the third allotment, with Themis' consent and not by force, another Titan, child of Earth, Phoebe, took her seat here." (Aeschylus, *Eumenides* 1–5)

"Such is the oracle recounted to me by my mother, Titan Themis, born long ago." (Aeschylus, *Prometheus Bound*, 875)

Apollo with violence took over the oracle.

"Apollo learned the art of prophecy from Pan,[1] the son of Zeus and Hybris, and came to Delphi where Themis at that time used to deliver oracles; and when the snake Python, which guarded the oracle, would have hindered him from approaching the chasm, he killed it and took over the oracle." (Apollodorus 1.4.1)[2]

Gaia, Themis' mother rebelled and expelled she gave prophetic dreams to humankind. (See Pythia Pisces)

"There is extant among the Greeks a hexameter poem, the name of which is Eumolpia, and it is assigned to Musaeus, son of Antiophemus. In it the poet states that the oracle belonged to Poseidon and Gaia in common; that Gaia gave her oracles herself, but Poseidon used Pyrcon as his mouthpiece in giving responses. The verses are these: 'Forthwith the voice of the Earth-goddess Gaia uttered a wise word, And with her Pyrcon, servant of the renowned Earth-shaker [Poseidon].'" *[Musaeus], Eumolpia*

"They say that afterwards Gaia gave her share to Themis, who gave it to Apollo as a gift. It is said that he gave to Poseidon Calaureia, that lies off Troezen in exchange for his oracle." (Pausanias *Descriptions of Greece* 10.5.6.)[3]

Themis fed the infant Apollo,

"Themis duly poured nectar and ambrosia with her divine hands: and Leto was glad ..." (*Homeric Hymn to Apollo* 3:125)

Themis was said to be the mother of the Titan Prometheus who is freed from his punishment for showing mankind fire, by using his knowledge from Themis' powers of prophecy.[4] (Fig. 44)

"Lofty-minded son of Themis who counsels straight." (Aeschylus, *Prometheus Bound*, 18)

"Often my mother Themis, or Gaia, though one form, she had many names, had foretold to me the way in which the future was fated to come to pass. That it was

Fig. 44 Themis and Nymphs, black figure dinos pot, 580–570 BCE.

not by brute strength nor through violence, but by guile that those who should gain the upper hand were destined to prevail." (Aeschylus, *Prometheus Bound*, 211–15)

Themis, as we have seen, is the mother of both the Fates, (Morai, Μοιραι) Clotho (spinner Κλωθω) who spins out the thread of life, Lachesis the disposer of lots (fate and destiny Λαχεσις) who measures the thread of life and Atropos, the inflexible (Ατροπος, the unchangeable, from τρεπω to turn) who cuts it off. Their actions are irrevocable and non-negotiable, you have your fate, your destiny, your time is finite, and it ends where fate decrees it must. Even Zeus must bow to the fates, however much he would prefer to control everything.[5]

Themis' other daughters are the Horae (Hours, Ωραι the seasons, spring, summer and winter⁶) (see Aphrodite) Eunomia (good order) Dikē (justice) Eirene (peace) goddesses who maintained the stability of society, they were also known in Athens as nature goddesses who controlled the growing of plants. Thallo, (blooming, Spring) Auxo, (increase, summer) and Carpo, (Fruiting autumn)⁷ guarded the entrance to Olympus. They served Hera (and may have reared her) and were followers of Aphrodite like the Graces; they were companions of Persephone, and were often depicted as three graceful maidens holding a plant or flower.

> "... Bright Themis who bore the Horae, the Seasons,⁸ and Eunomia (Order), Dikē (Justice) and blooming Eirene (Peace), who mind the works of mortal men, and the Moerae (Fates) to whom wise Zeus gave the greatest honour, Clotho, and Lachesis, and Atropos who give mortal men evil and good to have. And Eurynome, the daughter of Ocean, beautiful in form, bore him three fair-cheeked Charites (Graces), Aglaea, and Euphrosyne, and lovely Thaleia, from whose eyes as they glanced flowed love that unnerves the limbs: and beautiful is their glance beneath their brows." Hesiod *Theogony* (901–13)⁹
>
> "Next, he [Zeus] married bright Themis who bore the Horae (Hours), and Eunomia (Order), Dikē (Justice), and blooming Eirene (Peace), who mind the works of mortal men, and the Moerae (Fates) to whom wise Zeus gave the greatest honour, Clotho, and Lachesis, and Atropos who give mortal men evil and good to have." (*Theogony* 901–906)

We can speculate that all these attributes originally belonged to Themis alone, and that she was both goddess of Order, Justice and Peace and the Fate of individuals, spun out, measured and ended. She was also one of the original seers at Delphi and so had awesome prophetic powers. It was Themis who called assemblies and closed them, so her sense of justice and order brought fairness and calm to both gods and humankind. Both these attributes can be seen in the signs that Jupiter/Themis traditionally rules: Sagittarius and Pisces.

Sagittarius is often depicted as the wild party animal of the zodiac, but there is a serious and thoughtful side to the sign. Because she values her freedom she supports, Order, Justice and Peace. Which are prerequisites to all three. Without Order, Justice and Peace we have chaos and anarchy, which frees no one; rule by force rather than Justice only benefits the strong and Peace is only attained when all people (or the majority) are safe and well. For that reason, Sagittarians are often involved in justice and freedom movements and large organisations. Another aspect of Sagittarius is truth bearing, many political activists are found in this sign, this is due to her ruler Themis, (Jupiter) who demands justice and truthfulness. Speaking truth to power.

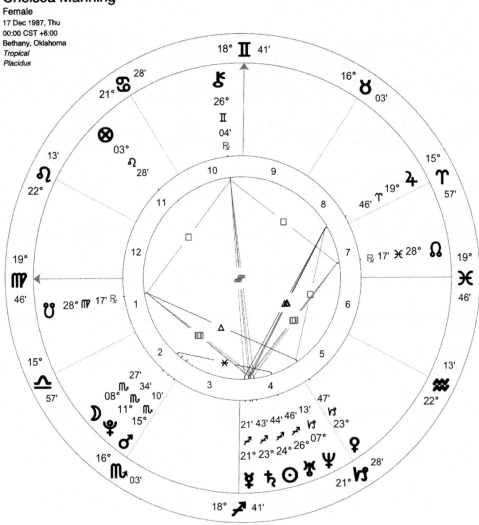

Chelsea Manning

Female
17 Dec 1987, Thu
00:00 CST +6:00
Bethany, Oklahoma
Tropical
Placidus

Chelsea Manning: Dealer in truths
17 December 1987. (No time) Crescent OK

"I want people to see the truth."[10]

Chelsea Manning, a trans-woman, was responsible for the greatest leak of classified data from the US army in 2013. She had a difficult childhood, the child of two alcoholics, she may have suffered from foetal alcohol syndrome. Born a boy, she knew at an early age she was female; she was subjected to bullying at school and later in the army. (Her Moon, Mars, Pluto conjunction in Scorpio shows again the hell that many Scorpios go through at a young age, which colours their choices in later life.)

"Sometimes you have to pay a heavy price to live in a free society."[11]

Her chart has Sun, Mercury, Saturn, Uranus in truth-seeking Sagittarius (ruled by Jupiter). She had to speak out and used technology (Uranus) spread the message of the war crimes the American army was committing. Jupiter has incredible courage when the cause is just.

Gifted in mathematics and computing, she joined the army as a way of coming to terms with her gender identity. While working as an intelligence analyst, she was horrified at what she encountered in Iraq. The video of the 12 July Baghdad airstrike where innocent civilians were massacred, shocked her and she leaked it,

> "The most alarming aspect of the video to me was the seeming delightful blood-lust the aerial weapons team happened to have. They dehumanized the individuals they were engaging and seemed to not value human life and referred to them as quote-unquote 'dead bastards,' and congratulated each other on their ability to kill in large numbers …. For me, this seemed similar to a child torturing ants with a magnifying glass …. I believed that if the general public, especially the American public, had access to the information contained [in the leaks], it could spark a domestic debate on the role of the military and our foreign policy in general as it related to Iraq and Afghanistan."[12]

Chelsea sent over 750,000 classified, or unclassified but sensitive, military and diplomatic documents to Wikileaks.

> "Once you come to realize that the co-ordinates in these records represent real places, that the dates are our recent history and that the numbers represent actual human lives—with all of the love, hope, dreams, hate, fear and nightmares with which we all live—then you cannot help but be reminded just how important it is for us to understand and, hopefully, prevent such tragedies in the future."[13]

261

"Chelsea Manning's most famous leak is arguably also WikiLeaks most famous leak, so it'll top this list. That would be the notorious *Collateral Murder* video, showing U.S. air crew gunning down unarmed Iraqi civilians with an enthusiasm that couldn't be matched by an eight year-old winning a five-foot-tall stuffed animal at the county fair. They murdered between 12 and 18 innocent people, two of them Reuters journalists. Zero people have been arrested for the collateral murders."[14]

In a letter to President Obama, requesting a pardon, and read out before sentencing at her trial, Chelsea wrote,

"It was not until I was in Iraq and reading secret military reports on a daily basis that I started to question the morality of what we were doing. It was at this time I realized that (in) our efforts to meet the risk posed to us by the enemy, we have forgotten our humanity. We consciously elected to devalue human life both in Iraq and Afghanistan. When we engaged those that we perceived were the enemy, we sometimes killed innocent civilians. Whenever we killed innocent civilians, instead of accepting responsibility for our conduct, we elected to hide behind the veil of national security and classified information in order to avoid any public accountability."[15]

"The release of the files brought to our doors the atrocities our governments carried out through media. It is my strong belief that this is the true essence of an activist … It is my great shame I live in an era where people like Julian Assange and Edward Snowdon, Chelsea Manning and anyone willing to open our eyes to the atrocities of war, is likely to be hunted like an animal by governments, punished and silenced." (14 April 2019)[16]

Chelsea was tried and found guilty, and was imprisoned from 2010 until 2017 when her sentence was commuted by Obama.

See also:

Shirley Chisholme, (30 November 1924. (No time) Brooklyn NY) First Black woman to enter Congress (Sun, Mercury and Jupiter in Sagittarius, Venus and Saturn in Scorpio).

Jane Fonda. (21 December 1937. (09:14) New York) Anti-war activist.

Margaret Chase Smith: 14 December 1897. (11:30) Skowhegan MA. First woman in both Congress and Senate, stood up to McCarthy-declaration of conscience) (Sun, Mars, Venus, Saturn and Uranus in Sagittarius)

The other side of Themis, the Seer or Sybil taps into the deep wellsprings of Spiritual wisdom. I associate this with what gifts, challenges, and opportunities we come in with, how we get to express these during our lifetime, and how long we have to do this work. Clotho, Lachesis, and Atropos.

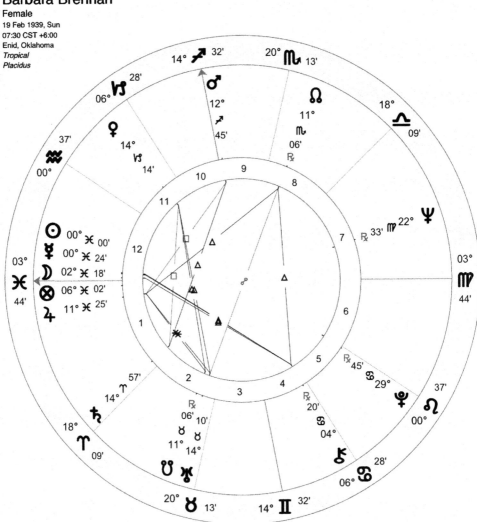

Barbara Brennan
Female
19 Feb 1939, Sun
07:30 CST +6:00
Enid, Oklahoma
Tropical
Placidus

Barbara Brennan: The Sybil
19 February 1939. (07:30) Drummond OK

"It is the one note with which you have drawn up your physical body from your mother the earth. Without the one note, you would not have a body." (p. 288, Light Emerging)[17]

Barbara has Mercury, Sun, Moon, Ascendant and Jupiter in Pisces, which Jupiter rules. She clearly has a massive connection to Spirit and is a conduit for messages and teachings from the Spiritual planes. Her Mars in Jupiter ruled Sagittarius conjunct her Midheaven shows her boldness and energy to spread her message to the wide world, via her career.

"If you follow your deepest longings it will lead you to your deepest pleasure."[18]

As a child, Barbara was able to see the auras of trees, animals and people. She did not say anything as she assumed everyone could see what she saw. Despite (or perhaps because of this) she decided to study physics, taking a BSc and then a Masters in Atmospheric Physics. She worked at NASA measuring the intensity of sunlight reflecting off the earth's surface and the effects of clouds, ice at the Arctic centre and light on the Pacific Ocean.

"The whole universe appears as a dynamic web of inseparable energy patterns … Thus we are not separated parts of a whole. We are a Whole."[19]

In 1971 she left NASA and travelled in a VW van to Mexico with her husband and began to reconnect with spirituality, meditating in the desert. Later, she studied bioenergetics and she began to see auras again and to have visions of clients' past lives. Studying with Eva Pierrakos in New York for nine years, she worked on understanding and integrating her healing and psychic gifts. She meditated for two years on unifying her life with Divine Will, another two on Divine Love then another two on Divine Truth.[20]

"Love is the face and body of the Universe."[21]

In Barbara's book, *Hands of Light, A Guide to Healing Through the Human Energy Field*[22] she claims to receive intuitive information about her clients during sessions, to see patterns in the energy fields of her clients which show there are common roots behind their issues. She describes the seven-layers of human energy field; each layer consists of different frequencies and types of energy which have different functions. Brennan views the chakras as receivers which process universal energy, which the person expresses physically, emotionally and physically. Barbara describes how to heal blockages of the chakras using her hands.[23]

"The gift of healing rests within everyone, it is not a gift given to a few, it is your birth-right as much as mine."[24]

Barbara Brennan encapsulates for me the Sybil side of Themis. She brings Divine messages to heal the physical, emotional and spiritual body of her clients and to give them guidance.

Notes

1. Who learned it from the Melissae (see Melissae/Mercury)
2. Aelian we learn that Apollo had to go to Tempe to be purified for the slaughter of the dragon, and that both the slaughter of the dragon and the purification of the god were represented every eighth year in a solemn festival at Delphi. See *Frazer, on Paus. 2.7.7* (*Paus. vol 3. pp. 53ff.*). The Pythian games at Delphi were instituted in honour of the dead dragon (Ovid and *Hyginus, Fab. 140*; compare *Clement of Alexandria, Protrept. 2, p. 29, ed. Potter*, probably to soothe his natural anger at being slain.
3. http://www.perseus.tufts.edu/hopper/text.jsp?doc=Perseus%3Atext%3A1999.01.01 60%3Abook%3D10%3Achapter%3D5%3Asection%3D6
4. March, 2002, p.376.
5. Morford, 2015, 135.
6. Autumn wasn't recognised as a season in Ancient Greece, Liddell & Scott, 1944, p.802
7. Although here, the three seasons exclude winter…
8. Suggesting the Hellenes took control of the calendar-which originally was a moon/ sun cycle based on women's menstrual and gestational rhythms, and later the wheel of the year see Grave, 2001, p.54
9. http://www.perseus.tufts.edu/hopper/text?doc=Perseus%3Atext%3A1999.01.0129 %3Acard%3D901 accessed 2.8.2020.
10. https://www.inspiringquotes.us/author/5080-chelsea-manning accessed 27.1.2021
11. Letter 22 August 2013. https://talkingpointsmemo.com/news/full-text-bradley-manning-s-letter-to-president-obama-requesting-pardon accessed 27.1.2021.
12. Goodman, Amy. 1.8.2013. *Manning, Snowden and Assange were the ones who took risks to expose crime.* The Guardian newspaper. https://www.theguardian.com/commentisfree/2013/aug/01/manning-snowden-assange-expose-wrongdoing accessed 27.1.2021.
13. https://www.theguardian.com/commentisfree/2015/may/27/anniversary-chelsea-manning-arrest-war-diaries accessed 27.1.2021.
14. Camp, Lee. https://www.mintpressnews.com/lee-camp18-ways-julian-assange-wikileaks-changed-the-world/258790/
15. Letter 22 August 2013. https://talkingpointsmemo.com/news/full-text-bradley-manning-s-letter-to-president-obama-requesting-pardon accessed 27.1.2021.
16. https://www.globalresearch.ca/mairead-maguire-requests-permission-visit-assange accessed 27.1.2021.

17. Brennan, Barbara. *Light Emerging, The Journey of Personal Healing*, Bantam, Berkley, CA.1993. p.288
18. www.Barbarabrennan.com
19. Hands of Light: A Guide to Healing Through the Human Energy Field (ed. Bantam, 2011) in https://libquotes.com/barbara-brennan/quote/lbs3q9b accessed 9.9.2020.
20. Angelo, Jean Marie. *Healing Ourselves with Hands of Light.* The Yoga Journal May–June 1993 p.72–75. https://www.yogajournal.com.
21. https://www.storemypic.com/album/barbara-brennan-quotes.RIN accessed 9.9.2020.
22. Brennan, Barbara. 1987. *Hands of Light: A Guide to Healing through the Human Energy Field*, Bantam, New York.
23. Angelo, Jean Marie. *Healing Ourselves with Hands of Light.* The Yoga Journal May–June 1993 p.72–75. https://www.yogajournal.com.
24. Angelo, Jean Marie. *Healing Ourselves with Hands of Light.* The Yoga Journal May–June 1993 p.73. https://www.yogajournal.com.

Saturn: Rhea

"Rhea ... goddess who holds the throne highest of all." (Pindar, *Nemean Ode* 9:8–9)

Rhea was another Titan (pre-Olympian) goddess. Known as 'Mother of the Gods' her name means flow and ease (ρεω). She was a goddess of the earth and the daughter of Ouranos and Ge/Gaia.

"Afterwards she [Gaia] lay with Heaven [Ouranos] and bore deep-swirling Oceanus, Coeus and Crius and Hyperion and Iapetus, Theia and Rhea, Themis and Mnemosyne and gold-crowned Phoebe and lovely Tethys." (Hesiod, *Theogony*:133)

Rhea was 'married' to Kronos and gave birth to Hestia, Demeter, Hera, Hades, Poseidon and Zeus.

"Rhea was subject in love to Kronos and bore splendid children, Hestia, Demeter, and gold-shod Hera and strong Hades, pitiless in heart, who dwells under the earth, and the loud-crashing Earth-Shaker, and wise Zeus, father of gods and men, by whose thunder the wide earth is shaken." (*Theogony*:453–9)

As we have seen previously, these 'marriages' are a way the father-god appropriated what was once the goddess' domain. Because they were stolen, the thief was ever mindful that they might be stolen from him. Kronos, fearful of a rival who would usurp him, swallowed all his children with the exception of Zeus. Rhea asked her parents for help.

269

"... He [Kronos] kept no blind outlook but watched and swallowed down his children: and unceasing grief seized Rhea ... she besought her own dear parents, Gaia and starry Ouranos, to devise some plan with her that the birth of her dear child [Zeus] might be concealed, and that retribution might overtake great, crafty Kronos." (*Theogony*:470–2)

Interestingly, the new-born Zeus is taken to Krete, which was 'undoubtedly the earliest seat of the worship of Rhea.' Diodorus (v.66) writing in the first century BCE described the site where her temple had once stood, near Knossus.[1]

"... They sent her to Lyktus, to the rich land of Krete, when she was ready to bear great Zeus, the youngest of her children. Gaia took him [Zeus] from Rhea in wide Krete to nourish and to rear. To that place came Gaia carrying him swiftly through the black night to Lyktus first, and then took him in her arms and hid him in a remote cave beneath the secret places of the holy earth on thick-wooded Mount Aegeum." (*Theogony*:479–484)

Rhea then is associated with the cave, specifically a cave in Krete. Oracles were often set in caves as they provide an ideal environment for trance states. It is well established that alteration of consciousness is brought about through sensory deprivation. Following the practices of their Palaeolithic forebears, the Greeks knew that caves provide a fertile environment for shamanic and spiritual experiences. To be in communion with the goddess, it was necessary to shed the physical shell and take the goddess within, to experience *enthusiasmos* (divine possession, ενθυσιασω) or mania (madness, frenzy μανια).[2] One of the easiest ways to do this was by fasting and silent vigil, perhaps ingesting hallucinogenic plants, within the silent, primeval darkness of a deep, deep, cave, accompanied by the hypnotic beat of a frame drum. The rhythmic beat of the frame drum was used for millennia by women priestesses to attain altered states.[3]

"The Titans had their home in the land of Knosos, where even today men point out foundations of the house of Rhea and a cypress grove which has been consecrated to her from ancient times." (Diodorus Siculus, *Library of History*:5.65.1)

There are many Kretan and Mycenaean ring seals showing worship on the mountainsides and divine possession there. (Fig. 45)

Rhea's worship involved ecstatic dance, rhythmic, chants beaten out on a *tympanon*, a wide handheld frame drum, which she is often shown holding. Her priests impersonated her mythical attendants, the *Curetes* and *Dactyls*, with a clashing of bronze shields and cymbals. (Fig. 46)

Graves (2011:30–1) writes that the Orphics said that Nux (night: Νυξ) the black winged goddess of whom even Zeus was afraid, lived in a cave; she represented Night, Order and Justice. In front of the cave, the goddess Rhea sat beating a bronze

Fig. 45 Mountain worship, seal, Minoan, Krete, 1500 BCE.

drum and calling attention to the oracles of the goddess. The drum was sounded to stop the sacred bees (see Mercury Melissae) from swarming in the wrong place and to ward off evil. It is possible that Rhea sitting outside her cave with her instruments suggests she is not prophesying but invoking or scaring off the profane from her sacred space, or alternatively calling the celebrants to the ritual. The drum, dance and chant are ancient methods of inducing altered states, which suggests her cult involved shamanic or ecstatic worship.

Rhea is sometimes associated with Cybele a near eastern goddess whose worship spread through Greece and later, Rome. Some Greeks saw Cybele as their own Rhea, who had deserted her original home on Mount Ida in Krete and fled to Mount Ida in the wilds of Phrygia to escape Kronos.[4]

Cybele's worship involved frenzied devotion and mysticism, her attendants the *Curetes* played wild music on the cymbals and drums. Rhea is often depicted holding a drum with lions by her side. Lions were sacred to Rhea because of her status as Goddess of the earth and the lion was the most powerful of all animals on that earth, and lions were believed to have been abundant in those places where Rhea was worshipped. This aspect of the Homeric hymn to *Mother of the Gods* probably relates to Rhea's worship,

> "Sing, clear voiced muses, daughter of great Zeus, to the mother of all gods and men. She who delights in the drums and tambourines, the piping of flutes and the howling of wolves, the roar of her bright-eyed lions, echoing through the mountains and the wooded forests."[5] *Homeric Hymn to the Mother of the Gods* 14. (Fig. 47)

Fig. 46 Rhea/Cybele and drum, terracotta mould, Olympus, 5thC BCE.

Mystical union with the goddess was realised through dance and music (see Historical Background). It may have been a din[6] or perhaps it was beautiful music, which induced trance and visions. Women traditionally played the frame drum, priestesses in Greece were depicted holding their drums on their grave markers. (Fig. 48)

"The frame drum was the primary tool of transformation that women and Priestesses of the ancient world used to access shamanic states of consciousness, facilitate

Fig. 47 Rhea/Cybele on lion, kylix fragment, 5thC BCE.

community rituals and to help lead community members across spiritual gateways in their indigenous birthing and dying rites."[7]

Shamanic drumming is found all over the world, women and their drums are depicted in statues, pottery and grave goods throughout the ancient world from Mesopotamia to Turkey, Egypt, Greece and India.

"In pre-classical Greece the women initiates called the *maenads* played the frame drum along with the priestesses of Demeter, Artemis, Aphrodite and the Muses. On the island of Crete, the frame drum was used in the rituals of Ariadne, Rhea and Dionysus. The frame drum was one of the main ceremonial instruments used by the Bee Priestesses or Melissae of the ancient Mediterranean world to access states of divination and oracular insight in dedication to the Bee Goddesses."[8]

Fig. 48 Funerary stele of woman and drum, Athens 5thC BCE.

Rhea as a mother goddess, and mother of all Gods and Humans, does not mean her realm was restricted to female fertility. She is Mistress of the Beasts. She is mostly shown seated, with lions flanking her throne. She is responsible for bringing the rivers into being. After giving birth to Zeus, Rhea looked in vain for sweet water to wash herself and the child, but all the water flowed in underground rivers.

> "So spoke the goddess and lifting her great arm she smote the mountain with her staff; and it was rent in two and a mighty flood poured forth, she then washed the body of infant Zeus."

Rhea then gave the child to the eldest Nymph Neda and named the stream after her. (Callimachus, *Hymn 1 to Zeus* 3rd C BCE)

Rhea is the daughter of Ouranos, god of the heavens, when she presented the stone to Kronos, pretending it was her child, he said she should feed it and her milk spurted out into the sky and formed the milky way. (Pseudo-Hyginus *Astronomica* 2.43)

The oak was sacred to Rhea;[9] her name maybe a variant of *Era* (earth), her spirit animal was the mountain lion and her bird the dove. When she saw how libidinous her son Zeus was, she forbade him to marry. Furious, he threatened to rape her; she turned into a fearsome serpent, he turned in a male snake wrapped himself around her and raped his own mother.[10] Again, showing the barbarity of the father-god.

Rhea saves her children from Kronos who swallowed them all, forcing him to regurgitate them and giving him a stone instead of the infant Zeus. It is said this stone was taken to Delphi where it was called the Omphalos or navel stone and was anointed with sacred oils by the priestesses there. This myth makes Rhea complicit in her subjection, but the takeover was brutal and fiercely fought.

Rhea saved the infant Dionysus who Hera had dismembered. He was boiled in a cauldron; the pomegranate sprouted from the earth where drop of his blood fell. Rhea re-assembled Dionysus and purified him for the many murders he committed while in Bacchic frenzy. Rhea afterwards initiated him into the Mysteries[11] and taught him the secret of the ivy, it is five-pointed like the vine, a sign of the goddess. Rhea was patroness of smiths who only worked in gold, silver, copper, lead and tin; when the iron-smelting Dorians invaded with their iron weapons, her worship declined.[12]

Rhea then shows cave, trance, wild animals, drumming, ecstatic dance, the Milky Way, rivers, deception, stones, prophecy, and the fierce power of the mother to protect her offspring. There is a toughness here that is found in the two expressions of Saturn/Rhea; Capricorn, and Aquarius, both women had to fight the patriarchy in order to fulfil their life's purpose.

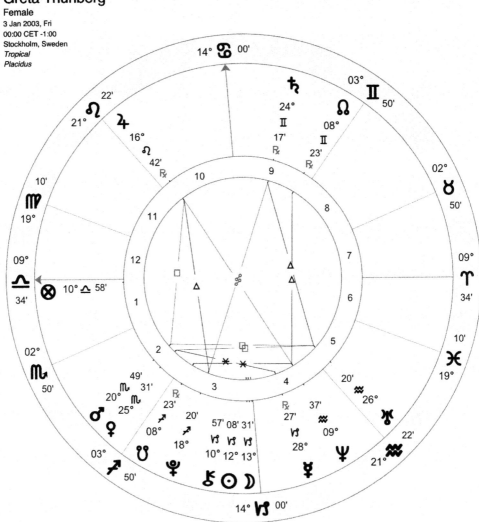

Greta Thunberg: Climate activist, Saving the Earth
3 Jan 2003. (No time) Stockholm Sweden

"My message is that we'll be watching you. This is all wrong. I shouldn't be up here. I should be back in school on the other side of the ocean. Yet you all come to us young people for hope. How dare you. You have stolen my dreams and my childhood with your empty words. Yet I am one of the lucky ones. People are suffering."[13]

Greta is a Swedish political activist working to stop global warming and climate change. She first heard about climate change in 2011 when she was eight and could not understand why so little was being done about it. She became depressed, stopped talking and eating and lost ten kilos in two months. Eventually she was diagnosed with Asperger syndrome, OCD, and selective mutism. She describes her mutism as, "Only speaking when necessary,"[14] and her Asperger's as her 'superpower.'

"I have Asperger's syndrome and that means I'm sometimes a bit different from the norm. And—given the right circumstances—being different is a superpower."[15]

Although we do not have her time of birth, she has a serious Sun, Moon, Mercury conjunction in Capricorn. Her Mercury is retrograde which may account for her selective mutism. Mercury in Capricorn gives great intelligence but also melancholy, exacerbated by the lights (Sun and Moon) in Capricorn also. But Capricorn has a mission, she needs to be heard and is outraged at the illogicality and ignorance of world leaders.

Greta struggled with depression for four years before she began her school strike. Her parents did not support her action, but agreed to let her go. Her father said, "We respect that she wants to make a stand. She can either sit at home and be really unhappy, or protest and be happy."[16] She persuaded her opera singer mother to stop flying, saying she was stealing her future and in effect ending her career. But Greta said this gave her hope that people could change.[17]

In August 2018, Greta decided to not attend school until the general election on 9 September in response to the heat wave and wildfires in the hottest summer for 260 years. News of her protest spread quickly on social media,[18] a representative of the Finish bank Nordea quoted one of her tweets to their 200,000 followers, and Greta received international coverage in less than a week.

In October 2018 she took part in protests all over Europe making high-profile speeches; in December 2018 over 20,000 students struck in 270 cities. She became a prominent figure for starting the first school strike for climate outside the Swedish parliament building. In November 2018, she spoke at TEDx Stockholm, and in December 2018 she addressed the United Nations Climate Change Conference after which there were student strikes all over the world, and in 2019 there were 'Fridays for a Future' marches, multiple coordinated protests involving over a million students each.[19]

"We are striking because we have done our homework, and they have not." Climate protest in Hamburg, Germany, 1 March 2019.[20]

Her Venus and Mars in Scorpio show her need to fight for her beliefs.

At the UN Climate Action Summit in her powerful speech, she said, "Our house is on Fire," and, "How dare you destroy my future."[21] "I want you to act as if the house is on fire because it is."[22]

The 'Greta effect'[23] has politicised a generation of young people and have galvanised support for Climate Change Action.

"The eyes of all future generations are upon you. And if you choose to fail us, I say—we will never forgive you." UN Climate Summit, New York, 23 September 2019.[24]

In the European elections, in May 2019 as Green parties recorded their best ever result boosting their MEP seat numbers from fifty to seventy-two.[25] Many of the gains came from northern European countries where young people have taken to the streets inspired by Thunberg. The *New Scientist* described 2019 as, "The Year the world woke up to climate change."[26] Greta is credited with increasing *'flying shame'*[27] which encourages people not to take flights and cause further damage to the environment.

"Change is coming, whether you like it or not."[28]

Ironically, 2020–1 has been the year that life has been locked down due to the Coronavirus. The drop in climate emissions and pollution perhaps will change our behaviour as there is a close link between pollution and the virus.[29,30]

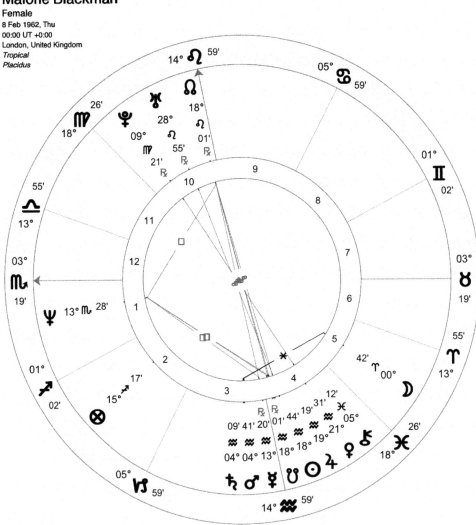

Malorie Blackman

Female
8 Feb 1962, Thu
00:00 UT +0:00
London, United Kingdom
Tropical
Placidus

Malorie Blackman OBE: Revolutionary creative
Aquarius—turning the tables on prejudice
8 February 1962 (No time) London

"All you need is an imagination, some ideas and some determination and you too,
can write stories."[31]

Malorie Blackman was Children's Laureate from 2013 to 2015. She writes fiction and
television drama for children and young adults and has used science fiction to explore
social and ethical issues, especially race. Her best known works are the *Noughts and
Crosses* series of books which explore racial prejudice in a fictional dystopia where
people of colour have the power and privilege and the white folks are discriminated
against. Concerning racism she said,

"I think it's very much a thing of the present. It's one of those things people have
to be ever vigilant about otherwise things will get worse. I think part of the way of
doing that is to have more culturally and ethnically diverse books and encourage
children to read as widely as possible. If children learn about different cultures, different religions and different races, you won't get the ignorance that leads to fear."[32]

In a 2007 interview for the BBC's *Blast* website, Blackman explained the title of the
series, *Noughts & Crosses* is,[33]

"One of those games that nobody ever plays after childhood, because nobody ever
wins it. At the risk of sounding 'arty', I wanted to say racism is a game no one is
ever going to win, so why bother playing it? And it's not even a game."[34]

Her stellium in Aquarius, Saturn, Mars, Mercury, Sun, Jupiter and Venus with a Moon
either in Pisces or Aries, shows someone with great intelligence (Saturn in his own
sign) with a huge drive to better her world through language (Mercury) new media
(Aquarius) pulling on her own experiences (Sun) with energy (Mars) a great deal of
good fortune (Jupiter conjunct the Sun) and humour (Mercury) and kindness (Venus).

Blackman was previously known as a Black author who didn't explore issues
around race; she published prize winning books including, *Pig-Heart Boy* and *Hacker*
where the character's ethnicity was not central to the plot.

"I wanted to show black children just getting on with their lives, having
adventures, and solving their dilemmas, like the characters in all the books I read
as a child."[35]

After eleven successful children's novels she felt the time was right to explore racism,
and in true Aquarian style she turned racism on its head. In the *Noughts & Crosses*

trilogy, the whites are the underclass who are seen as stupid and criminal and are called 'white bastards'. While the blacks are patronising, racist, oppressive and inhumane.

> "What I want to show was that once you start hating people for being different, that hate never stops."[36]

Her books have a deft, light touch dealing with this painful subject, turning everything upside down (Aquarius) the white people become the despised, low status people. I would guess there was some water in her chart (maybe the Moon or the Ascendant) as she writes with compassion and sensitivity.

Blackman used her own experience of injustice and prejudice. A Grammar school pupil, Malorie wanted to study English at Goldsmiths, but was told to do a business course at a polytechnic, a common experience among black women she later discovered. As well as little everyday aggressions which highlighted her 'difference' like needing a plaster and seeing the colour was designed to be inconspicuous on white people's skin.[37]

Her publisher expected to put Malorie in a 'black writers' box, but radically (Aquarius) she confounded their expectations,

> "A couple of editors did say, we want something for our multicultural list, and I'd think, 'Well, you're not getting one from me.'"[38]

Malorie said that the books were set in a dystopia which was an amalgam of Apartheid South Africa, the American Deep South and Northern Ireland during the troubles,[39]

> "The best science fiction is always about the present. Star Trek was a direct attack on McCarthyism."[40]

Publication of the *Noughts & Crosses* series was delayed in the USA because the main protagonist becomes a terrorist. Due to 9/11 there was resistance to having a children's book which described what might drive someone to become a terrorist.[41] Although Malorie's viewpoint was the opposite,

> "Callum is a Nought, he is automatically expected to go so far and no further. I wanted to talk about what other avenues are open to people if you start slamming doors on them. In Callum's case, he joins a liberation militia and becomes a terrorist."[42]

The books were eventually published in the USA in 2005. The irony is that in 2020 the FBI claimed the most severe terrorist threats now came from white supremacist groups.[43]

"Being an optimist I do believe that it is in the hands of the future generation to make things better, so let's hope it happens."[44]

Notes

1. https://www.theoi.com/Titan/TitanisRhea.html accessed 28.12.2020.
2. See Ustinova, Yulia. *Cave Experiences and Ancient Greek Oracles* in Time and Mind: The Journal of Archaeology, Consciousness and Culture. Vol.2, Issue 3. November 2009, p.266.
3. See Redmond, 2018, *When Drummers were Women*, for a history of women and the drum.
4. Jane Ellen Harrison, "Pandora's Box" *The Journal of Hellenic Studies* 20 (1900): 99–114.
5. http://www.perseus.tufts.edu/hopper/morph?l=au%29lw%3Dn&la=greek&can=au%29lw%3Dn0&prior=bro/mos&d=Perseus:text:1999.01.0137:hymn=14&i=1
6. In the myth of Zeus, he is protected from his murderous father, Cronus by the Curetes banging drums to hide his baby cries. Morford 2015:77. The suggestion is it was a discordant noise, but there is no reason to suppose this, it may have been beautiful music, for as the hymn relates, she delighted in it, which perhaps she would not have done if it was a racket.
7. https://www.sacreddrumming.com/drumming-history accessed 30.12.2020.
8. https://www.sacreddrumming.com/drumming-history accessed 30.12.2020.
9. Graves, 2011, p.39.
10. Graves, 2011, p.53.
11. Graves, pp.103–5.
12. Graves, p.186.
13. UN Summit in New York 2019. https://www.bbc.co.uk/newsround/49812183 accessed 7.8.2020.
14. *Thunberg, Greta* (24 November 2018). School strike for climate—save the world by changing the rules. *TEDx Stockholm. Event occurs at 1:46. via* YouTube. *'I was diagnosed with Asperger's syndrome, OCD, and selective mutism. That basically means I only speak when I think it's necessary. Now is one of those moments … I think that in many ways, we autistic are the normal ones, and the rest of the people are pretty strange, especially when it comes to the sustainability crisis, where everyone keeps saying that climate change is an existential threat and the most important issue of all and yet they just carry on like before.'* https://www.google.com/search?client=firefox-b-d&q=you+tube+greta+thunberg+speech+at+stockholm+tedx accessed 6.8.2020.
15. Instagram 1.8.2019. https://www.bbc.co.uk/newsround/49812183 accessed 7.8.2020.
16. https://www.theguardian.com/science/2018/sep/01/swedish-15-year-old-cutting-class-to-fight-the-climate-crisis accessed 6.8.2020.
17. *Crouch, David* (1 September 2018). *"The Swedish 15-year-old who's cutting class to fight the climate crisis". The Guardian.* https://www.theguardian.com/science/2018/sep/01/swedish-15-year-old-cutting-class-to-fight-the-climate-crisis accessed 6.8.2020.
18. Tweet, Greta Thunberg, Aug. 24. 2008. Reported in https://medium.com/@wedonthavetime/greta-thunberg-sweden-is-not-a-role-model-6ce96d6b5f8b accessed 6.8.2020.
19. *Haynes, Suyin* (24 May 2019). *"Students From 1,600 Cities Just Walked Out of School to Protest Climate Change. It Could Be Greta Thunberg's Biggest Strike Yet". Time. Archived from the original on 23 July 2019.*

20. Climate protest in Hamburg, Germany, 1 March 2019. https://www.bbc.co.uk/newsround/49812183 accessed 7.8.2020.

21. Transcript of her speech, https://www.npr.org/2019/09/23/763452863/transcript-greta-thunbergs-speech-at-the-u-n-climate-action-summit?t=1596711306328 accessed 6.8.2020.

22. World Economic Forum, Davos, 24 January 2019. https://www.bbc.co.uk/newsround/49812183 accessed 7.8.2020.

23. *Nevett, Joshua* (3 May 2019). *"The Greta effect? Meet the schoolgirl climate warriors"*. BBC *News*. https://www.bbc.co.uk/news/world-48114220 accessed 6.8.2020.

24. UN Climate Summit, New York, 23 September 2019. https://www.bbc.co.uk/newsround/49812183 accessed 6.7.2020.

25. *Henley, Jon* (27 May 2019). *"Five things we have learned from election results across Europe".* *The Guardian.* https://www.theguardian.com/politics/2019/may/27/five-things-we-have-learned-from-the-election-results-across-europe accessed 6.8.2020.

26. *Vaughan, Adam* (18 December 2019). *"The Year the World Woke up to Climate Change".* *New Scientist.* 244 (3261/62). pp.20–21 accessed 6.8.2020.

27. *Henley, Jon* (4 June 2019). *"#stayontheground: Swedes turn to trains amid climate 'flight shame'".* *The Guardian.* https://www.theguardian.com/world/2019/jun/04/stay-ontheground-swedes-turn-to-trains-amid-climate-flight-shame accessed 6.8.2020.

28. https://earth.org/greta-thunberg-quotes-speeches-to-inspire-climate-action/

29. Hernandez, Marco. *This is the effect the corona virus has had on air pollution all over the world.* The World Economic Forum, April 21st. 2020. https://www.weforum.org/agenda/2020/04/coronavirus-covid19-air-pollution-enviroment-nature-lockdown accessed 6.8.2020.

30. Brandon, Simon. *The Link between air pollution and Covid-19 deaths.* 29th April, 2020. World Economic Forum. https://www.weforum.org/agenda/2020/04/link-between-air-pollution-covid-19-deaths-coronavirus-pandemic/ accessed 6.8.2020.

31. http://www.bbc.co.uk/newsbeat/article/31541605/why-books-matter-by-malorie-blackman-marcus-sedgwick-and-holly-smale

32. https://web.archive.org/web/20081009021717/http://www.bbc.co.uk/blast/writing/people/malorie_blackman.shtml accessed 21.9.2020.

33. *Noughts & Crosses*, Doubleday, London, 2001.

34. http://www.bbc.co.uk/blast/writing/people/malorie_blackman.shtml accessed 21.9.2020.

35. Craig, Amanda. January 2004, *Malorie Blackman, the world in photographic negative.* The Times. https://web.archive.org/web/20061202031831/http://www.amandacraig.com/pages/journalism/interviews/malorie_blackman.htm accessed 21.9.2020.

36. Craig, Amanda. January 2004, *Malorie Blackman, the world in photographic negative.* The Times. https://web.archive.org/web/20061202031831/http://www.amandacraig.com/pages/journalism/interviews/malorie_blackman.htm accessed 21.9.2020.

37. Craig, Amanda. January 2004, *Malorie Blackman, the world in photographic negative.* The Times. https://web.archive.org/web/20061202031831/http://www.amandacraig.com/pages/journalism/interviews/malorie_blackman.htm accessed 21.9.2020.

38. Craig, Amanda. January 2004, *Malorie Blackman, the world in photographic negative.* The Times. https://web.archive.org/web/20061202031831/http://www.amandacraig.com/pages/journalism/interviews/malorie_blackman.htm accessed 21.9.2020.

39. https://web.archive.org/web/20081009021717/http://www.bbc.co.uk/blast/writing/people/malorie_blackman.shtml accessed 21.9.2020.

40. Craig, Amanda. January 2004, *Malorie Blackman, the world in photographic negative.* The Times. https://web.archive.org/web/20061202031831/http://www.amandacraig.com/pages/journalism/interviews/malorie_blackman.htm accessed 21.9.2020.

41. Craig, Amanda. January 2004, *Malorie Blackman, the world in photographic negative.* The Times. https://web.archive.org/web/20061202031831/http://www.amandacraig.com/pages/journalism/interviews/malorie_blackman.htm accessed 21.9.2020.

42. https://web.archive.org/web/20081009021717/http://www.bbc.co.uk/blast/writing/people/malorie_blackman.shtml accessed 21.9.2020.

43. https://www.fbi.gov/news/testimony/worldwide-threats-to-the-homeland-091720 accessed 29.12.2020.

44. https://web.archive.org/web/20081009021717/http://www.bbc.co.uk/blast/writing/people/malorie_blackman.shtml accessed 21.9.2020.

Areas of expression—the houses

See Appendix 1 for an alphabetical list of all the charts discussed previously.
Just as there are twelve signs of the zodiac, there are twelve houses of the horoscope. Is this a coincidence? No. Is there a connection? Yes. The houses of the horoscope mirror the meaning of the twelve signs in that they show the area of life the planets and signs are expressed through, be that family, money, health, career or education etc.

Remember the planets are the fundamental energies, and the signs how they are expressed; compare a Mars in Aries to a Mars in Pisces for example. The sphere in which Mars in Aries or Mars in Pisces is expressed is the house.

First house ascendant

I chose many of the charts because they have planets on the Ascendant which clearly demonstrates the nature of both the planet and the sign. The Ascendant is the person other people meet as you come into a room. How you look, how you interact with people. It is your public persona and also how you greet the world, and which is often how the world responds to you. It is not the 'real you' that is expressed via the Sun sign, your life's journey or essential nature. These can be quite different. Eventually we will all have to work through the lessons that our Sun signs present us with. The Ascendant also shows your health, vitality and general take on life.

In Beyonce's chart, even though she is a sun-Virgo, her sun is making no aspects to other planets. But she does have a stellium in Libra in her first and twelfth house, with Venus in Libra directly on her Ascendant. She will be seen and will experience the world

287

through that stunning Aphrodite Urania. She is beautiful, very feminine, dressed in extravagant and yet feminine clothing. She has that glow of glamour. Because Pluto is conjunct her Venus there is also something confronting and also absent; she is the image, the stunning image, but there is also nothing there, smoke and mirrors. It is in relation to the other that this goddess exists; with her fantastical and gorgeous stage sets, in her dance routines, through her elaborate costumes, the fantasy is created. It is ground-breaking, seductive and also confrontational. But as Beyonce has said herself, this is not who she is, it is a mask. (See Aphrodite Uranus, Venus)

Sharon Gannon has her Sun, Moon and Uranus conjunct her Ascendant, and Mercury in the first house. When the Sun and Moon are conjunct the Ascendant, the whole life path of the person is an expression of that sign. In Sharon's case, it is Cancer and it shows her compassion, kindness and speaking out on behalf of animals, protecting them. Her Veganism is compassion in action. Jivamukti yoga is like a big family, with annual meet-ups and a close connecting web (Cancer). Sharon's cooking and café show how she expresses her love, and also how she finds safety and community with her tribe.

Georgia O'Keeffe had Jupiter, Sun, Moon and Mercury conjunct her Ascendant in Scorpio. Her public persona was the same as her feeling life (Moon) and her true self (Sun). Scorpio is very secretive, she would have appeared as an enigma; mysterious, powerful, sexual and intense.

Second house

The second house relates to Taurus and is concerned with the material world. Money, possessions, values. It shows your relationship with that most emotionally charged of things—money, and what you value.

Isadora Duncan has a Stellium in the second house, Pluto in Taurus and Sun, Mercury and Venus in Gemini. Although she used her dance (Venus) to make money and felt that dancing for money was vulgar (second house), she argued against capitalism and the need to earn money. Isadora ran not for profit schools and spoke out on the failure of capitalism to support art and artists. She taught dance to earn a living (Gemini) and was rather notorious for living off her friends (Gemini); she also struggled financially (Pluto in Taurus).

Dolly Parton has Jupiter in Libra in the second house, showing her material abundance (Jupiter) which comes from the arts (Libra). Maya Angelou has the same Jupiter in Libra in the second house, and she also earned well (Jupiter) from her writing and poetry (Libra).

Jacqueline Onassis has Saturn in Sagittarius in the second house. Her father (Saturn ruling her fourth house) was a bon viveur (Sagittarius) who dissipated the family fortune (Saturn) which caused hardship. Her mother remarried into great wealth, but Saturn would have given Jacqueline a sense of shame and fear around money. It would also have ensured that, due to these early lessons, she arranged her life so she would not suffer in the same way again (she married into wealth twice).

Nina Simone had Uranus in Aries in the second house. She may well have been rash (Uranus Aries) with money and, although she earned a lot, she was never really financially secure (Uranus).

Third house

The third house corresponds to Gemini and traditionally relates to siblings, short journeys, communication such as letters and emails, and local community and neighbours.

Sybil Leek has Mercury, and Venus conjunct Uranus in Aquarius in the third house. Sybil was initiated into a local community of witches, and was also very active on television (Uranus).

Germaine Greer has Saturn in Aries in the third house. Her siblings may have felt like a burden to her (Saturn) and a restriction which she fought against (Aries) and, when she left Australia, they felt she abandoned them (Saturn).

Fourth house

Represents Cancer, our roots, our family or tribe, our home, one parent; it may be the father or the mother.

Germaine Greer has Moon conjunct Uranus in Taurus in the fourth house. She split (Uranus) from her home and family (Fourth house) to live in Britain. Her radicality (Uranus) is demonstrated by her purchase of land (Taurus) in the Australian rainforest to protect it (Taurus) for posterity.

Sybil Leek has Sun, Mars conjunct and Moon in Pisces in the fourth house. A lot of her early work was re-connecting with her ancestors and finding her people (Fourth house). Her psychic work (Pisces) is based on that shared heritage and gave Sybil her life's work (Sun).

Mary Shelley has her Sun, Uranus and Mars in her fourth house in Virgo suggesting she spent her life wondering where her home was (Sun). Uranus was the ruler of her midheaven (Aquarius) which may represent her mother dying shortly after she was born, and the trauma this caused later in life. Her Sun Uranus can also be seen to represent replacing or reanimating the mother figure by trying to engender new life (Sun) via electricity (Uranus) in her book *Frankenstein*.

Fifth house

Corresponds with Leo and so it rules children, creativity, lovers, acting and performing, and gambling.

Dolly Parton, has Sun, Venus and Mercury in the fifth house in hardworking and ambitious Capricorn. Her excellent business skills (keeping the rights to all her songs) have made her very wealthy (Capricorn loves the power and prestige money brings). She is creative and loves to perform, and the glitz and glamour of a superstar (Fifth house) while having the sober, farsighted business skills of a Capricorn. She has no children of her own but has raised her younger siblings and has several projects to support the well-being and future prosperity (Capricorn) of children with her Dolly's Book Club which sends out books to disadvantaged children to encourage literacy and hence later prosperity (Capricorn). Venus and Mercury in Capricorn in her fifth house show her creative success as a singer (Venus) and composer (Mercury), and also her longevity as a performer (Capricorn is always in for the long haul and often succeeds because these signs never give up).

Mary Wollstonecraft has Jupiter in the fifth house which is in a close square to Mars in Aries in the ninth house. This may show foreign lovers (Mars in the ninth) and Jupiter in the (fifth of lovers). Jupiter in her chart also rules the eighth house of death, which may show her death after childbirth (Fifth house).

Josephine Baker has Uranus (the radical) in her fifth house opposite a gentle, romantic Venus and Neptune in Cancer suggesting her lovers would be unusual (she was openly bi-sexual), and that her creativity was also radical and confronting. She experimented with radical ways to bring up children (Uranus in the Fifth) and had an unusual relationship with her children (Uranus).

Sixth house

Represents sickness, routine, work rather than career, meditation and yoga and other habitual disciplines, ritual magic and pets. The sixth is a hardworking house; people with several planets in the sixth work hard to develop skills, and work with repetition and schedules.

Valerie Solanas has an anxious Neptune in her sixth house in Virgo opposite a fearful, paranoid Saturn in Pisces, which may account for her later mental illness.

Seventh house

Libra's house represents our partners, romantic or otherwise, and open enemies (people who we know are our enemies).

Angela Merkel has a Stellium in the seventh house in Cancer, Sun, Uranus, Jupiter and Mercury. Other people are the way she finds her identity (Sun) and her caring nature (Cancer) is how others relate to her (the Mother). It shows how she takes great care to include the opinions of others (Mercury ruling the seventh house) before she acts. People expand her world (Jupiter) and also radicalise or transform (Uranus) her natural conservative nature (Cancer). Her career is not for self-aggrandisement or power but to care for her people (Cancer). This impulse to care has propelled her naturally shy and retiring nature (Cancer) into the world of others (seventh house). She dispatches her enemies by playing the long game and then going for the kill (Uranus) and then retreating and not crowing or boasting (Cancer).

Interestingly, AOC also has the same exalted Jupiter in Cancer in the seventh house and she does come over as caring (raising funds for the Texas snowstorm in 2021); she has a gentle, dignified and very feminine nature, which is deceptively soft (such as calling out abusive behaviour) but, like Angela, deadly to those who underestimate her. Her motivation again is to care for other people (Jupiter in the seventh). Jupiter rules her Ascendant (Sagittarius) so her search for justice (Jupiter/Sagittarius) is how she operates in the world and how people see her (Ascendant).

Eighth house

Scorpio's house of secrets, sex, death, other people's money-inheritance and debt, psychotherapy, the unconscious.

Maya Angelou has four planets in the eighth house; Mercury and Venus in Pisces and Uranus and the Sun in Aries. Death filled her life, from that of her friend MLK (on her birthday), Malcom X, and the man who raped her (Venus in the eighth) who was killed (eighth house) and which caused her muteness (Mercury in Pisces). Death and its aftermath marked her; she began writing after the death of MLK, perhaps using her creativity (Venus in Pisces) as a way of trying to make some sense of the bloodshed. With her writing she found her voice (Mercury) and her life's work (Sun, and Sun ruler of her Ascendant).

Ninth house

Sagittarius' house rules higher education, astrology, long distance travel, the law, publishing, philosophy, spirituality.

Mary Wollstonecraft had three planets in the ninth house; Mars in Aries and Sun and Moon in Taurus. She wrote ground-breaking books (Mars in Aries, ninth house publishing), and through her publishing she found emotional security (Moon Taurus), and her path in life (Sun). Her writing was fiery and innovative (Mars in Aries) she wrote on philosophical subjects and travel journals (ninth house).

Starhawk has Mars and Mercury in Gemini in the ninth house. She has written several books (Mercury) on women's spirituality (ninth house).

Jacqueline Kennedy-Onassis had her Sun and Mercury conjunct in the ninth house. In later life she embraced her true nature in publishing (ninth house). She expressed her Sun, Mercury overseas with Onassis, by being his queen (Leo).

Sybil Leek has Saturn and Neptune in her ninth house; she achieved fame on television (Neptune in Leo) in the United States (ninth house). Isadora Duncan (Jupiter in Capricorn) was famous and found her career overseas, embodying a new vision of dance (ninth house). Sharron Gannon (Jupiter in Aries) found her spirituality (yoga) overseas (ninth house).

Tenth house

Capricorn's house rules career, one parent, professional standing, lotteries, the government, and all public institutions. Many of the people I have written about are famous, so it is no surprise that they often have planets in the tenth house of renown.

Alexandria Ocasio-Cortez has three planets in the tenth house in articulate, combative and charming Libra. Mercury makes her intelligent, logical and finding delight in taking people down verbally, while her Sun, Mars conjunction shows a real fighter in the world of politics and social justice. If she hadn't been a lawmaker, she would have made an excellent lawyer.

Annie Oakley has Mercury and the Sun conjunct the midheaven and Saturn in the tenth house all in fiery, creative, dramatic Leo. She was a born performer and adored being centre stage, so much so that, when a woman sharp-shooter appeared to challenge her status, she withdrew rather than risk tarnishing her reputation.

Ella Fitzgerald has a lucky, rich Jupiter conjunct her Midheaven which show how her singing (Venus), with hard work (Taurus), and her optimistic and creative manner (Jupiter), allowed her to embody her Taurus Sun sign by becoming famous (tenth house), and to travel the world (Jupiter). Taurus rules the throat and singers; Ella was born to sing (and dance, her first love). Her Leo Ascendant would have made her a natural performer (or perhaps allowed her to hide behind the fire), owning the stage with glamour and power.

Eleventh house

The eleventh house rules groups and large organisations, co-operative endeavours, hopes and wishes, large friendship groups; it is Aquarius' house.

Margaret Mead has three planets in Sagittarius in the eleventh house, Mercury, Uranus and the Sun. Her research overseas (Sagittarius) resulted in writing books (Mercury) on how to socialise young people, and how traditional societies educated their youth to become responsible adults. It was radical at the time (Uranus) and caused a great deal of anger from traditionalist quarters and approval from feminist and liberal ones (opposing Pluto ruler of the tenth house of the establishment). Her works were used in theories of childrearing (Dr Spock) and to support the Womens Liberation Movement in the 1970s. Her Mars, Jupiter and Saturn conjunct her Capricorn Ascendant gave her the ambition (Mars, Jupiter) and gravitas (Saturn) to approach her task scientifically (Saturn) and to gain respect (Capricorn) and enduring fame (Jupiter Capricorn).

Dolly Parton has three planets in the eleventh house; Mars conjunct Saturn in Cancer and Pluto in Leo. Renowned for her charity work (eleventh house), one of her schemes was to get high school students in a deprived area to pair up. Dolly promised them each $500 dollars if they both graduated. By working together the pupils encouraged each other (Mars in Cancer), and a financial incentive (Saturn) is just the incentive the teenagers needed to persist and study (Saturn), and to succeed (Mars). Studies have shown how graduating from High School is the one factor which predicts success in later life (Saturn), and of course, an educated community benefits the whole community by raising the standards of everyone (eleventh house).

Twelfth house

The twelfth house is self-undoing, secrets, retreats, hidden enemies, karma. Often people with many planets in the twelfth have a karmic life which seems predestined and larger than their personality.

Germaine Greer has Sun and Mercury in the twelfth house. The Mercury in Capricorn shows her intelligence and academic work, and her writing life in solitude. Her Aquarius Sun suggests the same need for retreat to organise her radical thoughts. Her books tapped into a massive (as yet) unconscious yearning (twelfth house) for change for women, and she became the voice for her generation of women as they negotiated the various stages of a woman's life.

Dolly Parton has an un-aspected Moon in Virgo in the twelfth house which may suggest her emotional life (Moon) is kept well hidden. Moon in Virgo is nervous and can be critical of both self and others.

Nina Simone also had her Moon in the twelfth, (so perhaps a public persona needs this retreat to handle massive fame). The Moon was in lonely Capricorn, she would have needed solitude, but was also the tremendously powerful voice of the Black resistance movement; again like Germaine, the time was ripe for change and rebellion. Her Capricorn Moon suggests she may secretly (twelfth house) have wished to be accepted by the status quo (Capricorn). Her Moon was opposite her Pluto in Cancer in the sixth, suggesting her solitude and critical nature (Capricorn) may have impacted on her health and breakdowns (Pluto).

Aspects

In a horoscope, there are the planets in the Signs and Houses, but we also need to consider how the planets themselves interact within the chart. These connections are called Aspects.

Conjunction 0–9 degrees

The most obvious is when planets are grouped together; one planet next to another (or one of the angles) is called a conjunction, while more than three planets together are called a stellium. Clearly a stellium shows that the planets, signs and houses in this particular part of the horoscope are powerful and the focus for the life of the individual.

Malorie Blackman has a stellium in brilliant, radical, futuristic Aquarius, Mars, Saturn, Mercury, Sun, Jupiter and Venus. It is hard to imagine another life she could have had, which didn't involve writing, radical ideas, the collective, and fairness. Her books invent a world where the whites are treated as the blacks are today; a brilliant, unsentimental and radical take on black experience.

The nature of the Stellium depends on the nature of the planets. If the Sun or Moon is surrounded by difficult planets (infortunes or malefics[1]) they can temper or destroy the beneficial nature of the other planets.

Hannah Cockroft has Sun, Moon, Mercury and Venus in Leo, which shows her delight in being centre stage (Leo), her need to be the very best (Leo), her courage in overcoming adversity (Sun), and her glamourous appearance (Venus in Leo). Mercury in Leo makes the ideal performer and media star.

Lorena Bobbit's stellium in Scorpio, Sun, Mercury, Jupiter, Venus, Moon and Neptune show her life is about re-birth from her dark, violent past, and using her wisdom obtained from her ordeals to lift up others, while her Mars, Uranus conjunction in Taurus shows castration.

Chelsea Manning's chart shows two powerful examples of the lights (the Sun and Moon) besieged by malefics. Her strong, fiery Sagittarius Sun is part of a stellium of Sun-Mercury-Saturn-Uranus in Sagittarius, the need for the truth (Sun Sagittarius) is spoken (Mercury) in powerful (Saturn) and disruptive (Uranus) ways, using technology (Uranus) and spying (Mercury). The Stellium shows her speaking truth to power; Saturn rules the government. While her Moon-Mars-Pluto conjunction in Scorpio tells us secrets (Scorpio), they will be revealed in a powerful (Mars-Pluto) and explosive way—both her personal secrets (her gender identity) and State secrets about deaths (Pluto). Besieged as they are, the powerful Sun Sagittarius and Mars Pluto in Scorpio save her; she survives and perhaps flourishes under pressure and is lucky (Sagittarius). Although we do not have a birth time for Chelsea, so we cannot calculate the houses, her chart is so outstanding the aspects speak for themselves.

Georgia O'Keeffe has a Stellium in Scorpio conjunct her Ascendant, Jupiter, Sun, Moon and Mercury. This shows her whole life (Sun, Moon and Ascendant) are about expressing and embodying Scorpionic energies, or the life lesson of Scorpio, through her chosen means of communication (Mercury) which is closely opposite her artistic and hardworking Neptune in Taurus.

The orb for conjunctions is about 9° they are the more powerful the closer they are. Where you have a Stellium the orb counts for the planets next to each other, not all the planets.

Opposition 180 degrees

Oppositions are hard aspects because they involve signs of opposite natures: Aries-Libra (fire and air), Taurus-Scorpio (earth and water). There will be a pull in two directions in the chart, which can be harmonised or can create a locus of conflict and difficulty. People may at different times express one side of the opposition and then flip to embrace the opposite pole, or they can express one pole and then project the other side onto a partner or associate. As with all astrology, it depends on the level of awareness of the individual.

Where there are two oppositions, this major aspect is called the Grand Cross and, depending on the mode of the planets involved, it is called Cardinal (Aries, Cancer, Libra, Capricorn), Fixed (Taurus, Leo, Scorpio and Aquarius), or Mutable (Gemini, Virgo, Sagittarius, Pisces.). The Grand Cross is commonly seen with people who work at a collective level. The stress of the cross often propels the natives to work through the four arms of the cross to transmute or burn off Karma from previous lives.

Alexandria Ocasio Cortez has a Cardinal Grand Cross involving a cluster of planets on her Midheaven of career, Mercury, Mars, Sun, in cool, analytic and articulate Libra, opposite a trailblazing, feisty Moon in Aries, square an exalted, compassionate Jupiter in Cancer (promoting the needs of the people) in the 7th house of open enemies and friends, opposite an equally powerful Saturn, Uranus, Neptune in Capricorn, the sign of government in the first house. Her Saturn return (see Transits) catapulted her into public life, making her the youngest woman ever to serve in the US Congress. The area of expression, the houses, shows how she uses the planetary energies, and how they work together as a whole.

Isadora Duncan had a Fixed Grand Cross, deep Moon in Scorpio opposite Pluto in Taurus, square innovative Mars in Aquarius and radical and eccentric Uranus in Leo. The Moon and Pluto are in mutual reception (in each other's signs of exaltation and rulerships respectively). Uranus rules Aquarius and Mars has dignity in Leo. A fixed Grand Cross is harder to negotiate as fixed signs tend to dig their heels in and resist change. I feel her chart reflects the tragedies in her life, her issues with money and her need to shine and be recognised for her ground-breaking creativity.

Squares 90 degrees

Squares are two planets 90 degrees apart. A square is considered an aspect of stress. Maya Angelou had her sensitive, imaginative and gentle Mercury and Venus in Pisces square cruel, harsh Saturn in Sagittarius. This could point to her refusing to speak after she was raped (Mercury is said to be mute in Pisces); her fine sensitivity was over-whelmed and silenced, her mind (Mercury) retreated into her inner world (Pisces). (See also Houses and Transits).

T square: two squares and an opposition

Maya Angelou has a T square in cardinal signs, Sun Jupiter in Aries, opposite Moon in Libra; both are square Pluto in Cancer. Pluto squaring the lights (Sun and Moon) in the second and eighth houses respectively, shows violence (Pluto-classically rape) affect-ing the child (Moon) and her identity (Sun). Like Persephone in Hades, Pluto leads us to dark, powerless places in our psyche. Ultimately, though it can transform. Angelou refused to speak for the next five years. During this period of silence, she developed her extraordinary memory, her love for books and literature, and her ability to listen and observe the world around her.[2] In other words, Angelou found her true nature, retreating from this awful trauma and rebuilding her world from the inside out. Notice the Sun is also the Almuten of the chart. (See also Transits and Houses)

Hannah Cockroft has a Fixed T Square. All her Leo planets (Sun, Moon, Mercury, Venus) are square to Pluto in Scorpio and opposite Saturn in Aquarius which shows the physical restrictions (Saturn) which she needed to overcome to express all that brilliant Leo energy. Pluto represents the devastation which occurred at birth.

Although squares and oppositions are 'difficult' aspects they can make the native struggle through great obstacles, which brings its great rewards.

Trine 120 degrees

Trines are characterised as easy aspects, as the planets involved are in the same element; for example, Gemini, Libra and Aquarius make a trine in air. There are ordinary trines where two planets are involved, and Grand Trines where all three signs of the element are involved. Easy aspects mean the energy flows without interruption and the energies of these planets is easy to use and harmonious. Trines can make us lazy as the planets seem to work effortlessly, but they do also offer the opportunity for easy expression of these planetary forces.

Nina Simone had a hardworking and sometimes lonely Moon in Capricorn trine an equally detail oriented and skilful Jupiter in Virgo, which gave her the ambition, dedication and aptitude to surmount the obstacles which were in her way as a black woman classical musician. This would have helped to alleviate some of the tension caused by the Cardinal T square of Moon, square Uranus in Aries Square Pluto in Cancer.

Carlotta Perez has a Grand Trine in Earth, Sun, Mercury in Virgo, trine Uranus in Taurus trine Mars in Capricorn, as befits an economist (Taurus/Capricorn) who wished to revolutionise the economy (Uranus in Taurus) to make life sustainable (Virgo). She writes of the need to lift up the poor, and advises governments how to change (Mars Capricorn).

Sextile, sixty degrees

Like the trine, the sextile is a favourable aspect, less so than the Trine, but it helps flow and ease in the horoscope. Again, it can make certain difficult aspects easier or it can incline to laziness or taking the easy way out.

Greta Thunberg has powerful, forensic, combative Venus/Mars in Scorpio sextile highly intelligent and cautious Mercury in Capricorn (and perhaps her lonely and old-soul Capricorn Moon, depending on her birth time). This makes her more confident speaking out than would otherwise be the case, as Capricorn holds back and checks and rechecks their facts, lest they make an error and be shamed.

Kite: grand trine plus 2 sextiles

This major aspect is seen in many charts of famous people, I think the extra two sextiles on the grand trine seem to both temper the trines and also give focus for the grand trine, the apex of the figure.

Angela Davis has an Air Grand Trine Sun in forward looking, intelligent Aquarius, trine brilliant Mars, Uranus in Gemini (the classic radical academic or writer), and trine harmonious and collegiate Neptune in Libra. This speaks of her intellect, her ease in communicating, her great ideas, and her community focus. The Sextile of Pluto in Leo to Mars, Uranus and Neptune, speak of her addressing the issues of where

African Americans belong, their powerlessness (Pluto in Leo, their brilliance stolen), and the need to reconnect with their Black tribe (fourth house).

Rosalind Franklin had a grand kite in Water and Earth, combative and perceptive Mars in Scorpio, trine deep, soulful Pluto in Cancer, and trine scientific and deep reaching Uranus in Pisces. Saturn in scientific and detail oriented Virgo sextiles the Pluto and Mars giving her structure and great discipline. The watery Grand Trine suggests she was the warm, friendly and funny person her friends recalled, as well as her fierce intellect. Rosalind studied crystals (Saturn in Virgo) and was the first to photograph the deepest inner nature of humankind (Mars in Scorpio). Her Kite was also involved in a difficult mutable T square of Saturn in Virgo square her Moon in late Sagittarius or early Scorpio, square Uranus in Pisces. This suggests she cut people (Uranus) who did not come up to her high standards (Saturn), tried to restrict her freedom in any way (Moon in Sagittarius), or took her on in a power struggle (Moon in Scorpio). Her powerful Stellium in Leo would have made short work of them.

Another Brilliant scientist, Marie Curie, also has a Grand Trine in water, Sun in forensic Scorpio, trine radical Uranus in Cancer, trine deep and sensitive Moon in Pisces, both Uranus and the Moon are sextile to Pluto in Taurus (radium).

No aspect

As you would expect no aspect is also saying something about the horoscope. The most obvious is Beyonce. Her Sun is un-aspected. She describes her public persona (see Houses) as a mask and that the 'real' woman is a down to earth, uncomplicated person, who just wants a normal, Virgoan life.

Notes

1. Mars is the lesser Malefic and Saturn the greater Malefic, while the transpersonal planets, Uranus, Neptune and Pluto, together with Chiron may also be considered malefic. However, difficult aspects may make the individual stronger, rather than crush them, while easy aspects, the benefics are Venus and Jupiter, can make a person lazy and fail to develop their potential.
2. Gillespie, Marcia Ann, Rosa Johnson Butler, and Richard A. Long. (2008). *Maya Angelou: A Glorious Celebration*. New York: Random House. p.22.

Transits and cycles

The Moon

The Moon takes 28.3 days to go around the zodiac, so in one lunar month it will touch all the planets in your horoscope. You can watch as the Moon goes over each individual planet in your birth chart to get a sense of how each planet operates in your chart.

The Lunar Return is when the Moon is at the exact same degree as the Moon in your horoscope. You can draw up a chart for this moment, in the place you are in when this happens. You can then note the days of the month when it hits each individual planet and see for example how your Saturn reacts when the Moon hits, compared to your Venus. If you follow this for several cycles you will get a sense of how to use the energy of your chart most effectively on a day to day basis.

For example, Saturn days are good for paperwork, career advancement, but not so great for parties or creativity, the opposite being true for Venus days. Tracking the Moon through your horoscope can be like a great meditation on you, and how you react and operate in your world. It highlights weaknesses and strengths and allows you to pick the best time to do things; job interviews, travel, asking for favours etc.

Transits of the Moon are brief, but usually serve to energise other transits. Annie Oakley had the Moon going over her Ascendant the day she won the shooting competition which changed her life; on the same day Uranus was conjunct her Leo Sun and her Midheaven of career and fame highlighting her life's work (Sun).

The Sun

In the same way that you can do a Lunar Return, you can do a Solar Return, except now you pinpoint the day and time when the Sun is exactly over your Natal Sun; this may be your actual birthday or sometimes it is the day before or afterwards. You can then cast the horoscope for that time and again look at how your year is going to be. If you track the Sun around this chart in the same way as the Moon in the Lunar Return you can predict when are the best times to have holidays, work hard, look for a job, meet a partner etc.

Mary Wollstonecraft had the Sun transiting her Midheaven (mother) when she gave birth to Fanny (14.5.1794). This is a common connection, showing how the birth of a child allows the woman to connect to her mothering role. Of course, if there were no child, such a transit would suggest her career is highlighted.

Jupiter return

Jupiter's cycle is about twelve years. This means every twelve years Jupiter returns to the place it was when you were born. The Jupiter Return corresponds to the twelve-year cycle of Chinese astrology. Jupiter, being the planet of expansion, offers us a chance to enlarge our world. This is often a time when we grow; we may begin a course of study, travel, or get a little closer to realising our dreams. In the UK the first Jupiter return (around twelve years of age) coincides with the move to secondary education, which is a big leap up for most children. The second Jupiter Return is around age twenty-four, when we leave education and begin to build a life of our own. The third Jupiter return at age thirty-six is often the time we draw nearer to our dreams, or put them centre stage if we realise we have lost sight of them. The next Jupiter return at forty-eight, is part of the classical mid-life crisis (precipitated by Uranus, see below) where it is often felt this is a last ditch opportunity to grow and change (not true of course, but it often feels this way). Then comes the Jupiter return at sixty, when we may be retiring or at least thinking about what we plan to do with our later years. The sixties can be a time when people have a second flowering in their career. At seventy-two, we are in early old age, and often we settle down and spend time on our pleasures, and perhaps develop a spiritual practice or understanding of what our life has been about. The Jupiter return at eighty-four (also the time of the Uranus return, see below), gives us another opportunity to contemplate our lives, take up new interests.

How we experience our Jupiter returns depends on how Jupiter is placed in our natal charts, house, sign and aspects. If we are one of the signs ruled by Jupiter, Sagittarius and Pisces, the effects will be stronger.

Jupiter is a benefic (a helpful planet) whose main action is expansion, but of course problems can be expanded too. Some people, if they have gone off course in their lives, can find the Jupiter return unsettling as things get worse before they get better.

Angela Merkel had her Jupiter return in November 1989 when the Berlin Wall came down and the East Germans were set free (Jupiter). It also started her career as a politician, as the West Germans were looking for East Germans to join their political parties (luck and good timing-Jupiter).

Jupiter transits are when Jupiter touches planets in our horoscope, and they often bring about Jupiterian transformation.

Mary Wollstonecraft had Jupiter transit her natal ground-breaking Mars in Aries in the ninth house (publishing) when she published *Vindication of the Rights of Women* in 1792, and Jupiter (foreign travel) was transiting her natal Moon when she first went to France (December 1792), both of which launched her career, and her emotional life (Moon) was energised.

Lorena Bobbit had Jupiter conjunct her Mars when she castrated her husband, Mars (the knife) Taurus, (slow burning rage and then explosion), Mars the male genitals. As a Scorpio, Mars is her ruling planet, so the event led to her freedom (Jupiter) and finding her power (Mars).

Vera Wang had Jupiter conjunct her Saturn when she failed to make it into the Figure Skating Olympic team (Saturn, limitation) and decided instead to go into fashion. Jupiter to Saturn transits may seem like setbacks (Saturn) but they often lead to new growth in a different direction (Jupiter).

Louise Hay had an extraordinary lucky break (Jupiter) when in one week in March 1988, she appeared on both the Oprah and the Donahue shows which meant her book *You Can Heal Your Life* hit the best seller lists. Jupiter was conjunct her Aries Midheaven (career). She was invited because of her ground-breaking work with AIDs patients in *The Hay Ride* support group (Aries-courage); this was a time when AIDS patients were treated as though they had the plague.

Georgia O'Keeffe's life was transformed in 1908 when she won an art competition at art school and when her father was declared bankrupt (Saturn), when she was forced to leave college and get a job. The need to survive financially set her free (Jupiter) from her father's control (Saturn) and set her on her way to discovering her own path.

Saturn return

The Saturn cycle is around twenty-eight years, so when have our first Saturn return (where it hits your natal Saturn) at twenty-eight and thirty years, is the classic time for making commitments, like marriage, career, and establishing a stable life for ourselves. It is also a time for letting go of those things that no longer serve you. This may be lifestyle, relationships, careers, particularly where these things were done to please other people, living your life for your parents for example. Saturn is a hard taskmaster and the lessons can be very painful, especially if we resist the changes. Saturn will get its way; there is little negotiation. Because Saturn goes retrograde often, there are usually three or five contacts with your natal Saturn, so the whole process lasts a year or more. It is when we grow up (hopefully) and leave our childhood behind, which fits with Saturnine taking responsibility, getting serious and building for the future.

The second Saturn return happens at around fifty-six to fifty-eight years. This is when people begin thinking about retirement and, if they haven't already, they begin to do those things that they need to do. Second careers are common here, or late divorces or marriages. Saturn will make you look dispassionately at your life and cut out the dead wood.

The third Saturn return happens around age eighty-four (the same time as the Uranus return, see below) which may be when we contemplate our own mortality, or conversely, when we have another burst of life.

Although rarely pleasant, the Saturn return empowers us and guides us onto the right path for our life. Saturn Returns are easier for people with a strong natal Saturn, Capricorns and Aquarians.

AOC was elected to Congress on her first Saturn return, a classic assumption of responsibility (Saturn) in government (Saturn) for the greater good (Capricorn). Saturn is part of her Cardinal Grand Cross (see Aspects) which includes her Mercury, Moon, Midheaven, Jupiter, Uranus and Neptune. Therefore, any transits affecting any of these planets will in turn reverberate around the others connected by aspect.

Jane Goodall's Saturn return 1964–5 coincided with the time she was studying for her doctorate at Cambridge, which may have been a hard time (Saturn) away from her beloved animals, but also a time when she scientifically (Saturn in Aquarius) wrote up her ground-breaking research (Aquarius always ahead of the curve.)

Kino was accredited as an Ashtanga teacher (one of the youngest) in 2006, the year of her Saturn return. Her Saturn in Leo brought her international fame as a yoga teacher (Leo).

Saturn can also transit other planets in your horoscope with similar effects. Saturn transits can be both positive and or negative.

Ella Fitzgerald's life was suddenly (Uranus) transformed when she won a talent competition in November 1934. Saturn was conjunct her Uranus. Saturn Uranus transits can be incredibly disruptive unless you release the past (Saturn) and embrace the revolutionary. Ella's quick thinking (Uranus) changed her act from dancing to singing, and launched her stratospheric career (Saturn).

In a similar way, the life of Valerie Solanas was transformed when the *Scum Manifesto* was published (the first version was self-published in 1967). Saturn transited her Aries Mercury, Sun and Ascendant in 1968 bringing her fame (Sun of the Ascendant) for her radical (Aries) and confrontational (Aries) views.

When Maya Angelou was raped in 1935 and the rapist was killed, Saturn was conjunct her sensitive Venus and Mercury in Pisces. Maya withdrew into her imagination (Mercury in Pisces) and did not speak again until 1941 when Saturn was conjunct her Midheaven. Saturn can give terrible experiences but they ultimately offer great rewards. Maya used this time of retreat (Pisces) to read and develop her brilliant literary mind (Mercury in Pisces).

Jackie Kennedy married Onassis when Saturn was conjunct her Moon. He provided her with the protection and privacy money can buy (Saturn) and she was able to keep her children safe (Aries Moon in the fifth house); Bobby Kennedy had just been murdered and she was afraid for their lives.

Marie Curie received her second (solo) Nobel Prize when Saturn (reward for hard work, science) was conjunct her natal Pluto (radium).

Uranus returns

The Uranus cycle is around eighty-four years. So, the first major transit we see of Uranus is the Uranus half Return at around forty-two years. This is the archetypal midlife crisis, when we realise this might be the last chance to live the life we want. People leave unhappy marriages, undergo a dramatic career change, also the stereotypical buying of the sports car, having a face lift, taking a younger lover, or moving to a new country.

Uranus disrupts; sudden, drastic changes seem to come out of the blue. The house position of Uranus will give some indication which area of life is likely to be affected. As with Saturn, but more so, the best way to deal with Uranus transits is to surrender and let go gracefully of everything that is breaking up and moving away. This is easier said than done of course. But in my experience, things will change, whether we accept it or not, so the least painful choice is to surrender and trust; what lies the other side of the shock is progress.

Uranus transits generally last a year, as the planet will go retrograde at some point and will hit your natal Uranus three or five times. The first one breaks down the structure, the second (usually retrograde) allows for some adjustment, and the final hit will see the resolution or culmination of the experience. With five hits you have two retrograde periods and more opportunity to change.

For Sharon Gannon her Uranus half return coincided with her trip to India where she studied with the founder of Ashtanga Yoga, Sri Pattabhi Jois, which had a profound effect on her Yoga practice. Uranus transited the stellium on the Ascendant, so this was a time of great personal and professional transformation for her.

Maya Angelou's half Uranus return coincided with the writing and publication of *I Know Why the Caged Bird Sings* (1968–9) which brought her huge success. The book came about from a chance meeting (Uranus) with a publisher (Seventh house friends and colleagues) who dared her (Aries cannot resist a challenge) to write about her life. At the same time, Saturn (hard work and discipline) was conjunct her Sun (her life's work) and Jupiter (luck, publishing, success).

The Uranus half return is the second of the midlife challenges we face. Neptune quarter return at forty-one, Jupiter at forty-eight, Saturn at fifty-six. The Uranus return at eighty-four coincides with the third Saturn return, and many people will experience this as a last-ditch opportunity to do those things that they need to do to complete this life cycle. It may not be as dramatic as the half return, but it can be a deep, meaningful experience.

Uranus transits have a similar effect; they can be challenging, but they are easier for Aquarians, whose ruling planet it is.

Malorie Blackman had Uranus (radical) conjunct her Jupiter (publishing) and Venus in Aquarius when *Noughts and Crosses* was published (6 February 2001).

Neptune was also conjunct her Saturn (hard work) and Mars (drive) all in Aquarius (revolutionary).

Annie Oakley won the shooting competition (25 November 1875) when Uranus was conjunct her Sun and Midheaven. Her skill and showmanship (Leo) catapulted her (Uranus) into the public eye and transformed her life (Sun).

Hurricane Hannah had Uranus opposite her Jupiter when she did the trials at Loughborough in October 2007; her life was transformed (Uranus) and she discovered her passion for wheelchair racing.

Neptune

The Neptune cycle is around 165 years, so the only Neptune cycles we experience are the quarter return at around age fifty-one, and the half return at eighty-two years. As with Uranus, these are generational influences, your peers will be experiencing something similar, but the area highlighted will be shown by the house position of Neptune and any aspects it makes to other planets. Neptune brings confusion, exhaustion and sometimes spiritual awakening and creative outpouring. The quarter return may coincide with the Uranus half return which will be a twofold opportunity to realign your life (if it needs this). Neptune is mystifying, and the return is often experienced as a time of confusion, exhaustion and lack of motivation and focus. Neptune dissolves and for earthy and fiery types it is a hard energy to deal with. Like all the major transits, the general advice is to release, and especially to dream, vision and imagine a better life. This not the time for making decisions as often your judgement may be confused; it is a great time to be deceived and ripped off, so be very wary of new people or situations that seem too good to be true. For creative people though, this can be a time of great breakthrough in their work.

The Neptune half return at approximately eighty-two years, around the time of the Uranus return, may signify a deepening of spiritual life or a quest for meaning. Take care around gurus and teachers though; we can be duped at any age. Neptune is easier on the water signs and Pisces especially.

Neptune transits, where Neptune aspects other planets in your horoscope have a similar debilitating and possibly creative effect. Again, it may make three or five hits to the planet depending on periods of retrograde.

In 2011, when Greta Thunberg heard about climate change, she became depressed and stopped talking and eating, and lost ten kilograms in two months. Neptune was conjunct her Uranus. Neptune often causes depression, while Uranus is a shock to the system. Both Neptune and Uranus can cause silence, she was diagnosed with selective mutism and Asperger's. She cut herself off from the world (Uranus) but perhaps used this time to think through her vision (Neptune).

When Margaret Mead published *Coming of Age in Samoa* in 1928, Neptune was transiting her Moon in radical Aquarius (shocking the world) and Saturn (hard work, career) transited both her radical Mercury and Uranus in Sagittarius (philosophy) in the eleventh house of the collective (her work influenced culture, feminism and childrearing).

When *The Spiral Dance* was published in 1979, Starhawk had Neptune transit her Mercury (words, writing) and Venus (women, feminism, earth magic) in Gemini. This brought her fame and a spiritual following (Neptune).

Conversely, Georgia O'Keeffe's depression and admission to hospital coincided with Neptune on her midheaven in 1933.

Pluto

Pluto has a cycle of 248 years, so it is only the quarter return we are concerned with just after the second Saturn return, around age sixty-two. This time can be a time of drastic reorientation or endings in your life; death, devastation, destruction can all occur.

More important are Pluto transits which, because of the slow motion of the planet, can last for several years. It you have a stellium of planets, then a Pluto transit will be life changing, lasting for several years.

Again, it will be the house position of the planet that will show the area of influence, and in Pluto transits, the nature of the planet transited and its house position. For example, a Pluto transit to your Moon can mean emotional devastation, while to Mars, explosive anger and frustration.

Jacqueline Kennedy's husband was murdered when Pluto was conjunct her Mars, death (Pluto) by violence (Mars) publicly (Mars in the tenth house). Neptune was also coming up to the opposition of her Ascendant (change of public persona) and of course deep, deep, grief (Neptune).

Mary Shelley had her waking dream about the monster (Pluto) made by Dr Frankenstein when Pluto was conjunct her writerly Mercury in Virgo. Neptune (dreams) was also conjunct her Moon (16 June 1816 at 02:20 on Lake Geneva).

In April 1953 the report in *Nature* which contained Rosalind Franklin's ground-breaking photograph of DNA, Pluto (life changing) was transiting her brilliant Jupiter in Leo.

END NOTE

You might ask yourself, why does this matter? It was all so long ago. As I started this book, Australia was on fire, a global pandemic shut down the world for over a year and still rages on, the official death toll nearing three million worldwide. Those countries worst hit are those run by sons of the *father-god* who pursue brutalist, climate change denying policies.[1] Oregon and California are on fire, the sky turned red. Floods have devasted Ethiopia (300,000 displaced), Sudan, Burkina Faso, Algeria, Ghana, and Senegal, Nigeria. There have been flash floods in Pakistan, North Korea, Nepal, Chad, Republic of Ireland, India, Mexico, Afghanistan, Kenya and Uganda, Haiti, Dominican Republic, Thailand, and Vietnam.

Our world, the sacred world of Gaia is dying because of the mindset of the *father-god*. This is why it matters: We need urgently to change direction and ditch the ideology which has brought us to the edge of destruction. The world of the goddess is possible; it existed for thousands of years. We can live in harmony with nature and one another, where swords are turned into ploughshares, and we all share and delight in the infinite bounty of this beautiful blue planet.

Look to matriarchal societies elsewhere[2] and you will find a common thread. Matriarchal societies show a better way to organise society. Because the central cultural model is the mother and caring; everyone's needs are catered to for the greatest benefit to all. Difference is respected but not hierarchical. Society is organised by Clan, with respect for nature at the centre. Children are raised in common, biological motherhood and fatherhood is unnecessary for parenting. There is a subsistence economy where there is no private property, all property is controlled by the Clan Mother for the good of the whole Clan. It is a reciprocal economy based on gifts; Clans treat each other with food and celebrations. Decisions are made collectively; there is rule by consensus between individuals and their Clan and between different Clans. Spiritually, the Divine Mother is immanent, in all living things, not hierarchal or with an omnipotent, judgemental god, so nature is cherished and protected.[3]

There is another way. It is possible if we can dream it.

Notes

1. USA, India, Brazil, Russia, UK, China etc. https://ourworldindata.org/grapher/total-covid-deaths-region?year=latest&time=2020-01-11. latest accessed 12.9.2020.
2. For an excellent overview see, Gottner-Abendroth, Heide (Krause, Maureen, T. trans.) 1991. *The Dancing Goddess*. Beacon Press, Boston.
3. See https://feminismandreligion.com/2020/02/16/matriarchies-are-not-just-a-reversal-of-patriarchies-a-structural-analysis-by-heide-goettner-abendroth/ accessed 21.4.2021.

A–Z list of the horoscopes
(by surname)

Maya Angelou

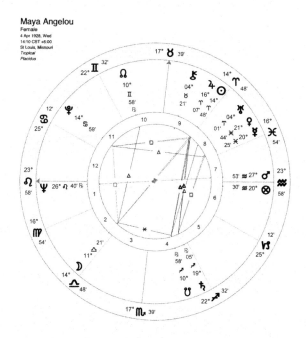

Josephine Baker

Beyonce

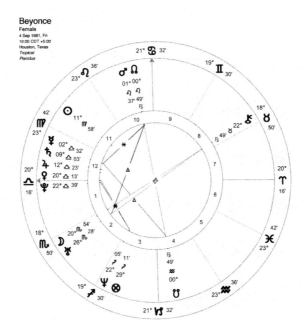

Malorie Blackman

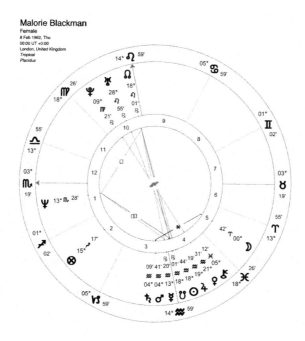

Lorena Bobbitt

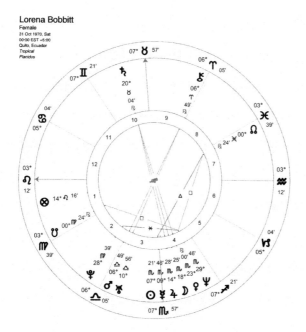

Barbara Brennan

Hannah Cockroft

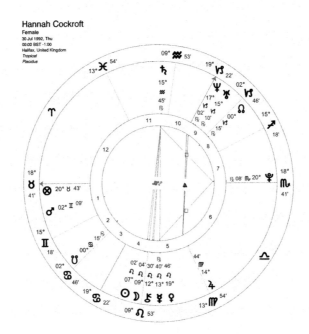

Marie Curie

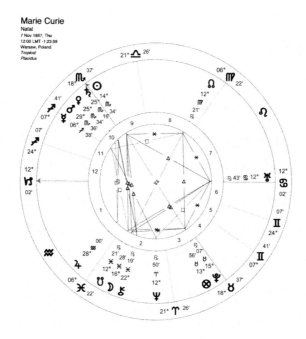

Angela Davis

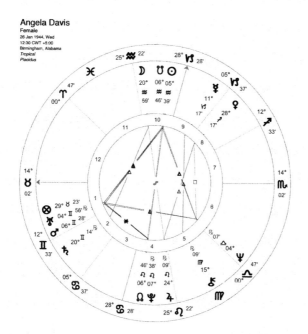

Isadora Duncan

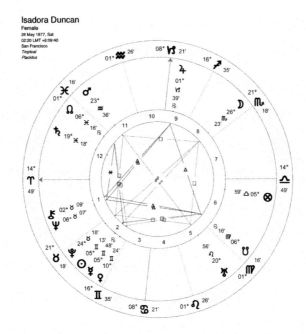

Ella Fitzgerald

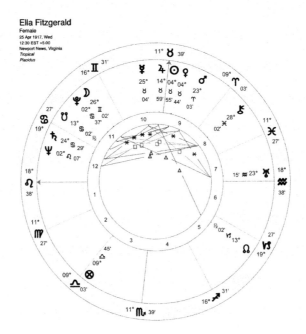

Rosalind Franklin

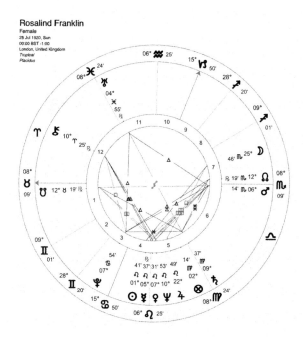

Sharon Gannon

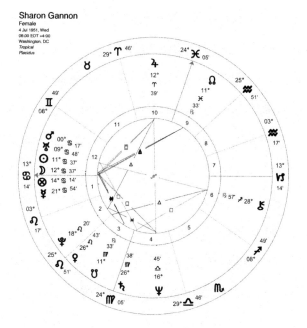

Jane Goodall

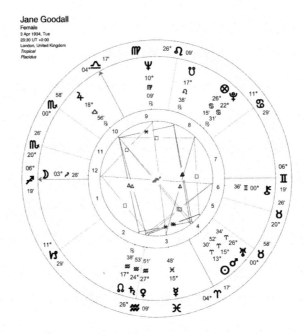

Germaine Greer

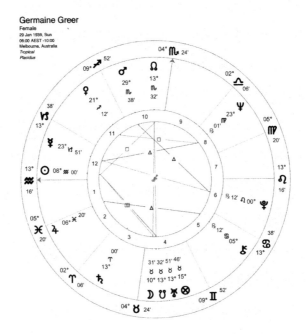

Louise Hay

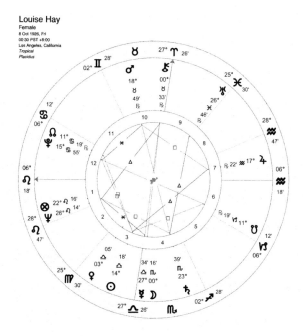

Jacqueline Kennedy Onassis

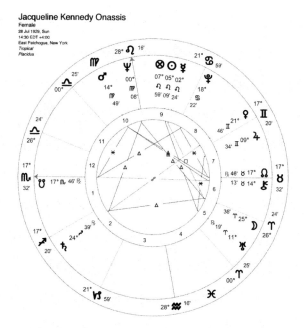

Kino

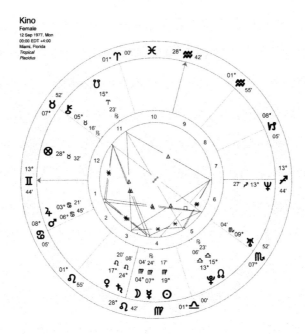

Sheila Kitzinger

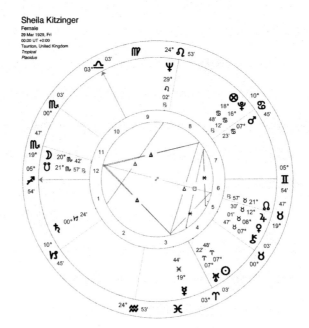

Lucy Lawless

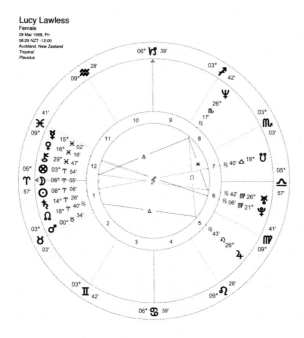

Sybil Leek

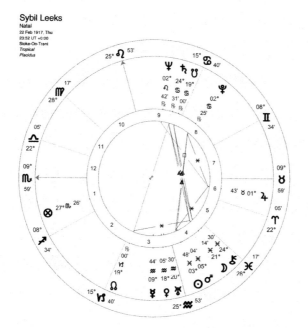

Maggie Lena Walker

Chelsea Manning

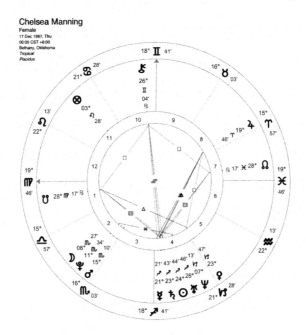

Margaret Mead

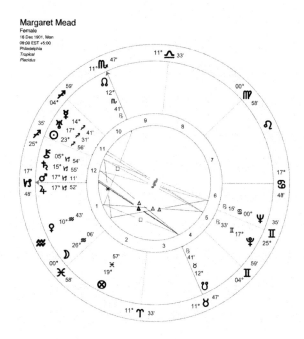

Angela Merkel

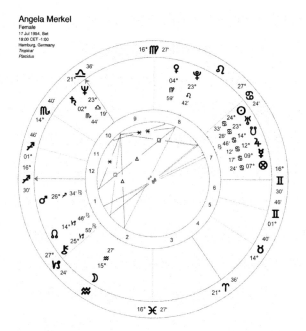

Georgia O'Keeffe

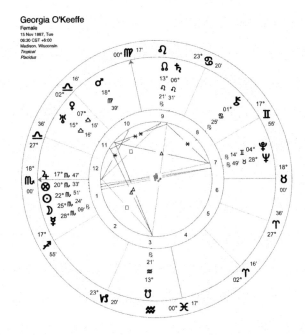

Annie Oakley

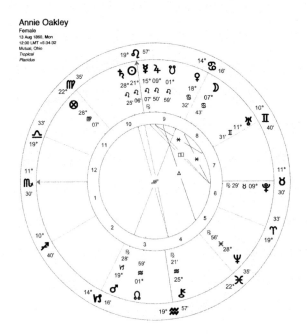

Alexandria Ocasio Cortez

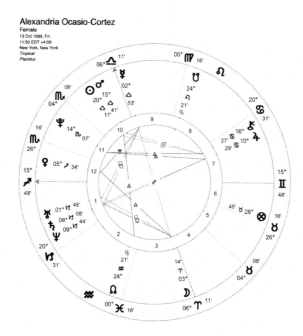

Dolly Parton

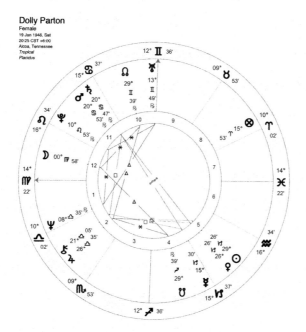

Carlotta Perez

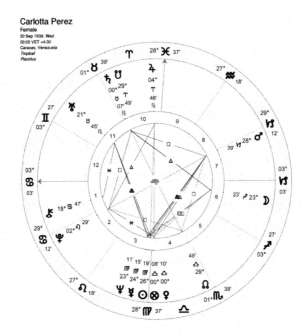

Helena Rubenstein

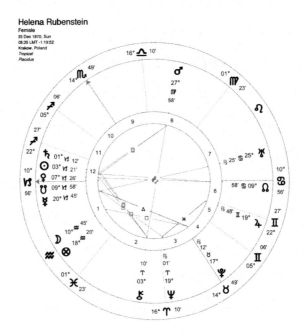

Mary Shelley

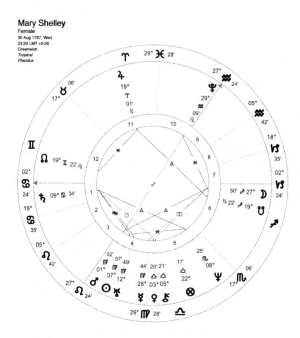

Nina Simone

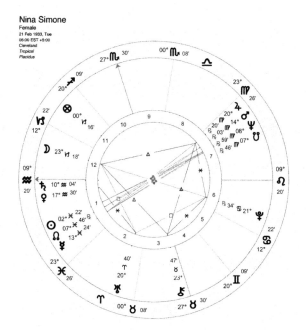

Valerie Solanas

Starhawk

Greta Thunberg

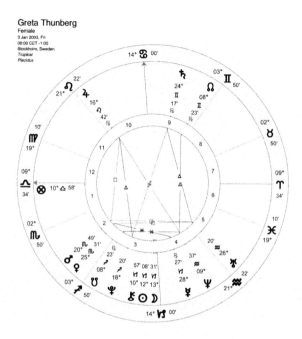

Vera Wang

Mary Wollstonecraft

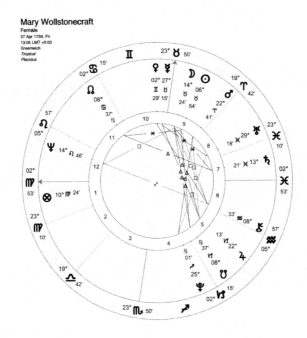

Key words

Sun: destiny, higher self, true self, life quest, Vital Spirit.[1]

Moon: emotional body, instincts, place of safety, mother(ing) comfort, habits.

Mercury: voice, communication, the mind, thoughts, reason.

Venus: money, sensuality, physicality, the natural world.

Mars: will, energy, focus, determination, stamina, desire, sex.

Jupiter: luck, expansion, travel, philosophy, higher education, spirituality, astrology.

Saturn: restriction, maturity, responsibility, the 'system,' boundaries, success, religion, the father.

Uranus: revolution, change, splitting apart, violence, irritability, brilliance.

Neptune: mysticism, creativity, dance, music, poetry, film, unboundedness, dissolving.

Pluto: violence, explosive change, the unconscious, power, wealth, sex, abuse.

The signs

<u>Aries</u>: Strengths: courage, enthusiasm, energy, can-do attitude, loyal, fearless, open-minded, future orientated, protective. Weaknesses: impatience, reckless, bad-tempered, selfish, dismissive, unco-operative, immature, spiteful, bullying.

<u>Taurus</u>: Strengths: calm, ordered, gentle, grounded, helpful, nature-loving, sensual, artistic, disciplined, reliable, modest. Weaknesses: lazy, greedy, slow, materialistic, mean, conventional, stubborn, jealous, ponderous.

<u>Gemini</u>: Strengths: chatty, inventive, speedy, funny, carefree, good communicator, sociable, adaptable, intelligent, open-minded. Weaknesses: irresponsible, fickle, liars, fantasists, superficial, dishonest, con artists, spendthrift, unfocussed, inconsistent.

<u>Cancer</u>: Strengths: warm, gentle, kind, caring, creative, protective, soft spoken, non-threatening, nurturing. Weaknesses: moody, passive, fearful, depressive, passive-aggressive, lazy, timid, hesitant, doubting, clannish.

<u>Leo</u>: Strengths: warm, entertaining, leadership, inspiring, child-like, protective, creative, extravert, big-hearted, open. Weaknesses: proud, vain, bullying, egocentric, bossy, domineering, selfish, sulking, childish, punishing, boastful.

<u>Virgo</u>: Strengths: meticulous, ritualistic, thoughtful, helpful, organised, health conscious, scientific, thinkers, modest, hardworking. Weaknesses: anxious, negative, worriers, timid, critical, depressive, obsessive, rigid, rule-bound, petty.

<u>Libra</u>: Strengths: articulate, charming, creative, artistic, loving, intelligent, analytical, scientific, cultured, demure, fair-minded. Weaknesses: vanity, dishonesty, argumentative, lazy, acquisitive, snobbish, inconsistent, dependant, superficial.

<u>Scorpio</u>: Strengths: deep, mystical, courageous, bold, perceptive, powerful, intense, truth-seekers, focused, persistent. Weaknesses: dishonest, jealous, vindictive, competitive, rancorous, melodramatic, loners, carnal, scheming.

<u>Sagittarius</u>: Strengths: honest, truth seeking, brave, freedom loving, open-minded, cheerful, fun, philosophical, spiritual, generous. Weaknesses, indulgent, greedy, libertines, commitment-phobes, inconstant, reckless, careless, impulsive, idealogues, immature.

<u>Capricorn</u>: Strengths: reliable, honest, logical, prudent, stable, organised, ambitious, caring, loyal, dogged. Weaknesses: critical, mean, conservative, depressive, rigid, cold, calculating, suspicious, negative, judgemental.

<u>Aquarius</u>: Strengths: visionary, intelligent, curious, accepting, unique, honest, funny, talkative, humanitarian, unpredictable. Weaknesses: fickle, disorganised, dismissive, idealogues, solitary, arrogant, ungrounded, impractical, gullible, odd looking.

<u>Pisces</u>: Strengths: kind, psychic, mystical, calm, open, loving, emotional, shape-shifters, beautiful, creative. Weaknesses: oblivious, indulgent, passive-aggressive, manipulative, dishonest, slippery, ungrounded, helpless, inconstant, selfish.

Note

1. See Brooke, Elisabeth. 2019. *Traditional Western Herbal Medicine*. Aeon Books, London. p.156.

Bibliography

Primary sources

Herodotus, *The Histories*. Holland, Tom (trans.) 2014. Penguin Books, London.

Hesiod, *Theogonia Opera et Dies Scutum*. (Greek). Solmsen, Friedrich. (ed.) 1952. Larendon Press, Oxford.

The Homeric Hymns Allen, W, Thomas (trans.) 1811. Clarendon Press, Oxford.

Homer, *The Iliad*. (trans. Lattimore, Richmond.) 2011. University of Chicago Press, London.

Homer, *The Odyssey*. Rieu, E, V. (trans.) 1991, Penguin Books, London. Wilson, Emily. 2018. W. W. Norton & Co. New York.

Lilly, William, *Christian Astrology*, 1647, 1985. Regulus Publishing. A. Wheaton & C. Ltd. Exeter.

Ovid, *Metamorphoses*, Raeburn, David, (trans) 2004. Penguin Books, London.

Ovid, *Metamorphoses* (Latin) Tarrant, R.J. 2004. Clarendon Press, Oxford.

Sappho. Poochigian, Aaron (trans.) *Sung with Love: Poems and Fragments*. 2015. Penguin Books, London. Lombardo, Stanley. *Complete Poems and Fragments*. 2016. Hackett, Indianapolis.

Virgil, *The Aeneid*. West, David (trans.) 1991. Penguin Books, London.

Secondary sources

Bachofen, J.J. *Myth, Religion and Mother Right*. 1992. Princetown University Press, Princetown. NJ.

Baring, Anne & Cashford, Jules. *The Myth of the Goddess*. 1993. Arkana, London.

Blundell, Sue. *Women in Ancient Greece*. 1995. British Museum Press, London.

333

Blundell, Sue. Williamson, Margaret. *The Sacred and the Feminine in Ancient Greece*. 1998. Routledge, London.

Boardman, John. *Early Greek Vase Painting*. 1998. Thames and Hudson, London.

Brennan, Barbara. *Light Emerging, The Journey of Personal Healing*. 1993. Bantam, Berkley, CA.

Brooke, Elisabeth. *Herbal Therapy for Women*. 1992, 2018. Aeon Press, London.

Brooke, Elisabeth. *A Woman's Herbal*. 1992, 2019. Aeon Press, London.

Brooke, Elisabeth. *Women Healers through History*. 1993, 2018. Aeon Press, London.

Brooke, Elisabeth. *Traditional Western Herbal Medicine*. 2019. Aeon Press, London.

Campbell, Joseph. 2nd edition *A Hero with a Thousand Faces*. 1972. Bollingen Series XVII, Princeton University Press, Princeton NJ.

Chulup, Radek. *The Semantics of Fertility: Levels of meaning in the Thesmorphoria*. 2007.

Connelly, Joan, Breton. *Portrait of A Priestess: Women and Ritual in Ancient Greece*. 2007. Oxford University Press, Oxford.

Connelly, Joan, Breton. *Ritual Movement through Greek Sacred Space: towards an Archaeology of Performance*. in A. Chaniotis, ed., *Ritual Dynamics in the Ancient Mediterranean: Agency, Emotion, Gender, Reception*. 2011. Stuttgart, 313–346.

Dillion, Matthew. *Girls and Women in Classical Greek Religion*. 2002. Routledge, London.

Eisler, Riane. *The Chalice and the Blade*. 1987. Harper & Row, San Francisco.

Eliade, Mircea. Trask, W.F. (trans.). *The Sacred and the Profane*. 1959. Harcourt Brace, London.

Victor Frankl. *Man's Search for Meaning*. 1984. Simon and Schuster, New York.

Frazer, J.G. *The Golden Bough*. 1983. Macmillan Press, London.

Gimbutas, Marija. 'The First Wave of Eurasian Steppe Pastoralists into Copper Age Europe,' *Journal of Indo European Studies 5*. 1 Jan 1977.

Gimbutas, Marija. *The Language of the Goddess*. 1989. Harper and Row, San Francisco.

Gimbutas, Marija. *The Goddesses and Gods of Old Europe, 6500–3500 BC*. 1982. Thames and Hudson, London.

Goff, Barbara. *Citizen Bacchae-Women's Ritual Practice in Ancient Greece*. 2004. University of California Press, Berkeley.

Goodison, Lucy. *Death, Women and the Sun, Symbolism of Regeneration in Early Aegean Religion*. 1989. University of London Institute of Classical Studies, London.

Gottner-Abendroth, Heide. *The Dancing Goddess*. 1991. Beacon Press, Boston.

Graves, Robert. *The Greek Myths*. 2011. Penguin Books, London.

Grimal, Pierre. Maxwell-Hyslop, A.R. (trans.). *The Dictionary of Classical Mythology*. 1987. Blackwell, Oxford.

Harrison, Jane. *Themis: A study of the Social Origins of Greek Religion*. 1912. Cambridge University Press. Cambridge.

Harrison, Jane. *The Religion of Ancient Greece*. 1921. Constable & Co. London.

Harrison, Jane. *Myths of Greece and Rome*. 1927. Earnest Benn, London.

Jacobsen, Thorkild. *The Treasures of Darkness: A History of Mesopotamian Religion*. 1976. Yale University Press, New Haven.

Kernos, 20. Pdf: http://ufar.ff.cuni.cz/sites/default/files/u15/chlup_-_the_semantics_of_fertility.pdf

Leek, Sybil. *The Diary of a Witch*. 1968. Prentice-Hall, Englewood Cliffs, New Jersey.

Liddell, Henry. Scott, Roger. *A Lexicon* abridged *Liddell and Scott's Greek English Lexicon*. 1944. Clarendon Press, London.

March, Jenny. *Dictionary of Classical Mythology*. 2002. Cassell, London.

Marinatos, Nanno. *Minoan Kingship and the Solar Goddess*. 2010. University of Illinois Press, Chicago.

Morford, Mark, P.O., Lenardon, Robert, J. Sham, Michael. *Classical Mythology*. 2015. Oxford University Press, Oxford.

Nilsson, Martin, P. *Minoan-Mycenaean Religion and its Survival in Greek Religion*. 1968. C.W.K. Gleerup. Lund.

Piggott, Stuart. *Prehistoric India*. 1950. Penguin Books, Harmondsworth.

Radice, Betty. *Who's who in the Ancient World*. 1973. Penguin Books, London.

Redmond, Layne. *When Drummers were Women: A Spiritual History of Rhythm*. 1997, 2018. Echo Point Books & Media. Brattleboro, Vermont.

Scott, Michael. *Delphi*. 2014. Princeton University Press, Princeton.

Spretnak, Charlene. *Lost Goddesses of Early Greece- A collection of Pre-Hellenic Myths*. 1992. Beacon Press. Boston.

Strolonga, Polyxeni. *The Foundation of the Oracle at Delphi in the Homeric Hymn to Apollo*. 2011. Greek, Roman and Byzantine Studies 51.

Summer, Amanda. *Goddesses in the Dirt: Travels with Persephone*, Jan 10th. 2011. https://travelswithpersephone.blogspot.com/2011/01/goddesses-in-dirt_3954.html accessed 22.7.2020.

Willetts, R.F. *Cretan Cults and Festivals*. 1962. Routledge and Kegan Paul. London.

Williams, Terry Tempest. *When Women were Birds, Fifty-Four Variations on Voice*. 2013. Picador, London.

INDEX

Printed by Printforce, United Kingdom